FLORA BRITANNICA

FLORA BRITANNICA
THE CONCISE EDITION

RICHARD MABEY

Supported by Common Ground

With photographs by
Bob Gibbons and Gareth Lovett Jones

CHATTO & WINDUS
LONDON

Half-title page: wild teasel, p. 135.
Frontispiece: the Aston on Clun Flag Tree, p. 106.
Title page: ivy, p. 225.

First published 1998

© Richard Mabey 1998

Richard Mabey has asserted his right under the Copyright,
Designs and Patents Act 1988 to be identified as the author of
this work.

First published in the United Kingdom in 1998 by
Chatto & Windus
Random House, 20 Vauxhall Bridge Road,
London SW1V 2SA

Random House Australia (Pty) Limited
20 Alfred Street, Milsons Point, Sydney,
New South Wales 2061, Australia

Random House New Zealand Limited
18 Poland Road, Glenfield,
Auckland 10, New Zealand

Random House South Africa (Pty) Limited
Endulini, 5A Jubilee Road, Parktown 2193, South Africa

Random House UK Limited Reg. No. 954009

A CIP catalogue record for this book is available from the
British Library

Papers used by Random House UK Limited are natural,
recyclable products made from wood grown in sustainable
forests. The manufacturing processes conform to the
environmental regulations of the country of origin.

ISBN 0–7011–6731–9

Design by Ian Muggeridge

Printed and bound in Singapore
by Tien Wah Press

Contents

Introduction

ON THE 50th anniversary of VE Day, many of the world's leaders gathered in London's Hyde Park for a memorial ceremony and, in the spring sunshine, laid posies of their national flowers around a large globe. It seemed a touching and ingenuous tribute, a rediscovery of one of the oldest spring rituals of reparation. Many of the blooms were traditional: red roses for England, thistles for Scotland and daffodils for Wales; Austria had edelweiss, Canada the sugar maple and South Africa the king protea. There were odd coincidences and improvisations, too, evidence of the momentous changes in the status of many nations over the previous decades. Cornflowers were laid by France, Germany, Estonia, Belarus and the Czech Republic; and formal bouquets of florists' cut-flowers – roses, tulips and carnations – by countries from Albania to Uzbekistan.[1] For many poor and unstable countries, it was clear that the idea of a 'national flower' was unfamiliar, maybe even artifical. But during the ceremony something serendipitous and enchanting happened. In the gusting May breezes, drifts of windblown Japanese cherry blossom – the international flower of peace – blew across Hyde Park like confetti, a reminder that nature makes its own unscripted gestures of renewal.

Plants have had symbolic as well as utilitarian meanings since the beginnings of civilisation. They have been tokens of birth, death, harvest and celebration, and omens of good (and bad) luck. They are powerful emblems of place and identity, too, not just of nations, but of villages, neighbourhoods, even personal retreats. Yet, as at Hyde Park, they are different from any other kind of symbol in having independent existences

Beechwoods: the symbol of the Chiltern Hills, though many plantations date only from the nineteenth century.

The symbolic use of plants is widespread in Europe. This sundial on a farmhouse wall in the Cévennes in France represents a carline thistle – the 'chardon soleil' – whose dried flower-heads are often nailed to doors for good luck.

of their own. Primroses and the last roses of summer still announce the seasons when *they* decide, with no respect for our calendars.

In Britain, wild species have an even more central role in national and local cultures than those from gardens. We pick sprigs of heather for luck, munch blackberries in autumn, remember Wordsworth's lines when the daffodils are in flower, and link hands around threatened trees. Our children still make daisy chains, whack conkers, and stick goosegrass stems on each other's backs. Despite being one of the most industrialised and urbanised countries on earth, we cling to plant rituals and mystical gestures whose roots stretch back into prehistory: holly decoration for the winter solstice, kisses under the mistletoe, the wearing of red poppies to remember the casualties of war. We name our houses, streets and settlements after plants, and use them as the most prolific source of decorative motifs on everything from stained glass to serviettes. From the outside, it must look as if we are botanical aboriginals, still in thrall to the spirits of vegetation.

But is this just the dying stages of an obstinate habit, the outward signs of a longing for the rural life that most of us have lost? Do we really still believe in the bad luck that may-blossom can bring into a house, and in the efficacy of the increasing numbers of herbal nostrums crowding onto chemists' shelves? Or is our seeming respect now a touch tongue-in-cheek? When wild flowers are dragged willy-nilly into shampoo advertisements and state rituals, maybe it is time to ask whether the particular plants themselves have any meaning left for us, or whether they have become purely notional, registers of a fashionably Green 'life-style'.

When work started on *Flora Britannica* in 1992, this was the question which underpinned all others. We were aware of surviving crafts and cottage wisdom, and of the familiarity expressed in our immense legacy of vernacular plant names. But we didn't know whether, as a people (or collection of peoples), we could still be said to have an intimacy with wild plants that was not purely nostalgic and backward-looking. Did people still meet under meeting-place trees? Were children inventing new games for the new, exotic species constantly escaping into the wild, as they did centuries ago for horse-chestnut and sycamore seeds; and was that two-way traffic of wild and cultivated plants over the garden wall still busy? Did plants continue to play any role in our senses of place and season, those fundamental aspects of everyday life that seem everywhere to be under threat from regimentation and the ironing out of local difference? And what names did we use for them now, to ourselves and to each other?

Most traditional local names seem more or less confined to books these days and the worry was that the whole of our plant culture might have become equally moribund. Certainly it has suffered much attrition over the past three centuries. Cromwell's Commonwealth, for instance, suppressed many of the festive parish ceremonies that involved plants (e.g. Beating the Bounds, and May garlands) on the grounds that they were pagan relics.[2] The Victorian era passed on a mixed legacy, too. The practice of using plants as the subject of Christian moral parables added quaint new meanings to a few species but also hastened the end of many of the older and more deep-rooted associations.[3] The so-called 'Language of Flowers' (bay as an emblem for 'glory', acacia for 'platonic love', etc) had no real popular roots at all and was invented from scratch by a group of mid-nineteenth-century French writers.[4]

Yet what we have found in the field research for *Flora Britannica*, and in the multitude of public contributions to it, is that Britain still has a lively popular culture of plants. Although wilder superstitions have faded, and other social groupings – family, friends, schools – are given the loyalty once reserved for the parish, the ancient engagements between plants, people and places continue unabated. What is fascinating is how they are now informed by popular ecology and a sense of social history. The belief, for example, that many of our most interesting plants, from crab-apple to wild garlic, were introduced by the Romans is being replaced by a curiosity about their real origins and uses. And trees with local and historical associations – native lime and black-poplar, yew, wild service – are increasingly being planted as landmarks and memorials in preference to exotic species.

The growing affection for trees has doubtless been strengthened by the growing range of threats to them. Around the country they have been symbolic and physical rallying posts for resistance to the 'great car economy'. One in particular, a 250-year-old sweet chestnut on George Green in Wanstead, became the focal point for those fighting the M11 link road through east London. It was occupied by protesters from June 1993 until it was felled amidst scenes of fierce local resistance on 6 December that year. During those months, 400 letters of support were addressed to the tree and its inhabitants.[5] Yet it may be an even sharper sign of how deeply trees have returned to our consciousness that another one could be scapegoated and attacked in an episode that could have come out of the Dark Ages. In Tamworth, Staffordshire, after the funeral of a young man who died after his car crashed into a tree in 1991, ten of the mourners went to the scene of the accident and hacked down the flower-decked tree with axes and a chainsaw.[6] It makes for a rich and sometimes contradictory mixture of science and superstition, communal custom and individual whim; but perhaps this is the shape that folklore is taking on today.

Flora Britannica was launched in the winter of 1991–2, and over the years since it has been regularly publicised on television and in the press, as well as through schools, community groups and amenity societies (more than a hundred at local and national levels). The many thousands of responses have come in all manner of forms – postcards, tapes of discussions, snapshots and family reminiscences, as well as long and detailed essays on the botanical folklore of individual parishes and individual species. We did not ask for biographical details, so there is no way of statistically breaking down the contributors into young or old, male or female, rural resident or urban newcomer. But on the surface there are no clear biases – except that many contributions came from people who found that talking about their experiences of familiar and commonplace plants enabled them to articulate their feelings about place and nature in general.

Geographically, there are slight biases. Contributions have arrived from all over England, Scotland and Wales, but are densest from areas which have both rich landscapes and a tradition of interest in natural and social history, e.g. Devon, the Welsh Marches, the Sussex Weald and east Suffolk. The big industrial cities are well represented, too, especially Glasgow, Liverpool, Sheffield and Bristol. The only significant gap occurs over central Scotland. There are explanations for this in the history of the region. The infamous Clearances and the long history of sheep and deer ranching impoverished much of the flora, and Presbyterianism frowned on the celebration of what was left. In parts of Scotland, even Christmas trees are still banned from primary schools.[7]

There seems to be little evidence of nationalism in our modern cultural attitudes to plants. What comes across time and time again is the overriding importance contributors attach to their neighbourhood, their local patch. Yet there are feelings shared across Britain which seem to be determined by the kind of place people live in, and sometimes there is more in common between a village in Scotland and a village in Norfolk than there is between two adjacent Welsh settlements. These have been among the most encouraging revelations of the project, echoing as they do the insistence of the 1991 Rio Earth Summit that the future of life on earth depends crucially on local understanding and action.

Many of our contributors would go further than this. For them, an intimate and equal relationship with nature is not so much a path to conservation as its goal. Local plants – which Ronald Blythe once described as 'a form of permanent geography'[8] – are markers not just of their landscapes, but of their autobiographies, as a contributor from Sussex demonstrates:
'Every year on Good Friday we would set off after lunch (boiled cod), each with our basket and a good stock of small balls of wool, for the woods, where we would sink down on the mossy grass and pick bunch after bunch of primroses to decorate the Priory Church on the next morning for Easter Sunday. If Easter was late the woods would be full of the sound of cuckoos and perhaps we might even see a swallow. We might come on a plant of stinking hellebore in the chalky soil but these were rare. White violets had their Special Places. The ones I remember best were at the base of the old flint walls round the churchyard or by the footpath to the Goodwood Dairy which we passed along weekly to fetch our two pounds of butter handed to us by the red-cheeked Mrs Miller, the Scottish dairymaid. Several miles of these walls had been built by prisoners from the Napoleonic Wars round parts of the Goodwood Estate. Purple violets were more common but no less cherished, and were followed a few weeks later by masses of pale mauve dog-violets. We did not find wild daffodils in Sussex, though my mother has once bicycled as far as West Dean Woods and seen them there (as I have in the last ten years). Years later, when our children were small and we lived at Bridport in Dorset, we would discover them in the fields near Powerstock and in the Marshwood Vale. The banks of the little Rivers Brit and Asker would be lined with snowdrops here in February, too, and that odd flower butterbur would appear in damp meadows.'[9]

Flora Britannica does not claim to be the last word on the current role of plants in British culture. My hope is that this concise edition (and the other volumes in the series, *Wild Herbs* and *Spring Flowers*), arranged according to some of the great themes of plant–human relationships, will trigger as many responses as it records.

A note on the text

The text includes species of ferns and flowering plants from England, Scotland and Wales. Ireland and the Channel Isles are not included. The species are to some extent self-selected by whether they have figured in local cultures and

Flora Britannica – high-summer flowers on a Dorset cliff.

whether contributors reported this. By British botanists' standards there is an inordinate number of introduced and naturalised species, which are often found more fascinating; but then these *started* with a cultural profile, often by already being in trade or in gardens.

Clive Stace's comprehensive *New Flora of the British Isles* has been invaluable. I have, for the most part, followed his nomenclature in both English and Latin, his ordering of families, and often, where there is doubt or disagreement, his verdicts on the status of species.

The vernacular names (indicated as 'VN') are all ones that were contributed to the project as being in current use, and they are usually printed in the spellings in which they were submitted. I have tried to eliminate obvious copying from previous printed sources, though there are inevitably some borderline cases. Except in special circumstances, I have not indicated particular areas where particular names prevail. The geographical mobility of contributors, who are often

writing from one place and remembering another, and the mobility of the names themselves through the mass media would have made this a misleading and potentially inaccurate qualification.

The notes from contributors are printed as they were sent in. Editing has been confined to selection of passages and occasional changes in spelling and punctuation to assist clarity. Editorial additions are indicated by square brackets. As many of the contributions were handwritten, I must apologise if I have made any errors in transcription either in the text itself or the names of contributors. If notified we will do everything we can to remedy such mistakes in any future editions.

Reference numbers refer to the Source Notes section. First-hand evidence is indicated by name, parish and county of the contributor. Book references appear in the notes under author and year of publication with full references being given in the Select Bibliography.

Children explore a fallen plane in Russell Square, London. The damage wrought by the 1987 storm awakened old affections for and new interests in trees.

Giant hogweed framing Ringwood church, Hampshire.

Local Names

Cheddar pink, safe from pickers, on a limestone outcrop in the Cheddar Gorge.

THE COMMON NAMES of wild plants are the fullest and most revealing register of the part they have played in our lives. Often they indicate aspects that have touched people's imaginations – a time of flowering perhaps, or a likeness, a use, a scent, an attachment to a particular habitat. So we have Lent lily (wild daffodil) and May-flower (hawthorn); lady's-slipper and foxglove; spindle and self-heal; wood anemones and field poppy. Beyond these is the great lexicon of purely local names. Some species have acquired more than a hundred over the centuries, an extraordinary testament to parish curiosity and inventiveness. Many of these vernacular names record quirks of local geography or custom, or how a particular dialect found its way around a more conventional naming. In South Devon for instance, furze was 'fuzz', wild plums 'bullums', and cleavers 'cliders'. One of the most impressive tallies is for cuckoo-pint or lords-and-ladies (*Arum maculatum*), for which Geoffrey Grigson records some 90 different local tags, all of which say something about the plant's history or associations.[1] Starch-wort, for example, recalls the era when the dried and ground-up tubers were used as a substitute for starch in laundries. The majority are some kind of comment on the appearance of the plant's flowering parts in spring: the long, dull purple or yellow spadix, partially cloaked by a pale green sheath. Many names – even cuckoo-pint itself (pint is short for pintle or penis) – are, perhaps not surprisingly, rather rude: dog's cock (Wiltshire) and priest's pilly (Westmorland), for instance. Others make more genteel reference to the contrasting form and colour of the two parts of the flower shoot, for example Jack in the pulpit (Cornwall) and sucky calves (Somerset). Cuckoo-flower (many locations) probably refers

Lords-and-ladies or cuckoo-pint has a host of other evocative common names.

to the time the flower-sheath appears, but may be another euphemistic dubbing and derive from *cucu*, Anglo-Saxon for 'quick' or 'lively'. The commonly used lords-and-ladies is probably a Victorian invention, coined as a polite alternative to this great catalogue of vulgarities.

But are all of them bookish names now? How many of these local terms actually survive in modern usage, in the regions that coined them? And where they do, are their origins and meanings understood?

Common ragwort, *Senecio jacobaea* (VN: St James' wort, Staggerwort, Stammerwort, Yellow tops, Stinking Willie, Mare's fart). Ragwort is regarded as the great enemy by those who keep horses, and summer weekends spent laboriously hand-pulling and removing the plants are a regular chore to check the plant's spread. Neither horses nor other grazing animals will normally eat the growing plant, unless it is so dense that it is difficult to graze without ingesting some, but they will when it has died and dried out. Green or dry, it causes insidious and irreversible cirrhosis of the liver.[2] A Ministry of Agriculture adviser has seen its effects at close quarters: 'The plant is responsible for half the cases of stock poisoning in Britain. It is susceptible to spraying and cutting, but when wilting or distorted by the spray, cattle will eat it with fatal results. But sheep can consume small quantities of the mature plant with impunity and apparent relish. Coming to this area [Montgomeryshire] of few cattle and thousands of sheep I was impressed by the total absence of ragwort except in those places inaccessible to grazing sheep. By contrast, in North Staffs, a dairy farming area with few sheep, ragwort posed the principal weed problem, many fields being heavily infested.'[3]

The still-used local names of mare's fart in adjacent North Shropshire and Cheshire and of stinking Willie in Scotland suggest how loathed the malodorous foliage is by cattle farmers.[4] Ironically, paddocks and pastures full of the golden flowers, with swallows dipping amongst the ragged-edged leaves, are one of the most beautiful sights of high summer and have become more common with the spread of set-aside schemes on arable land. It is no real surprise that, as the farming writer Robin Page reported, at least one farmer found a more positive way of dealing with ragwort in the hot summer of 1993: 'I have discovered a farmer in the West Country who has solved his ragwort problems. He has been picking it and selling it in his farm-shop as "summer gold". The townies love it. Can you imagine visiting a flat in Birmingham and seeing a tasteful vase of ragwort on the sideboard – bought here for a very modest price. He surely deserves a diversification award.'[5]

It is not such a preposterous idea. John Clare, very familiar with the tribulations weeds caused to farmers, could also see the beauty of 'summer gold':

Ragwort thou humble flower with tattered
leaves
I love to see thee come & litter gold ...
Thy waste of shining blossoms richly shields
The sun tanned sward in splendid hues that
burn
So bright & glaring that the very light
Of the rich sunshine doth to paleness turn
& seems but very shadows in thy sight
(c. 1831)[6]

In the Isle of Man, ragwort is called 'Cushag' and is the national flower, though its ambivalent reputation in the countryside is reflected in the fact that it is also used as a satirical emblem: 'Among the many Manx exiles living in America and elsewhere there was an expression used to curb over-enthusiastic and nostalgic praise of the "li'l island": "We know – Ta airh er ny Cushaghyn er shen" (There's gold on the Cushags there).'[7]

Oxford ragwort, *S. squalidus*. Although it is now the most abundant ragwort in most British cities, this south European species has a fair claim to its Oxford title. A plant (reputedly gathered from the volcanic rocks of Mount Etna) was certainly growing in the University Botanic Garden in the eighteenth century, and was noticed there by Sir Joseph Banks in the 1770s. Linnaeus is believed to have described and named the species from specimens sent to him from Oxford.[8] But by the turn of the century its downy seeds had wafted out of the Garden and begun to colonise the city's old walls. By the 1830s it had arrived at Oxford Railway Station, and from there it set off down the Great Western Railway. It found the granite chips and clinker of the permanent way a congenial substitute for its natural dry habitats in the southern European mountains, and by the end of the nineteenth century it was well established in many southern English counties. The slipstream of trains seemed to help the seeds on their way. George Claridge Druce described a

journey he took with some of them, which floated into his carriage at Oxford and out again at Tilehurst, in Berkshire.[9] Now it is distributed over almost the whole of England and Wales, even down to the tip of Cornwall: 'Oxford ragwort has long since reached the end of the [old] GWR line, growing all along the track on the last couple of miles to Penzance.'[10]

Yet it has remained very much an urban plant, sticking close to railways, factory walls, motorway verges, building sites and car parks, and rarely invading village walls, for instance, or grasslands where common ragwort grows; for example, in Herefordshire: 'The main railway line runs from Abergavenny to Hereford and any ragwort growing on waste ground within a quarter of a mile on each side of the track is usually Oxford ragwort. Further afield it is common ragwort.'[11]

Perhaps this taste in habitats lay behind the specific scientific name *squalidus*, for the plant

Oxford ragwort, putting on a show in its own city.

itself is anything but squalid. It is smaller and more compact than common ragwort and brightens all the wastelands it graces, especially in the company (as it so often is) of rosebay willowherb.

London ragwort, *S. × subnebrodensis*, is a hybrid between Oxford ragwort and sticky groundsel (below) which crops up occasionally on wasteland in the south-east. J. E. Lousley first discovered it in London in 1944, when he named it *S. × londinensis*.[12] **Sticky groundsel**, *S. viscosus*, is a similar plant to common groundsel, but unpleasant-smelling and covered with very sticky hairs. It may be native on sandy and gravelly soils. (John Ray first recorded it in Britain in 1660 as plentiful in the Isle of Ely.)[13] But in this century it has behaved very like an alien, spreading rapidly across the country in a similar pattern – and into similar wasteland habitats – to Oxford ragwort.

Corn marigold or **Gold**, *Chrysanthemum segetum* (VN: Dunwich Buddle, Johnny Buddle). It is ironic that for centuries corn marigold was commonly named after the most precious of metals at the same time as being regarded as one of the most noxious of cornfield weeds. In the twelfth century, Henry II issued an ordinance against 'Guilde Weed', which was probably the earliest enactment requiring the destruction of a weed. In *A Boke of Husbandry*, 1523, John Fitzherbert included 'Gouldes' in his blacklist of plants that 'doe moche harme'. A few parishes in arable England – Golder, Oxfordshire, Goldhanger, Essex, and Goltho, Lincolnshire – may even have been named after it.[14] (It is also tempting to wonder if the still-used East Anglian names of 'Boodle' and 'Buddle' have any connection with the slang word for money or burgled jewellery.)

In the late nineteenth century, when bright colours came into vogue, corn marigolds became briefly fashionable for table decoration. Matthew Arnold wrote to his sister in 1883: 'I thought of

Corn marigold, an arable weed which is recovering in some areas. The Black Isle, Scotland.

you in passing through a cleared cornfield full of marigolds. I send you one of them. Nelly gathered a handful, and they are very effective in a vase in the drawing-room.'[15]

Gold was common on light soils throughout Britain until after the war. A Welsh farmer remembers: 'teams of women in the fields towards Hereford with special long-handled tools with a sort of fork on the end, walking along the rows of corn and hooking out "the yeller daisies". They are a more disliked weed because they don't dry out easily and tend to rot the straw in the bales.'[16]

Between the 1950s and 80s corn marigold retreated in the face of modern weedkillers. But, more recently, set-aside policies and reduced spraying on field edges have resulted in some localised resurgence, often from long-dormant seed, as in Corby Hill, Cumbria: 'In 1983 there was an explosion of corn marigold growing in short barley in a field near my home. How long the seeds have remained dormant, God only knows, as I have not seen this before during my lifetime – 59 years.'[17]

It has been most successful in the sandy soils of East Anglia, by Sizewell B nuclear power station for instance: 'The rough verges on the side of the road were bright with corn marigolds,

Butterbur by a Peak District river. The pale flower-spikes, which appear before the leaves, were once known as 'early mushrooms'.

right up to the power-station fence. How's that for ancient and modern?'[18]

Butterbur, *Petasites hybridus* (VN: Wild rhubarb, Butcher's rhubarb). The huge rhubarb-like leaves of butterbur really were used for wrapping butter in the days before refrigeration. Handle a leaf and you will understand why. It is not only large and pliable enough to fold without breaking, and thick enough to cushion butter from bruising and soak up any seepage, but actually feels cool to the touch because of the soft grey down on the underside. It can still make a serviceable wrapping for picnic left-overs or a cache of wild berries.

But butterbur leaves are most often used today as umbrellas or sunshades – as their scientific name suggests: *Petasites* derives from the Greek *petasos*, meaning a broad-brimmed felt hat. Gerard agreed that the leaves were 'of such a widenesse, as that of it selfe it is bigge and large inough to keepe a mans head from raine, and from the heate of the sunne'.[19]

By the River Dove in Derbyshire I have seen quite young children spontaneously picking butterbur leaves to protect themselves from a summer downpour, as have contributors in many parts of the country.[20] One botanist's grandchildren regularly dress up entirely in butterbur leaves when playing in their hop-vine wigwams.[21]

Like colt's-foot, butterbur's flowers appear before its leaves, often as early as February. When they first push through the soil the spikes look sufficiently like flushed button mushrooms to have earned the now obsolete country name of 'early mushrooms'. When fully emerged, the tassled blooms give the flower-spike the look of a dwarf pink conifer. Butterbur is a species of stream-banks and damp waysides almost throughout Britain, and is evocative of shady places by water in high summer: 'There is a fine patch of [butterbur] along the River Lea near Hertford. I identified it as a child (as so much else) from Brooke Bond tea-cards. I find it often grows in a haunting situation.'[22]

Lords-and-ladies, *Arum maculatum* (VN: Cuckoo-pint, Cuckoo flower, Jack in the pulpit, Parson in the pulpit, Devils and angels, Red-hot-poker, Willy lily, Snake's meat, Cows and bulls). As I discuss in the introduction to this chapter, the bizarre form of this abundant plant of woods and hedgerows (the shiny arrow-shaped leaves, often speckled with black, and the pale green sheath, sometimes streaked with purple, hooding the purple or yellow spadix, which eventually produces a spike of bright orange berries) has generated a huge number of imaginative local names over the centuries. A few (see above) still survive, and there are even some new coinings. 'Willy lily' is as splendidly ribald as anything from the first Elizabethan era; and one family's tag, 'soldier in a sentry box',[23] catches the

Lords-and-ladies or cuckoo-pint, a very common species.

sheathed effect of the flower structure as well as any of the traditional names. There are new interpretations of old names, too:

'I am surprised by the suggestion that Lords and Ladies is a polite Victorian convention. It seems more likely to me that it is a bit of downstairs vulgarity in the ancient tradition, i.e. "The Lord's and the Lady's".'[24]

'I understood the [common] name went back further to the days of powder and patch, when Lords and Ladies sported "beauty spots", sometimes to be seen on the leaves of the wild arum.'[25]

'My father used to pronounce "pint" to rhyme with mint, not with pint as in pint of milk. Maybe

an abbreviation of pintle [slang for penis].'[26]

But, for all its bawdy associations, the plant itself is a handsome and modest one, pale and sculptural in the spring. There is a fifteenth-century carving of it in berry in Westminster Abbey, and an exceptional representation on a choir-stall in St Paul's Church at Four Elms in Kent, done by Evelyn Chambers of the Art Workers' Guild in about 1917.[27] And, perhaps with unintentional irony, wild arum is still used instead of its extravagant cousin, altar-lily, at Methodist funeral services in some Cornish communities.[28]

It was also associated with St Withburga in Cambridgeshire:

Bog asphodel in the New Forest.

'Old Fenmen in the last century … held the traditional belief that when the nuns came over from Normandy to build a convent at Thetford in Norfolk they brought with them the wild arum or cuckoo-pint. When the monks of Ely stole the body of St Withburga from East Dereham and paused, on their way back, to rest at Brandon, tradition has it that the nuns of Thetford came down to the riverside and covered the saint's body with the flowers. During the long journey down the Little Ouse of the barge bearing St Withburga several of the lily flowers fell into the river, where they threw out roots. Within an hour they had covered all the banks as far as Ely with a carpet of blooms, and more remarkable still, these flowers glowed radiantly at night … The pollen of the flowers does, in fact, throw off a faint light at dusk and when the Irish labourers came in large numbers to find work on the Fens during the famines in their own country during the last century, they named the lilies Fairy Lamps. The Fen lightermen had long called them Shiners.'[29]

The baked and ground roots of lords-and-ladies were once in demand as a home-grown substitute for arrowroot (normally from the West Indian species *Maranta arundinacea*), under the name of Portland sago. But the resulting gruel tended to be bitter, and the crushed roots were more often employed as a domestic starch (especially for ruffs), though they often produced severe blistering of the launderers' hands.

Bog asphodel, *Narthecium ossifragum*. The yellow star-flowers of bog asphodel, ranged in short spikes on leafless stems, are often the brightest flecks of colour on peat-bogs and damp heaths. In autumn the whole plant turns tawny and can colour large patches of valley bog in places such as the New Forest. At one time it was regarded as a true, miniature asphodel, a lily of the field, and early botanical names were *Asphodelus luteus* and *A. Lancastriae*.

The modern scientific name *ossifragum* – bone-breaker – is more down-to-earth. It derives from the belief that grazing the plant made the bones of sheep brittle – though it was not bog asphodel that caused this, but the sour, calcium-

Plymouth pear, confined to the outskirts of the city and to a few hedges over the Cornish border.

poor pastures in which it occurs. It is confined to such habitats and is a species chiefly of western and northern Britain, where it was occasionally used as a substitute for saffron and as a yellow hair-dye. There are colonies on the wet heaths of west Norfolk and south-east England, especially Sussex, Surrey and Hampshire, but bog asphodel is declining throughout the lowlands as wetlands are drained.

'Plants, places and names'. Plants often derive their names from close association with a particular place. It may be the place where the species was first discovered, or first named, or to which it is exclusively confined. Oxford ragwort grows all over Britain now, but it began its spread from the Oxford Botanic Garden. Bath asparagus was sold in Bath, as well as growing chiefly in woods within a 20-mile radius of the city. Plymouth pear has been known in hedges near Plymouth since 1870 but was found near Truro in 1989. Tunbridge filmy-fern still grows near Tunbridge Wells, though its distribution in the British Isles is mainly western. The endemic Arran service-tree and Lundy cabbage are still confined to the islands commemorated in their names. Cheddar pink, though it is quite common further south in Europe, in Britain grows wild only in the Cheddar Gorge. There is even a 'Rottingdean sea-

Tunbridge filmy-fern – first named at Tunbridge Wells, Kent, but also found in several areas of western Britain.

But it is dangerous to assume that a place-name component which resembles the name of a plant necessarily derives from one. Buckhurst, Essex, is a 'beech-wooded hill', but Buckingham is 'river-bend land held by Bucca's people'. Holmstone Beach, Kent, is named from the Old English *holm*, meaning holly; but Holme in Huntingdonshire is from the Old Norse *holm*, meaning 'island' or 'raised ground in a marsh'. It is always essential to trace the name back step by step to its first use and spelling to be sure of its origins and meaning.[30]

Plants also appear frequently in field and street names. The latter are only occasionally named after genuine botanical residents; the former almost invariably were. Some straightforward Oxfordshire field names are Primrose Shaw, Thistle Field, Broom Hill, Hazeley Mead, Blewbottle Coppice (after an old name for the cornflower) and Gorsty Mead; more obscure are Chesscroft ('chess' is an old Oxfordshire name for the grass *Bromus secalinus*, which grows amongst wheat) and Guldfurlong, named after another arable weed – the corn marigold.[31]

Caroline Giddens, of the Exmoor Natural History Society, drawing in part on N. V. Allen's work, has compiled a list of botanically influ-

lavender', a plant from Sicily naturalised on the cliffs of the Sussex seaside town.

Conversely, places are frequently named after the plants that grow there: odd and noticeable plants (such as box); abundant plants (such as beech and fern); economically useful plants (such as cress, as in Kersey, Suffolk); and old, isolated and conspicuous oaks, thorns and pear-trees.

Cheddar pink. In Britain it is found only on a few cliffs in the Cheddar Gorge, Somerset.

enced Exmoor place names. Here is her selection of names based on shrubs and smaller plants: 'Brompton Regis in the Domesday Book is Brunetone and Gerard said "the country hereabout is strewn with Broom". I should think this meant gorse (*Ulex* spp.) rather than broom (*Cytisus scoparius*). We also have Broomstreet. Gorse here is locally known as furze, which gave rise to Furzebury Brake and Furzehill Common, which was Furshulle in 1270. Most hill farms have their furze brake, i.e. gorse-covered hill.

The blackberries give us Bramblecombe and Brimblecombe, and Brendon comes from Bramble Hill.

Ferny Ball is a bracken-covered hill to this day, and Ivystone Rock is an ivy-covered promontory into the Bristol Channel.

Billbrook, a village with the longest ford in England, derives its name from bilders, an old name for water-cress.

It is thought that an area named Cowlings derives from ling fields for cattle – the area was heather-covered until enclosed in the nineteenth century.

Cuckolds Combe is interesting, cuckold being an old name for burdock, and Riscombe means rushy combe, from the Old English *rysc*, meaning rushes.

Nettlecombe is obvious, as is Snowdrop Valley [see p. 138], which is still visited in spring for its carpets of white flowers.'[32]

Cheddar pink, *Dianthus gratianopolitanus*, is in Britain confined to limestone ledges in and near the Cheddar Gorge. The Cheddar pink is an exceptionally attractive plant – tufted, grey-leaved, topped with rose-coloured, clove-scented flowers – and, after its discovery in the early eighteenth century, it became as famous as Cheddar cheese. It was dug up by tourists and locals alike, transplanted to rockeries, sold to alpine plant merchants. By the late nineteenth century, some guidebooks to the Mendips were declaring it extinct. But the plant clung on in the more inaccessible corners and crevices in the Gorge, and it is now thoroughly protected. It can nor-

Spiked star-of-Bethlehem in its heartland in Wiltshire. The young shoots were sold as 'Bath asparagus'.

mally be seen through field-glasses, and, for those who strike up a fancy for it in their alpine gardens, there is a range of cultivated varieties on the market.

Spiked star-of-Bethlehem or **Bath asparagus**, *Ornithogalum pyrenaicum*. Bath asparagus earned its commoner name in the most straightforward of ways. Its young, unopened flower-spikes were gathered from the wild in May and sold in the markets of Bath, for cooking as asparagus. Bath is close to the centre of its distribution in Britain, which is concentrated in the counties of Avon and Wiltshire (though small colonies occur in some other localities, including Bedfordshire). In the Avon Valley, especially, and on the Bradford-on-Avon plain, it occurs in almost every hedge-bank, green lane and copse. In ancient woodland, it can be as abundant as the bluebell, and in this habitat has all the appearance of a long-established native.

Yet its somewhat odd distribution (it is happiest and most widespread in the Mediterranean region) has raised the possibility that it is an introduction. David Green has speculated that its abundance around Bath may be a legacy of the Roman occupation of this area: 'I wonder whether the bulb of *O. pyrenaicum* arrived via the earth ball of a Roman vine, or whether it was deliberately introduced for its own culinary value.'[33]

But its tall spikes of greenish-yellow flowers are a handsome and distinctive feature of the limestone countryside around Bath and look thoroughly native. It is good that commercial picking of the shoots ended some years ago – though good, too, that the tradition of eating the shoots is kept up by a few locals.

Summer snowflake, *Leucojum aestivum* (VN: Loddon lily, Snowflakes). As with the fritillary, there has been a lingering suspicion as to why this exquisite and conspicuous lily should have remained apparently 'undiscovered' until the late eighteenth century. It is two or three feet tall, with gracious sprays of iris-like leaves and clusters of white bell-flowers as big as acorn-cups. They hang at the end of long stalks, each petal daubed with an emerald beauty-spot near the tip. When the flowers nod towards you in the breeze, you catch a flash of gold from the stamens. In its favoured habitats it grows in great, sweeping

Summer snowflakes – Loddon lilies – in Berkshire.

beds. And Gerard, writing at the end of the sixteenth century, remarked: 'These plants do grow wilde in Italy and the places adiacent, notwithstanding our London gardens haue taken possession of them all, many yeeres past.'[34] Not a plant, in short, that was likely to be overlooked.

Yet it was not until the 1780s that William Curtis found the first wild colony, 'betwixt *Greenwich* and *Woolwich* ... close by the Thames side, just above high water mark, growing ... where no garden, in all probability, could ever have existed'. He went on to ask how 'so ornamental a plant, growing in so public a place, could have escaped the prying eyes of the many Botanists who have resided in London for such a length of time'.[35] A fair question, to which Geoffrey Grigson (though not Curtis himself) responded with a resounding 'Impossible', suggesting instead that the seeds had floated down-river from gardens – presumably in the snowflake's current heartland beside the tributaries of the Thames in Oxfordshire, Berkshire and Wiltshire.

Yet in these places it grows in identical situations to those of indisputably wild populations on the continent, in winter-flooded, wooded swamps. To see the plant *en masse* in damp willow carr by the River Loddon in Berkshire, or the Wiltshire Avon, north of Salisbury, is to be both strongly persuaded of its native status and to understand why early botanists might have missed it in the wild. By the Loddon south of Twyford, for instance, the isolated clumps at the corners of riverside gardens have all the look of escapes, quite possibly the Mediterranean variety (ssp. *pulchellum*) favoured by gardeners. Then, south of Sandford Mill, the river-edge grows wilder. There are bigger, taller stands of snowflake growing amongst marsh marigolds under the trees. Follow their trail through the dark alders and nettles, and you enter a quite different habitat, a shifting, humid swamp, caked with a flood-wrack of willow branches and leaf litter. And amongst this debris are sheaves upon sheaves of snowflake, in patches sometimes hundreds of yards square. It is an astonishing sight, but an inhospitable place and not one likely to

tempt an early botanist in a wet April.

At the close of the nineteenth century George Claridge Druce noted that summer snowflakes were used for decorating the altar in Wargrave Church, Berkshire, and that 'large quantities from Shillingford have been sold in the Oxford streets recently'.[36] In Long Wittenham, Oxfordshire, they were anciently included in May Garlands (perhaps circumstantial evidence of their being indigenous in the Upper Thames region): 'The ceremony of crowning the May Queen, which includes a parade through the village in period costume and maypole dancing, was revived in 1968. The posies carried are mainly of wild flowers, and by custom they included Loddon lilies. They are known locally as snowflakes.'[37]

Summer snowflake, an exquisite flower, yet not 'discovered' in the wild until the late eighteenth century.

Plants as Emblems

PLANTS DO NOT just figure in place names; they can form strong associations with places. Sherwood Forest is known for its oaks, the Cotswolds and Chilterns for their beeches, Dymock in Gloucestershire for its wild daffodils. Beyond these specific links, plants can be more general indicators – familiars, if you like – of particular habitats. Bluebell is the classic species of old woodland, heather of moorland and old-man's-beard the most conspicuous plant of chalk country. Geoffrey Grigson once proposed that each English county should have its own emblematic flower and suggested meadow crane's-bill for Wiltshire and bird's-eye primrose for Yorkshire. His criteria were simply that the plants should be locally abundant or frequent and showy, ('Cornish moneywort would not do for Cornwall.')[1]

More parochially, plants have been adopted as emblems of villages, schools, football clubs and individual families. Plants also form associations with seasons or moments of the year – the primrose with Easter, dog-rose with midsummer, holly and mistletoe with Christmas. The corn poppy conjures up two moments – high summer in arable country and then November, when imitation poppies are worn in remembrance of the dead in two world wars.

Field poppies, east Suffolk, now largely confined to the edges of fields.

Ferns are evocative plants, redolent of landscapes of humidity and shade. They conjure up dappled woodland, West Country lanes, old stone walls, even Victorian grottoes. This isn't just romantic fancy. Ferns prosper in moist conditions and reproduce not by seed but by minute spores, which need damp for successful fertilisation.

Their aesthetic and ecological associations mean that ferns have had more than their share of tribulations over the past two centuries. In the Victorian era there was a fashion for collecting them, for the purpose of pressing, producing spore-prints, or especially for 'growing on' in the miniature indoor glasshouses known as 'Wardian cases'. The scale and effects of the 'Victorian Fern Craze' have been graphically documented by David Elliston Allen.[2] Yet, despite the plunder, it is doubtful if any species was made even locally extinct. In fact a number of ferns from rocky places in the north and west have actually expanded their range over the past few centuries, by taking to substitute habitats, particularly walls and the sheltered stonework of old buildings.

But such places are no longer the refuges they once were. The passing of steam has dried out railway cuttings and tunnels. Central heating is doing the same to houses and factories. And everywhere, walls are subject to repointing,

A screen from Wallington: ferns, including royal fern, by Pauline Trevelyan (and grasses and cornflower by John Ruskin).

A depiction of moonwort on a canvas-work panel in Hardwick Hall, Derbyshire.

weatherproofing and the eradication of hapless plants of any group.

Adder's-tongue, *Ophioglossum vulgatum*, and its relative **moonwort**, *Botrychium lunaria*, are small, scarce ferns of old grassland whose oddity of appearance once made them much in demand by herbalists. They are still special and mysterious plants to discover, barely standing clear of the late spring grass.

Adder's-tongue is the more southerly species. One single short frond grows each year, which divides to form an oval 'leaf' encasing a tongue-like spike (which carries the spore-cases) in something of the manner of lords-and-ladies (see p. 21). In the days of sympathetic magic it was believed to be a cure for snake-bite.

Moonwort is a plant chiefly of dry upland pastures and rock ledges in north and west Britain. Its 'leaf' is fringed with half-moons. It was once believed to be capable of opening locks and unshoeing horses. The seventeenth-century herbalist and astrologer Nicholas Culpeper passed on a Civil War legend about its power: 'On the White Down in Devonshire, near Tiverton, there was found thirty Horse-shoes pulled off from the Feet of the Earl of Essex his Horses, being there drawn up into a body, many of them newly shod, and no reason known, which caused much admiration … and the herb usually grows upon Heaths.'[3]

Royal fern, *Osmunda regalis*. A fern which merits its name, growing occasionally up to 10 feet tall, with fronds that are cut into broad and elegant leaflets. It is a species of fens and wet woods, and was one of the most frequently plundered by Victorian collectors. It is now making something of a comeback, in the West Country at least, by escaping from the ornamental lakes and shrubberies where it was introduced a century or so ago, and recolonising woods and riverbanks. It is also plentiful in the fens around the Norfolk Broads. An unusual site (1991) was in a crack about seven feet up in a high retaining wall in central Lancaster.[4]

Tunbridge filmy-fern, *Hymenophyllum tunbrigense*, is a delicate, almost translucent species found on damp rock-faces and tree-trunks in shady coombes in western Britain. It was first discovered, outside its main range, near Tunbridge Wells in Kent, in 1696. It is still to be found in the village of Eridge, two miles outside the town (though also over the county border, in Sussex). **Polypody**, *Polypodium vulgare*, is named from the numerous foot-like divisions of its root system. It is typically found growing on the trunks and branches of trees, and is one of those species which helps give an ancient forest feel to the banked and wooded landscapes of the west and north. It is only scattered in middle England. As a native, **maidenhair fern**, *Adiantum capillus-veneris*, is a rare plant of sheltered limestone cliffs near the sea, in west and south-west Britain (excluding Scotland). It has beautiful fan-shaped leaflets on wiry stalks, which rather fancifully suggested female pubic hair to those who named the plant. In the nineteenth century it formed the basis of *capillaire*, a flavouring made by simmering the fronds in water for many hours.

Bracken, *Pteridium aquilinum* (VN: Fern). Like all abundant and aggressive plants, bracken has an ambivalent image. Stock farmers resent the way it can take over and sterilise good grazing land. Many naturalists regard it as dull and oppressive, inimical to other species. Yet for those who have lived in brackeny places, its

Polypody, often found growing on the trunks of older trees.

sharp almond scent and the first splashes of yellow on its fronds in autumn can evoke powerful feelings: 'There is a sprig of bracken in the final journal of my late father. To him bracken encapsulated the essence of the countryside. On every walk he went through the same ritual – he would push finger and thumb up the stem of a bracken frond, crush the leaves and inhale the released fragrance … It evoked for him memories of his first holiday spent by the River Severn. He and his friends slept on the floor of a wooden hut strewn with bracken, listening to the nightingale, wishing he hadn't got to go back to the industrial town of Smethwick.'[5]

Bracken – abundant, durable, versatile and free – has provided many people, from town and country alike, with some of their first *physical* engagements with nature:

'Bracken fronds we plaited, folding mini-leaflets over each other until a strong straight strip design was formed.'[6]

'Another frustrating task [during a childhood in the Lake District] was the making of bracken sandals. Plaits of fern or bracken are, of course, easily made. But joining them together to form soles, using grass or rushes as threads, is more difficult. Sometimes we managed this, but the cool footwear this produced was not very durable.'[7]

'Ideal for thatching a bivouac, if the fronds are laid like tiles on a roof. Has kept generations of tentless scouts warm and dry overnight in bad weather.'[8]

But bracken has also played a more serious role in the rural economy. It has been used for manuring and covering potato beds, for dressing chamois and kid leather, and as fuel and tinder. ('Dead bracken shoved up the chimney and ignited, sets light to the soot and saves bothering with sweeps.')[9] In eighteenth-century Scotland, the naturalist John Lightfoot reported, 'the inhabitants mow it green, and, burning it to ashes, make those ashes up into balls with a little

Bracken taking on its autumn colours on a Chiltern common.

water, which they dry in the sun, and make use of them to wash their linen instead of soap. In many of the western isles the people gain a considerable profit from the sale of the ashes to soap and glass makers.'[10] In the Highlands in the late nineteenth century there were experiments in making bracken silage. Stock ate it greedily, without any apparent ill effects, but the practice never caught on.[11]

Chiefly, though, it was a universal packing and padding stuff. It provided winter bedding for cattle, a cool lining for baskets of fruit and fish, and cushioning for the transport of slate and earthenware.

A glimpse of just how important bracken was in local economies is given by an order made in 1764 for the conservation of fern on Berkhamsted Common in Hertfordshire: 'No person whatsoever shall cut or cause to be cut any fern on the common called Berkhamsted Common from the first day of June until the first day of September yearly under pain of forfeiting and paying for every offence the sum of forty shillings.' (Local legend has it that bracken-cutters used to line up on the common, waiting for midnight to chime from the Parish Church and then staking out their patches, like gold prospectors.) This was not an order imposed by the Lord of the Manor; it was an act of self-regulation drawn up by the commoners themselves, to prevent damage to the recuperative powers of the bracken, and to increase the value of their rights in the future.[12]

Most of these traditional uses became obsolete with the invention of the pneumatic tyre, and later with the development of modern packaging techniques. But farm animals are, here and there, still bedded on bracken, along the Welsh borders for instance. 'I have seen it cut and baled on Titterstone Clee, in Shropshire. I have used it myself instead of straw in my chicken run.'[13] In the Yorkshire Dales the cut fern was 'loaded on a wooden sledge and slid down the fell with the aid of a horse'.[14] In the Forest of Dean one smallholder cuts it for garden mulch: 'I have about one and a half acres of the stuff, some of which I make use of: it is an excellent bedding for the

donkey throughout the winter. The soiled bedding, stacked until the spring, is then useful as a mulch around the garden. I also regularly cut fronds in the early autumn. Spread around loosely, about nine inches deep, they make a very effective weed-suppressing mulch.'[15]

But in most areas these practices have died out. And where bracken is no longer needed, it is no longer cut and begins to spread remorselessly. It is reckoned that, by 1990, the extent of bracken cover in Britain was between 1.2 and 2.7 per cent of the total land surface, and maybe up to 15 per cent in areas of rough upland grazing in northern England.[16] This has meant an increase in the incidence of bracken-grazing by animals, in Gwent for instance: 'Bracken is not eaten much by animals, but in recent dry summers when the grass has dried up so much [1993], there has been little else to eat.'[17] The grazing of bracken is not a trivial matter, as it is toxic to all animals, causing serious changes in the composition of the blood. It has also been suspected recently of being carcinogenic in humans if eaten to excess (the young shoots are used as food in the Far East) and even from continued inhalation of the spores.

Despite these problems, bracken is still not regarded as an entirely verminous plant. It has an honourable place on the badges of the Robertson and Chisholm clans, and is figured as one of the defining plants of Ashdown Forest on an embroidered kneeler in Nutley Church, Sussex.[18] Enormous fronds are still measured (13 feet being recorded in Savernake Forest, Wiltshire),[19] and everywhere people still welcome the exquisite young 'fiddleheads' in May and the paperlacework of fading gold fronds in autumn, picked out by the first air-frosts.

Many of the more familiar wall-ferns belong to the spleenwort family, *Aspleniaceae*. Their native homes are amongst rocks in the high rainfall areas of the west and north. But there have been colonies on old stonework, particularly churches, since botanical records began. And the coming of the railways provided more opportunities for spread. The railway system supplied (and still does to some extent) a range of damp, sheltered habitats for ferns to colonise and a means for ferrying their lightweight spores about. Max Walters, Director of the University Botanic Garden at Cambridge until 1983, has compared how ferns have adapted to church and railway habitats – he calls the two life-styles 'ecclesiastic' and 'ferroviatic' – in the dry, windswept flats of what is probably the least congenial county for ferns in England.

At Old North Road Station, on the disused Cambridge–Bedford line, he discovered (in 1968) a dark fern 'cave' under one of the platforms, where there were plants of **wall-rue**, *Asplenium ruta-muraria*, and 'the largest **Hart's-tongue** (*Phyllitis scolopendrium*) which I have seen in Cambridgeshire'. More remarkable was the appearance of the first recorded colony in the county of **brittle bladder-fern**, *Cystopteris fragilis*, which is entirely dependent on artificial habitats outside its natural range, mainly in the limestone uplands. From about 1920 till 1953 this same platform was also home to one of the very few colonies of maidenhair fern (see above) in inland Britain. 'In Cambridgeshire,' writes Dr Walters, 'the most "continental" part of Britain, a shaded overhang or pit can provide a higher humidity, which may crucially determine the ability of ferns to thrive there.' In more open railside locations, there is **black spleenwort**, *A. adiantum-nigrum*. Of the ten new Cambridgeshire records since 1860 (before which it was found almost exclusively on churches) four were on railway walls, including the one separating Cambridge Station Goods Yard from the Cattle Market.[20]

This is by no means the end of the story of Cambridge's spleenwort familiars. The most celebrated fern patch in the city is an ancient colony of wall-rue on the steps of the Senate House, exactly where it was first recorded by Charles Babington in 1860.[21] (Oxford's more mundane, but far more out-of-place, academic fern is the bracken that grows in small embattled patches around the ancient walls of the Bodleian Library and Sheldonian Theatre.)

Most of these species can be found in similar situations elsewhere in lowland Britain. (And they grow in artificial habitats in the west and

Hard shield-fern, growing in a limestone gryke at Gait Barrows, Lancashire.

north, too. Charles Kingsley's daughter, Charlotte Chanter, reckoned the most luxuriant wall-rue she ever saw was 'growing inside the tower of Morwinstowe Church' in Cornwall.)[22] With them may be **maidenhair spleenwort**, *A. trichomanes*, and **rustyback**, *Ceterach officinarum*, so called from the dense, rust-coloured, almost felt-like layer of scales on the underside of the fronds.

Species from the buckler-fern family, *Dryopteridaceae*, are the main contributors to the texture of the woodland vegetation in May and June, after the spring flowers have gone.

Hard and **soft shield-ferns** (*Polystichum aculeatum* and *P. setiferum*) are named from the shape of the spore-cases on the underside of the fronds. The soft shield-fern is one of the most 'sportive' species, and more than sixty sports or varieties were found in the wild and taken into gardens in Victorian times. Many are still in cultivation. In the variety *cristatum*, the tips of the fronds subdivide into tassels or crests; in *decompositum* the leaflets are cut down to the midrib; *abruptum* is remarkable for the way the branches are cut short; *biserratum* has large, broad leaflets; and *proliferum* bears miniature fernlets at the angles formed by the branches with the midrib. 'The handsomest of all,' according to one Victorian guidebook, 'is undoubtedly *plumosum*, in which the fronds will reach nine inches in width and nearly three feet in length. It has a spreading, plume-like habit, but is unfortunately a gem which is "rare" as well as "rich".'[23]

Martin Rickard has traced the origin of this last sport and argues that the collecting fad was not entirely harmful. Without it, many remarkable varieties would have gone unnoticed and would quite likely have quickly disappeared,

never to be seen again either in gardens or in the wild. 'Plumosum Bevis', for example, 'is sterile in most seasons, and it was not until several years after its discovery in 1876 that any sporangia were noticed. The few spores produced subsequently gave rise to some of the most wonderful hardy British ferns in cultivation today: these are 'Plumosum Drueryi', 'Gracillimum' and the cream of the crop, 'Plumosum Green'. Yet the parent of these marvellous plants was only ever found once, in a lane bank at Hawkchurch on the Devon/Dorset border. It was discovered by a labourer, Jon Bevis, who recognised it as different and pulled it from the hedge and delivered it to a local fern enthusiast, a Dr Wills. Would that hedge-bank and that fern still be there today? Possibly, but I doubt it.'[24]

Broad or **common buckler-fern**, *Dryopteris dilatata*, and **male-fern**, *D. filix-mas*, are the most common and widespread woodland species. The latter's closest relative (with which it often

Maidenhair spleenwort is quite common on old walls.

hybridises), **scaly** (or **golden-scaled**) **male-fern**, *D. affinis*, has splendid, shiny ginger scales up its main stems. **Lady-fern**, *Athyrium filix-femina*, is in fact from a different family, but was named in contrast to the male-fern because of its greater elegance and delicacy. It is another 'sportive' species, with some 60 to 70 varieties discovered by the end of the nineteenth century. The first, 'Kalothrix' ('beautiful hair'), was found in the mountains of Mourne at the end of the seventeenth century by Sherard.[25]

Lady-fern prefers slightly more acid soils than the male-fern, but Walter Scott's rhapsodic description of its haunts could apply to the whole fern tribe:

> *Where the copse-wood is the greenest,*
> *Where the fountain glistens sheenest,*
> *Where the morning lies the longest,*
> *There the lady-fern grows strongest.*[26]

Common poppy, *Papaver rhoeas* (VN: Corn-poppy, Field poppy). Feelings about the meaning of plants can run deep, in many ways. Once, writing about the persistence of plant symbolism, I mentioned that the red poppy, which we wear on Remembrance Day, had been 'an emblem of blood and new life since the Egyptians'.[27] A few days later I received a letter from a London man who had lost two cousins in the First World War and who thought it strange that I 'should apparently be unaware of the English habit of wearing poppies on 11th November each year by way of remembering the Englishmen who died'.[28]

I do understand the English origins of this tradition and my correspondent's sense of grievance that a powerful symbol of personal loss had been seemingly diluted or appropriated. Yet the scarlet poppy's association with death and new life, with corn and harvest, is as old as agriculture, and maybe as civilisation itself. It has been one of the world's most successful 'weeds', and has followed and exploited the spread of farming across the globe so comprehensively that no one is sure of its native home. It is a plant which belongs not so much to a particular home as to a way of life – to the tilling and disturbance of the

'Fiddleheads' of scaly male-fern

soil, and to the building (and razing) of communities. The archaeologist Flinders Petrie found poppy seeds mixed up with grains of barley in relics from the Twelfth Dynasty at Kahun in Egypt, which prospered before 2500 BC.[29] There, and maybe across much of the Middle East and the Mediterranean, poppies must have gone through the same evocative cycle: growing up unbidden in the fields, their blood-red petals cut down with the corn, only to spring up again, in numberless quantities, the following summer. No wonder they became such complex symbols of growth, blood and new life. The Assyrians called them 'the daughters of the field'. For the

Romans they were the sacred plant of their crop goddess Ceres. Garlands for her statues were made from poppies interwoven with barley or bearded wheat, and poppy seeds were offered up in rituals to ensure the fertility of the crops.[30]

Corn-poppies probably reached Britain mixed up with the seed-corn of the first Neolithic settlers, and even here were soon regarded as ambivalent signs of fertility and death. In the late medieval period they were called 'corn-roses', but often confused with the opium poppy and believed to induce sleep or headaches (though they have no such properties). Many of the early vernacular names – 'thundercup', 'thunderflower', 'lightnings' – reflect the ancient belief that poppies must not be picked, for fear of provoking storms; and conversely, perhaps, that whilst they were unpicked the crops were safe from summer downpours. And two centuries before the slaughter on Flanders Field, the scarlet troops massed amongst the wheatfields of southern England were being nicknamed 'soldiers' and 'redcaps'.[31]

Some of these old beliefs found a Victorian echo in the brief but heady fashionability of the cliff-top landscapes of Cromer and Overstrand in Norfolk, which were immortalised as 'Poppyland' by the *Daily Telegraph*'s drama critic, Clement Scott. Scott had taken to visiting these new seaside resorts in the 1880s and had fallen in love not just with the local miller's daughter, Louie Jermy, but with the sight of waves of scarlet blossoms in fields and lonely churchyards, sweeping down to the very edge of the cliffs, and set against the sparkle of the North Sea in high summer. He began to write ecstatic columns about Poppy-land in August 1883, and started a fad that brought thousands of visitors to the little villages on what the Great Eastern Railway rapidly renamed 'The Poppy Line'. Scott also wrote a popular but painfully sentimental poem

The poppy 'is the most transparent and delicate of all the blossoms of the field ... [it] is painted glass; it never glows so brightly as when the sun shines through it' (John Ruskin).

about his East Anglian Arcadia, entitled 'The Garden of Sleep', which recalled the flower's soporific reputation: ' 'Neath the blue of the sky, in the green of the corn/ It is there that the regal red poppies are born!/ Brief days of desire, and long dreams of delight,/ They are mine when my Poppy-land cometh in sight.'[32]

The obscene sea of mud and broken bodies that stretched around Ypres and the Somme thirty years later was a very different kind of 'Garden of Sleep'. Millions of soldiers and animals were simply churned into the earth, like so much compost. The men who had been persuaded to fight 'in order to preserve and somehow possess the beauties of the English countryside' were busily engaged, as the poet Ivor Gurney saw, in turning France, a 'darling land ... blessed with a merciful spirit founded on centuries of beautiful living', into a wasteland 'of mud and swamp and brimming shell-holes'.[33] Edmund Blunden saw the terrible irony clearly, and in his bitter poem 'Rural economy' he becomes a farmer, planting seeds of iron, which, manured with 'bone-fed loam/ Shot up a roaring harvest home'.[34]

Yet the real harvest had an ironic and paradoxical healing power. Not everything could be killed. The war artist William Orpen visited the battlefield in the summer of 1917, six months after the carnage of the Somme, and was mesmerised by it: 'No words could express the beauty of it. The dreary dismal mud was baked white and pure – dazzling white. White daisies, red poppies and a blue flower [probably cornflowers], great masses of them, stretched for miles and miles. The sky a pure, dark blue, and the whole air, up to a height of about forty feet, thick with white butterflies: your clothes were covered with butterflies. It was like an enchanted land, but in the place of fairies there were thousands of little white crosses, marked "Unknown British Soldier" for the most part.'[35]

The explosion of the poppies, seemingly coloured by blood but also healing the land, had struck writers at the front since the first summer after the war's outbreak. In the early winter of 1915, Colonel John McRae, a Canadian academic and volunteer medical officer, was treating the

'Shirley' could be found in surrounding fields until the late 1980s, despite the village now being part of greater Croydon, and the fields turned into golf-courses.[42] But there is a permanent bed of Shirley poppies in the large garden of what was once Wilks's vicarage (now an old people's home), and a pub named 'The Poppy' (the Shirley was dropped from the name quite recently) not far down the road.

Shirley poppies bring the poppy's story, always full of ironies, full circle. White Shirley poppies, or white artificials, are worn by peace movement supporters on Armistice Day, to honour the dead without condoning war.

Common duckweed, *Lemna minor*. This is the most frequent of the small water plants which can cover areas of stagnant water with mats of green. Lesser duckweed's leaves are only 2 to 4 mm in diameter, with a clove-like, three-lobed shape; packed tightly, they can make the surface of the water appear solid. In the north-west of England, a region of abundant flooded marl- and brick-pits and derelict canals, duck-weed gave rise to the myth of Jenny Greenteeth, a lurking, amorphous monster that would suck naughty children into the depths if they ventured too close.

At the beginning of this century, Jenny was sometimes used as a threat to children who did-n't keep their teeth clean. But most frequently she seemed to be a lurid, coded warning to chil-dren to stay away from dangerous water. The folklorist Roy Vickery found that the myth had survived in Cheshire and Lancashire at least until the 1980s. Occasionally, Jenny was described as having an actual physical form. A 68-year-old woman from Fazakerley was told as a child that Jenny inhabited two pools beside Moss Pitts Lane and 'had a pale green skin, green teeth, very long green locks of hair, long green fingers with long nails, and she was very thin with a pointed chin and very big eyes'.[43] Normally, though, she was a shapeless and invisible threat, as described to Vickery by a 34-year-old woman in 1980:
'I remember, as a very small child, being told by my mother to stay away from ponds as Ginny Greenteeth lived in them. However, I only recall

Ginny living in ponds which were covered in a green weed of the type which has tiny leaves and covers the entire surface of the pond. The theory was that Ginny enticed little children into the ponds by making them look like grass and safe to walk on. As soon as the child stepped onto the green, it, of course, parted and the child fell through into Ginny's clutches and was drowned. The green weed then closed over, hiding all traces of the child ever being there. This last point was the one which really terrified me and kept me away from ponds, and indeed my own children have also been told about Ginny, although ponds aren't as numerous these days.'[44]

A duckweed 'lawn' in a Dorset waterway.

THE SPRING

The spring is the flower world's crowning moment. Indeed, the opening of flowers is a major part of the definition of spring. Botanists even have a measure of the advance of the season across the land, based on the time common and widespread flowers first come into bloom. Different species flower at times determined by a combination of daylight length and temperature, and in general bloom later the higher and further north they are. The lines joining points where a given species blooms on the same day are called isophenes, and from them it is possible to calculate that spring travels north and inland at roughly two miles per hour – very close to strolling pace! But the surfaces of Britain are so intimately convoluted that at a local level the principle breaks down. Spring flowering remains an intensely local affair, celebrated nationally, but with a different focus in every wood and parish.

'Spring festivals'. To say that most spring ceremonies and traditions involve plants would be true, but would be to miss the point: the encouragement and celebration of new growth – both wild and cultivated – is what these ceremonies are for. They are, to use that much misused phrase, fertility rites.

A surprisingly large number survive in modern Britain, yet because of religious, political and commercial pressures they have tended to coalesce around a few key dates, pagan quarter days and Christian festivals merging for convenience with twentieth-century bank holidays. The sacred and secular elements become blurred in a similar way. Only one occasion has no ceremonials attached to it and that, ironically, is the most 'natural' of all – the spring equinox of 21 March, optimistically called 'the first day of spring'.

One key historical factor must be taken into account in considering the match between the dates of various festivals and the 'natural' calendar. Up until the mid-eighteenth century two different calendars had been operating simultaneously in Britain, the 'Old Style' Julian calendar and the 'New Style' Gregorian calendar. In 1751, Lord Chesterfield's Act provided that the

Primroses and other 'first flowers' of the spring.

Gregorian calendar should become the norm throughout Great Britain and its dominions. By this time the discrepancy between the Old and New Styles had reached 11 days and, to normalise affairs, Parliament decreed that the days between 2 and 14 September 1752 should be omitted. From then on, natural events were tagged with a calendar date of 11 days later. So, if primroses traditionally flowered on 21 March in a village, they now bloomed on April Fool's Day.

The various species associated with spring festivals are discussed under their individual entries, but the following are some of the chief festivals that involve plants.

The Christian festival of Eastertide begins with Palm Sunday, when sprays of pussy willow or yew are sometimes used as substitutes for true palm. Primroses have become the flower of Easter itself and are often used to decorate churches.

May Day is the occasion of the old Celtic festival of Beltane, which is echoed in dozens of ceremonies across Britain: in Padstow, Cornwall, cowslips are worn in the Obby Oss procession; in Oxford, a Jack-in-the-Green cloaked in hawthorn leaves careers through the city. 'May birching' is largely obsolete, but involved fixing sprigs of plants to people's doors. The plants were chosen either because of their symbolic associations or because their names rhymed with the epithet regarded as most apt for the householder. So,

plum, holly or briar meant, respectively, glum, folly or liar.[45] May garlands are still made on May Day in many country schools (and, more traditionally, in a few villages). At Charlton-on-Otmoor, there is a belief that the local May Day garland ceremony is an almost thoroughly Christianised relic of an old pagan festival. The Rector writes:

'With the coming of Christianity the missionaries had two choices with this, as with other customs – they could suppress it or adapt it. It would seem that they adopted the second course. It was clearly impossible to continue a pagan spring festival, so that ended; instead a Christian festival was held in honour of the Blessed Virgin Mary. This was, or became, associated with the figure on the rood in the church, representing the Lord's Mother. With

'The Vuz Dance of Flowers', a spring 'trade dance' revived in West Torrington, Devon in 1994.

the coming of Christianity, therefore, the pagan mother-goddess was no longer worshipped … It is a traditional custom, from time immemorial in the village, that children make little crosses covered with flowers … Since 1963 they bring them in procession to the church, where a service takes place, followed by dancing in the village street. The verse makes it clear that [the carol they sing] relates not to the May garlands carried by the children, but to the decorated "garland" on the north end of the screen, which indeed stood "at the Lord's right hand".' [16]

The more secular garland ceremony at the Oxfordshire village of Bampton has, ironically, migrated to the more overtly Christian festival of Whitsuntide. The flowers used in what is a partly competitive ceremony must be wild: 'The fields belonging to the old Busby brothers were filled with every flower you could think of – Moondaisies, Harebells, Goozie Ganders, Pots and Pans, Clovers, Ragged Robins and Quaker Grass. We picked yellow flags from the brook, because these went on the top of the garland. The flowers were usually kept in a tin bath until Sunday evening. To make the garlands, two willow sticks were tied in circles and placed one inside the other, tied at the top. The grown-ups, mainly Mums, would then tie the flowers (which by this time we had bunched in small bunches) in identical order up each side of the hoops. When all the sides were covered, the garland would be hung on the line, splashed with water and left till morning.' [47]

Other festivals which doubtless began as May Day rites for encouraging growth in fields and woods have also moved towards the end of the month, often joining the civic commemoration of the Restoration of Charles II on 29 May (e.g. Oak Apple Day and Grovely, and Arbor Day at Aston on Clun). Rather more have clustered around the movable feast of Rogationtide (the fifth week after Easter, leading up to Ascension Day). Rogation Sunday became officially sanctioned by the Church for the blessing of crops, which was combined with the social business of reaffirming land boundaries and common rights in the ceremony known as Beating the Bounds or

The Garland King, covered in flowers and foliage, like a Green Man, is carried on horseback throughout the Garland Day celebration in Castleton, Derbyshire, on 29 May

Perambulation. Plants were invariably involved in this, being amongst the most frequent natural features marking boundaries, as well as instruments (in the form of elm or willow wands) for beating them. The seventeenth-century poet and populist preacher George Herbert, Rector of Bemerton in Somerset, listed the benefits of the ceremony, including 'a blessing of God for the fruits of the field; Justice in the preservation of bounds; Charitie in living walking and neighbourly accompanying one another'. [48]

Games and Rituals

A NUMBER of children's games are based on plants, the most familiar being conkers. For centuries children have passed on the tricks of making dandelion clocks, ribwort plantain guns, goosegrass stickers and rose-hip seed itching powder. Some of the games require a sophisticated knowledge of the plants, as with the Wiltshire children who played with the seed-heads of smooth sow-thistle: 'We played a game called "silver and gold". Each child would choose a seed-head and at the given sign slit it open with their finger nails. The one who had chosen a head where the seeds were yellow (gold) and the other part silver was the winner. Too young and the flights would be green and the seeds a greeny yellow; too old and the seeds would be brown. We always called the plant "silver and gold".'[1]

In several areas of Britain, field horsetail is known as 'Lego plant' because of the way that the stem can be pulled apart in sections and then reassembled. Similarly, burdock is occasionally called 'the Velcro plant' because of the way its burs, with their curved tips, cling to each other and to any rough surfaces. (It is a compliment returned, since the inventor of Velcro was reputedly inspired by the plant.)

The inventiveness of children is perhaps best demonstrated with the superficially unpromising families of rushes and grasses. Soft-rush pith has been made into fake cigarettes, arrows, a levitating 'worm' and the frames for toy lorgnettes. Wall barley is made into 'flea-darts' and 'crawly-wallies' that make their way up the backs of jumpers. Even species comparatively new to Britain have their games, like snowberries, which are stamped on to produce miniature explosions, and the pods of Indian balsam, which are used in seed-hurling competitions.

Edinburgh's Burry Man – entirely clothed in burs – sets out for his day-long procession around the city.

Greater plantain, *Plantago major* (VN: Rat's tails, Angels' harps, Banjos). 'Rat's tail' is a perfect description of the flowering spike of this very common perennial of paths, pavement cracks, waysides, lawns, short grassland and field edges. The rosette of leaves, lying flush with the ground, also gave it a name when it migrated to North America with the early settlers. Amongst the Indians it was known as 'English-Mans Foot', not so much because its leaves are flat and broad, but because they seemed to dog the settlers' tracks, 'as though produced by their treading'.[2]

Plantain's leaves are tough, elastic and resilient, and exceptionally tolerant of trampling. This quality, interpreted according to the principles of sympathetic magic, suggested that it would be a healing herb for bruising and crushing wounds. As 'waybread' (and there could not be a more basic or reverent description than that) it was included amongst the Anglo-Saxons' nine sacred herbs:

> *And you, Waybread, mother of worts,*
> *Open from eastward, powerful within,*
> *Over you chariots rolled, over you queens*
> *   rode,*
> *Over you brides cried, over you bulls belled;*
> *All these you withstood, and these you*
> *   confounded,*
> *So withstand now the venom that flies*
> *   through the air,*
> *And the loathed thing which through the*
> *   land roves.*[3]

The healing powers of plantain aren't entirely fanciful. The leaves contain tannins and astringent chemicals, which can make them useful styptics if crushed and applied to small cuts, and an alternative to dock leaves in the relief of nettle stings.

The elasticity of the leaves has also made them natural subjects for children's games:

'The stalks or leaves, if broken gently, retained a few strong fibres, which are slightly elastic, allowing one to "milk a cow" by pulling the leaf gently out, then relaxing it. Or seeing who could get the longest fibre before the leaf finally parted.'[4]

'I remember we used to pull off the leaves of ratstail plantain, and from the number of ribs or threads which pulled out and hung down, and by the length of them, that was an indication of how many, and how lengthy, had been the lies we had told that day.'[5]

'They were known as "Angels' Harps", because when you pull the leaves apart you get the fibres showing between.'[6]

This name has many secular – and more contemporary – variations, from 'banjos' to 'Beatles' guitars', some of which are probably confined to individual schools or even gangs.[7]

Ribwort plantain, *P. lanceolata* (VN: Fighting cocks, Short bobs, Soldiers and sailors, Black Jacks, Hard-heads, Carl doddies; Fire-weed, Fire-leaf). Ribwort plantain (also abundant in grassy places) has, in contrast with Englishman's foot, lance-shaped leaves and a short, stubby flowerhead on top of a long wiry stem. This is still used in the game of 'soldiers'. The stem is wound once round itself, like a noose, just below the head. Then, by tightening the noose and pulling it sharply forward, the plantain's head is yanked off and hurled forward like a catapulted stone.

A variant is to use the plantain on its long stem as a substitute for a conker and attempt to knock a rival's flower-head off. In Kent this game is known as 'dongers'[8] and in Scotland (along with the plant itself) as 'Carl doddies': 'Carl and Doddie are diminutives of Charles and George, and the name of the game is an obvious memory of the '45 Jacobite Rebellion, with Bonnie Prince Charlie and King George III trying to knock each other's heads off.'[9]

'We had a game for two with ribwort plantains, when they were in bloom. Each person pulled a stalk with a strong "head", held it out and recited:

> *Ma faither and your faither*
> *Were sitting supping brose.*
> *Ma faither said to your faither*
> *Ah'll hit off your nose.*

Then one struck a sharp blow on the rival's plantain head hoping to knock it off and so be the winner.'[10]

Cleavers or goosegrass – which children still stick to coats and hair and long-suffering pets.

'As in conkers, some plantain heads are much tougher than others, and a champion soldier is greatly prized. Some veterans were like grizzled warriors and would knock out hundreds.'[11]

In hayricks, the brittleness and dryness of ribwort plantain leaves is still used by some farmers as a clue to the likelihood of the stack catching fire. It is, presumably, a rough measure of the amount of moisture in the hay itself, though one farmer, at least, believes the plantain leaves themselves could set the rick afire: 'A farmer in south Shropshire told me that ribwort plantain is called fire-weed or fire-leaf because, if not thoroughly dried, it can cause spontaneous combustion of hay.'[12]

Cleavers, *Galium aparine* (VN: Bobby Buttons, Clyders, Clydon, Clivvers, Goosegrass, Gosling weed, Goose bumps, Gollenweed, Herriff, Hairiff, Sweet-hearts, Kisses, Sticky Willy, Sticky grass, Sticky weed, Stickleback, Stick-a-back, Sticky bobs, Sticky buds, Sticky William, Claggy Meggies, Robin-run-the-hedge). Cleavers is the abundant scrambling annual (it can grow 10 feet in a season) which children still wield and stick to each other's coats and hair. The whole plant is covered with hooked bristles that make it difficult to detach from any slightly rough surface. Hence the great majority of its surviving local names, from cleavers itself to kisses. ('It is known as sweetheart because of its clinging habits.')[13] In Scotland there is a game called 'Bleedy Tongues', in which anyone foolish enough to stick out his tongue has it cut by the rough leaves.[14]

Snowberry, *Symphoricarpos albus* (VN for fruit: Lardy balls). This North American shrub was introduced to Britain in 1817. It is extensively planted in shrubberies and plantations, especially as cover for game, and widely naturalised by suckering. The flowers are pink and inconspicuous, and the shrub is best known for its marble-sized white berries:

'They are known as "Lardy balls" in Wiltshire. My grandmother told my mother that this is because lard used to be packed in pigs' bladders which looked perfectly white and spherical, like the autumn berries on this shrub.'[15]

'Local children pop snowberries beneath their feet on footpaths. They make a surprisingly loud noise.'[16]

Snowberries are readily eaten by blackbirds in hard weather. They are edible by humans, too, though they are hardly worth the effort and can cause digestive upsets in sensitive individuals and especially in children.

Burdock, *Arctium minus* and related species (VN: Bachelor's buttons, Button sourees, Beggar's buttons, Love leaves, Sticklebacks, Sticky bobs, Sticky Jack, Sticky Willy, Cleavers, Velcro plant). The inventor of Velcro fastening reput-

Burdock's large leaves were, like butterbur's, popular foreground fillers with seventeenth- and eighteenth-century landscape painters.

edly got the idea from the seed-heads of burdock, the familiar 'burs' whose hooked bristles clamp them to any rough surface they come in contact with, including each other. Modern children have returned the compliment by nicknaming burdock 'the Velcro plant'.[17] Many older local names survive, and testify to the plant's adhesive reputation. (Some are shared, incidentally, with that other clinging plant, cleavers, see p. 49.)

The games played with burdock are usually quite basic. Children throw them at each other and stick them surreptitiously on the backs of shirts and jumpers or onto the fur of tolerant pets. (Giving the seeds a chance to hitchhike on passing mammals is the chief function of the hooks.) But in Lancashire a more elaborate game was devised: 'They were of course individually used in fights, but we also used to collect them and construct large balls, also thrown at each other or rolled around like sticky bowls. We would also coat our jumpers with them, much to the annoyance of our Mums of course, because getting them off again could pull a jumper to shreds.'[18]

This game echoes one of the most extraordinary and elaborate plant-based rituals in Britain – the Burry Man parade held each summer in the Royal Burgh of Queensferry, Edinburgh. No one knows how old the ceremony is, but since 1687 it has been associated with the annual Ferry Fair, now held on the second Friday in August. On that day a man dressed from head to ankle in burs perambulates about the town, visiting houses and receiving gifts and greetings. The following notes are condensed from an account prepared by the Edinburgh City Museum: 'For some days before the festival, large numbers of burs are gathered locally (though they are increasingly hard to find in the developing edges of cities). They are spread out on tables and allowed to dry. This also makes it easier to extract pieces of stalk, leaves and grass and encourages the departure of various hedgerow insects which the Burry Man has no desire to carry with him in his costume. A couple of days later, the process of making the "patches" begins. These are rectangular panels, each composed of 500 or so burs, and of course require no adhesive to stick to each other, or to the Burry Man's clothing.

The Burry Man's day begins at around 6 a.m. in the Town Hall, where the making of his costume takes place. Onto undergarments made of white flannel, the dresser fits the patches from the ankle upwards, and sensitive areas, such as the back of the knees, the crotch and the armpits, are filled in by the careful placement of individual burs. The process, which takes two hours, continues until the Burry Man's entire body is encased in bur-patches. The overall effect is of a suit of chain-mail. The only exceptions are his hands and his shoes, and the crown of his head, which is covered by a hat garlanded with flowers. Apertures in his face-mask are made for his eyes and mouth. The costume is completed by small sprays of flowers being pushed between the burs at the shoulders, hips and outside of the knees, and by a folded Scottish standard being wound round his waist.

At 9 a.m. the Burry Man emerges into Queensferry High Street, carrying two staves bedecked with flowers. He walks slowly and awkwardly with his arms outstretched sideways, carrying the two staves, and two attendants, one on each side, help him to keep his balance by also holding on to the staves. Led by a boy ringing a bell, the Burry Man and his supporters begin their nine-hour perambulation of South Queensferry.

The first stop is traditionally outside the Provost's house, where the Burry Man receives a drink of whisky through a straw.

Occasional offerings like this must keep him going throughout the day. At about 6 p.m., the Burry Man returns to the Town Hall, exhausted by his efforts and usually somewhat inebriated by his intake of neat whisky. Although it occurs only once a year, the task of being Burry Man is extremely demanding, requiring stamina, a strong bladder, an indifference to the discomfort caused by the more penetrative burs, and a conviction that this ancient custom should not die out.'[19]

The origins of this custom are not known for certain. It has obvious affinities with the May-time fertility rites, especially the parades of the Green Man. But it is possible that the Burry Man also played the part of the ritual scapegoat, a fig-ure who wore an exaggerated 'hair-shirt' for the rest of the community and carried away on his clinging back any evils afflicting them. At Fraser-burgh, until the middle of the nineteenth cen-tury, an almost identical Burry Man ritual was

enacted to 'raise the herring'. And at Buckie on the Moray Firth, when the fishing season was bad, a man wearing a flannel shirt stuck all over with burs was paraded through the village in a hand-barrow, to bring better luck to the fishing.[20] (There are suggestions of sympathetic magic here, with the burs representing both fish-scales and fish-hooks.)

Burdock has had many more immediately practical uses. Its large leaves have been used as butter-wrappings, like butterbur (see p. 21), and as alfresco lavatory paper.[21] Its young shoots, peeled of their outer skin, can be eaten raw and have a taste reminiscent of young new potatoes. The roots can be roasted or stir-fried (as related species are in Japan) but are better known in this country as an ingredient in various 'near-beers'. The burdock for that one-time favourite fizzy drink 'Dandelion and Burdock' is these days imported in the form of hot-water extracts from eastern Europe.[22] But similar brews are still occa-sionally home-made. In Tredegar, for example, one mother used a concoction of burdock, cleavers, dandelion, blackberry tops and nettles.[23]

Although burdock is a rather gawky plant, it has the virtue of being sturdy, upright and large-leaved, and it has been a favourite foreground filling for landscape painters, George Stubbs for example. Claude Lorrain, one of the fathers of pastoral painting, insinuated its leaves into many shady corners.

Mugwort, *Artemisia vulgaris* (VN: Gipsy's tobacco, Muggar). A very common perennial of waysides and waste places, growing to four feet tall, mugwort's leaves are deep-cut, greyish below and glossy green above, smell only faintly of wormwood, and often have a rather dusty and bedraggled look when growing close to roads. (It is called 'Council weed' in the Bickerstaffe/ Melling area of Lancashire, as 'it always appears after the Council have been out'.)[24] Once *Mater Herbarum* (the Mother of Herbs), it was in widespread use as a charm and medicinal plant (stuffed in the shoes to prevent travel weariness, for instance). But today it is chiefly used as a children's smoking leaf.

'Village boys said they knew how to make

cigarettes, but this was just rolling mugwort ("muggar") flowerets inside newspaper strips.'[25]

'We would gather mugwort, which we called "cosi", to dry and smoke in big acorn cups, making a hole in the side and putting a stout straw through for the stem. Many a time we went home feeling groggy but never telling why. Our dear old Mum would have had a fit.'[26]

Mugwort is still an important symbolic plant in Manx folklore, where it is known as Bollan Bane or Bollan Feaill:

'Sprigs are worn at the July 4th annual openair parliamentary assembly on Tynwald Hill. (Tynwald, the Manx Parliament, has survived continuously from the period of the Norse kingdom of Man.) The wearing of mugwort was revived about 1924, having gone into abeyance in the latter nineteenth century. It is now a conspicuous feature of this National Day, although some born-again Christians objected to it in the mid-1980s on the grounds that it was a pagan idea.'[27]

'Until quite recently no law had force until it had been read from the Tynwald Hill. The turves of the hill are said to have been taken from each Parish on the Island. It is the most revered spot in Man to Manxmen all over the world. Bollan Bane (the Manx name means "White Wort", referring to the white underside to the leaves) is worn as a charm by almost everybody present.'[28]

Soft-rush, *Juncus effusus*. This is a thin rush, growing in tufts up to three feet high in damp woods, waterlogged ground, marshes and ditches. It has glossy green cylindrical stems and yellowish flowers, but is best known for its pith, which, with care, can be extracted in quite long strips. Well into the nineteenth century this was used in making the basic source of illumination in most country cottages – the rushlight. These ancient vegetable tapers were simply lengths of peeled rush, soaked in fat or some other inflammable substance and then burned like disembodied wicks. In his great tract on self-sufficiency, *Cottage Economy*, William Cobbett placed his entry on them between goats and mustard, and obviously regarded them as one of the staples of life: 'I was bred and brought up mostly by *Rushlight*, and I do not find that I see less clearly than

other people. Candles certainly were not much used in English labourers' dwellings in the days when they had meat dinners and Sunday coats.'[29]

Fifty years previously, his near neighbour, the Revd Gilbert White of Selborne, had written the classic account of the preparation and economics of the rushlight, a tribute to the ingenuity and frugality of eighteenth-century cottagers: 'The rushes are in best condition in the height of summer; but they may be gathered, so as to serve the purpose well, quite on to autumn. It would be needless to add that the largest and longest are best. Decayed labourers, women and children, make it their business to procure and prepare them. As soon as they are cut they must be flung into water, and kept there; for otherwise they will dry and shrink, and the peel will not run. At first a person would find it no easy matter to divest a rush of its peel or rind, so as to leave one regular, even rib from top to bottom that may support the pith: but this, like other feats, soon becomes familiar even to children; and we have seen an old woman, stone-blind, performing this business with great dispatch, and seldom failing to strip them with the nicest regularity. When these *junci* are thus prepared, they must lie out on the grass to be bleached, and take the dew for some nights, and afterwards be dried in the sun.

Some address is required in dipping these rushes in the scalding fat or grease; but this knack also is to be attained by practice. The careful wife of an industrious Hampshire labourer obtains all her fat for nothing; for she saves the scummings of her bacon-pot for this use; and, if the grease abounds with salt, she causes the salt to precipitate to the bottom, by setting the scummings in a warm oven … A pound of common grease may be procured for four pence; and about six pounds of grease will dip a pound of rushes …

If men that keep bees will mix a little wax with the grease, it will give it a consistency, and render it more cleanly, and make the rushes burn longer: mutton suet would have the same effect. A good rush, which measured in length two feet four inches and a half, being minuted, burnt only three minutes short of an hour: and a rush still of greater length has been known to burn one hour and a quarter. These rushes give a good clear light …'[30]

Rushlights may not be as quaint and anachronistic as they sound. They are easy to make, as White points out, once you have the knack of peeling the rushes. They have the advantage over candles of not dripping scalding tallow, so they can be held and carried without a holder; and they burn with a clear, almost smokeless flame, which is surprisingly bright. (In the nineteenth century a single rushlight would often serve several people sitting round one table. Those doing fine work, such as lace-making, would use a globe of water as a lens, to produce a concentrated spotlight.) Their economic use of waste fat was not forgotten during the dark days of the

Soft-rush. Its pith was once soaked in fat and used in household lamps.

Second World War, when they had a temporary revival in rural areas.[31]

The pith's absorbency (due to its fine cellular structure) also means that it is exceptionally lightweight, and this has been noticed – and exploited – by children:

'While walking home from school in the Lake District we frequently paused to make "cigarettes" from rushes. This called for delicate handling of the rushes, which we peeled, trying to manage as long a piece of peeled rush as possible. There was no question of trying to light the cigarette; you simply held it in your mouth as if holding a real cigarette. The texture of the plant was such that it held easily to the lips, even when you talked.'[32]

'Take a piece of rush, strip the green from it and liberate the pith with your thumbnail – producing an almost weightless white worm, up to a foot in length. Then introduce this to the updraft of an outdoor fire. The result is uncanny – it shoots heavenwards, spiralling as it goes, then gently drifts downwards only to be sucked up again by the draft.'[33]

'Make arrows out of soft-rush stems, by half-peeling a strip of the outer skin away from the pith of a section of rush stem, balancing the stem across the top of one's hand, then pulling sharply on the half-peeled strip – which propels the arrow at a suitable target.'[34]

'We used to peel soft-rushes to put on little leaf "plates" as "bananas", with rowan berries as "oranges".'[35]

'The girls in this area used to plait soft rush so as to make what they called "Ladies' Hand-mirrors". This was done by bending the stem sharply at the middle at two points about quarter of an inch apart. The stem was then plaited by bending each side in turn sharply over the other at right angles. When this had been done along almost the whole length, the ends were pushed through the starting loop to make a small circle with a lorgnette-type handle. An adequate supply of saliva was then needed to persuade the loop to take on a saliva lens, which formed the mirror surface.'[36]

'A recent craze among local primary (and

early secondary) schoolgirls in the Forest of Dean is for "friendship bracelets" usually of cotton threads, occasionally wool. My daughters have also tried soft rush, and often say "We're going for the record, plaiting three strands-long lengths with it." ' [37]

Although grasses dominate the rural landscape, as crops and as the ground-cover of most open countryside, they do not in the main have sufficient individuality to have found a place in popular culture. The exception has been children's games. Here, the grasses' round-the-year accessibility and abundance have worked in their favour. And while not much discrimination is used when sucking stems for sweetness or whistling through leaf-blades, children have spotted and ingeniously exploited many of the fine differences between species.

Perennial rye-grass, *Lolium perenne*, is a tough-stemmed native of waysides, rough ground and pastures, which is also one of the most widely used species for reseeding grasslands. Its distinct, well-spaced spikelets have made it the grass of choice for a children's prediction game in the Yorkshire Dales: 'Each spikelet was pulled off in turn to fit the rhyme till it was used up. And so we chanted "This year, next year, sometime, never; silk, satin, muslin, rags; boots, shoes, slippers, clogs (this latter footwear was normal in the village); the Big House, little house, pigsty, barn", and so on.' [38]

Annual meadow-grass, *Poa annua*, **rough meadow-grass**, *P. trivialis*, and **smooth meadow-grass**, *P. pratensis*, are abundant in grassy places. Their loose heads of flowers and seeds are used to illustrate a seasonal rhyme. This version is from Somerset: 'We used meadow grass to demonstrate the four seasons, saying "Here is the tree in springtime" (pushing the grass into a bunch). "Here's the tree in summer" (letting the spikes go). "Here is the tree in autumn" (brushing all the seeds off). "And here's the tree in winter …" ' [39]

Mixed meadow-grasses in the early morning, Monewden Meadow, Suffolk.

It is still made into serviceable brushes by us.'[48]

But its importance in stabilising dunes has made the harvesting of marram for thatch and plaiting illegal in some western coastal areas. This is perhaps an over-reaction, as marram is a true pioneer plant, needing space. Once it has completely covered a dune, it begins mysteriously to die out.

Meadow foxtail, *Alopecurus pratensis*, is common in grasslands, preferring rich, damp soils. Once the spikelets or seeds have been stripped off, this is the favourite species for giving 'Chinese haircuts'. The flowers would be stripped off the stem, leaving only their short, wiry stalks. These would then be twiddled into another child's hair (or, with older boys, hairs on the legs) – usually of the child sitting at the desk in front.

A sharp pull would then remove all the hair tangled up in the stalks.[49]

Timothy, *Phleum pratense*, and **smaller cat's-tail**, *P. bertolonii*, are both common throughout Britain and notable for their long, silky heads. (Curiously, for a common native grass, *P. pratense* has acquired an American name: 'Timothy' is after Timothy Hanson, a farmer who introduced its seed to Carolina in about 1720.)[50]

'We used cat's-tails to make rabbits. The large heads would provide ears, arms and feet, with the heads wrapped round another one for the body.'[51]

Common couch, *Elytrigia repens* (VN: Squitch, Twitch, Wickens, Stroggle, Grandmother grass). This is an abundant perennial of cultivated places and rough ground, with long, complicated and obstinate roots.

Marram grass on Gibraltar Point, Lincolnshire. Marram is one of the chief natural agents for stabilising sand-dunes.

'My mother, born in 1891, introduced me and my daughter (and through us her daughter) to "grandmother grass" or couch grass. One plucks off the head of the grass and sticks it in another head, still on its stem. A flip of the hand holding the stem and "Grandmother, grandmother, jump out of bed" is recited as the first head springs out of its nest.'[52]

Couch-grass roots are an effective mild diuretic and were gathered for this purpose by the National Herb Committee during the Second World War.

Wall barley, *Hordeum murinum*, is a common annual of walls, waste and rough ground, and bare patches in dry grassland. Its bearded heads are as clinging as burdock burs and have found their way into numerous games. (Some of these are reminders that the Latin specific name, *murinum*, is derived from *mus*, a mouse, not *murus*, a wall!)

'In school we throw "flea-darts" at each other. They stick to hair and clothing. They are the flowers of wall barley and wild oats.'[53]

'We played "crawly-wallies" by picking spikes of wall barley, holding them upside down within one's closed fist; then, by making small movements with one's fingers, the wall barley spike climbs out and escapes.'[54]

'A variation was to put a head of wall barley beneath the ribbing of the jumper of the person sitting in front of you at school and then wait for it to work its way up their back and start them scratching.'[55]

Wall barley, one of the commonest grasses of town streets.

Plants as Resources

MANY WILD PLANTS have had some kind of domestic use. The following examples show the inventiveness and familiarity with plants of our ancestors:

Lady's bedstraw is a coagulent and was once used as a substitute for rennet in setting cheese.

Cottongrass's downy seed-heads have been used as a home-grown cotton wool substitute and for stuffing pillows.

Butcher's-broom. Otherwise known as 'knee-holly', its spiny shoots were used for scrubbing butchers' blocks and for making mouse-proof cages for meat.

Butterbur's large leaves were once used as a cooling wrapping for butter and other perishable foods; it is also still useful as an emergency umbrella.

Horsetail stems contain silica crystals and were used for scouring and polishing pewter.

Soapwort's leaves, boiled in water, make a mild detergent, which is still sometimes employed by museum conservation departments for cleaning fragile fabrics.

Colt's-foot's dried leaves are the main ingredient of herbal tobacco.

Many of the trees that are used for commercial timber also have traditions of small-scale domestic use. Walking sticks are made from deliberately bent ash saplings and from branches twisted by honeysuckle. Sycamore is carved into love-spoons in Wales, elder into paper-knives and birch twigs bound into whisks. There has been resourcefulness too in the *parts* of trees that are used: the young willow twigs (often coloured more brightly in late winter and spring) that are used in basket-weaving; the richly grained knots and burrs from cherry, elm and yew that are sought out by turners.

'When gorse is in blossom, kissing's in season.' Western gorse and heather in full bloom, South Stack, Anglesey.

Silver birch, *Betula pendula*. Birch was one of the first trees to recolonise Britain after the retreat of the glaciers, and it remains an opportunist, pioneering species today. Its seeds are produced in huge numbers and are blown about like dust in the wind. On areas of open woodland or heath, the frizzy seedlings can carpet the ground in a matter of months. In this respect birch plays the same role on slightly acidic ground as ash does on calcareous soils, and where there is not much competition from other species – as in parts of the Scottish Highlands – it can form pure woods, even though the individual trees rarely live more than 80 years.

Its powers of regeneration and rapid growth have inevitably made it unpopular with foresters, who mostly regard it as a worthless competitor with spruces and other commercial trees. So they slash and spray the seedlings and ring-bark mature trees. Nature conservationists do the same to birch that invades heathland and fens.

But silver birches – white-trunked, airily leafed, rich in bird-life – are exquisite trees, and the official hostility that is shown towards any that appear in the 'wrong place' is not always popular with the public. In Ashdown Forest, 'the clearing of invading birch on the heathland areas caused such untoward comment by visitors and local dwellers that it has been decided to mount an exhibition portraying the birch's life from seedling to use – covering distribution, management, natural history, poetry, folklore and a big section on woodworking. Birch wine, which is still made as a home brew on a small scale, will be exhibited. A small trade exists making besom brooms with birch and hazel handles.'[1]

These vestigial uses in Sussex reflect the enormous versatility of this prolific raw material. Writing of the great Scottish birchwoods in the 1840s (birch – usually as the prefix birk – is the commonest place-name prefix in Scotland),[2] J. C. Loudon pointed out that the local inhabitants hadn't many other trees to turn to:
'The Highlanders of Scotland make everything of it; they build their houses, make their beds and chairs, tables, dishes and spoons; construct their mills; make their carts, ploughs, harrows, gates and fences, and even manufacture ropes of it. The branches are employed as fuel in the distillation of whisky, the spray is used for smoking hams and herrings, for which last purpose it is preferred to every other kind of wood. The bark is used for tanning leather, and sometimes, when dried and twisted into a rope, instead of candles. The spray is used for thatching houses; and, dried in summer, with the leaves on, makes a good bed when heath is scarce.'[3]

Young silver birches, rapid colonisers of open areas on acid soils.

Birches on a steep slope in Glen Strathfarrar. Birchwoods are one of Scotland's 'signature' plant communities.

Subsistence is hardly an issue in the Highlands today, and birch is now more often
employed as the favoured fuel for smoking had-
docks, and as a source of sap for fermenting into
wine (an increasingly popular speciality of Deeside).[4] Besoms made from birch spray are still
quite popular with gardeners, but the Forestry
Commission has stopped using them for beating
out fires – not surprisingly perhaps, since young
birches are amongst the few deciduous trees that
will burn standing.

South of the Border, omelette whisks are fashionable: 'We make whisks by cutting a bunch of
birch twigs in spring around bud-burst. Hold
each twig at the cut end with a piece of rag and
strip off the bark in one pull. Bundle the stripped
sticks together and bind with another long

stripped birch twig.'[5]

(The adjective 'silver' for birch, from the satin
lustre of the papery white bark, is also a comparatively recent Sassenach invention. It is not in
any of the editions of Evelyn's *Sylva*, and seemingly first appeared in a poem by Tennyson.)[6]

Recently, birch has begun to be looked at
more respectfully by commercial foresters, as an
alternative to exotic conifers on poor moorland
soils. It is just as good as a source of pulpwood
and has the virtue of actually improving the soil
rather than acidifying it, as conifers do.

This would have been thought a quite unnec-
essary and utilitarian defence of the tree by
medieval Celtic poets, who loved the birch for its
spring greenery and dappled summer light, more
golden than under any other native tree. The

Ancient birch trunk in Glen Strathfarrar, Inverness.

Hazel catkins, widely known as 'lamb's-tails'. (The red female flower is also just visible.)

fourteenth-century Welsh poet Gruffydd ap Dafydd wrote an elegy 'To a Birch-tree Cut Down, and Set Up in Llanidloes for a Maypole': 'Long are you exiled from the wooded slope, birch-tree, with your green hair in a wretched state; you who were the majestic sceptre of the wood where you were reared, a green veil, and now turned traitress to your grove ... You were made, it seems, for huckstering, as you stand there like a market-woman; and in the cheerful babble at the fair all will point their fingers at your suffering, in your one grey shirt and your old fur, amid the petty merchandise. No more will the bracken hide your urgent seedlings, where your sister stays; no more will there be mysteries and secrets shared, and shade, under your dear eaves; you will not conceal the April primroses, with their gaze directed upwards; you will not think now to inquire, fair poet tree, after the birds of the glen.'[7]

But there is still a vestige of magic around upland birches: 'Near Balmaclellan [Kircudbrightshire] lies the lonely village of Dunscore. One of the houses there is called Letterick, and some years ago the owner died. His last instructions were that his body should be placed in a basket and he should be buried upright near a birch tree. He asserted that he would return regularly in the guise of a crow to keep an eye on

things. Needless to say a lone crow does come to sit in the tree at intervals.'[8]

Hazel, *Corylus avellana* (VN: Halse, Hezzel, Ranger; Lamb's-tails [catkins]). These days hazel is known for its catkins, universally called 'lamb's-tails', its late summer nuts, and occasionally for providing water diviners with their forked twigs. But for much of the past 6,000 years it was a more utilitarian resource. Its foliage was used for cattle food, and its whippy shoots for making the framework for houses and fences.

Hazel was one of the first trees to recolonise Britain after the last Ice Age, coming soon after birch, and for a while it was the most abundant shrubby species. But it is a bush more than a tree, rarely growing above 30 feet in height, and does not tolerate deep shade. When the bigger forest trees began to cover Britain, hazel retreated to more open areas, on cliffs, unstable rocks, riverbanks and the like. It was the opening out of the wildwood by early settlers that gave it the chance to spread again.

In the wild, hazel will occasionally grow into a single-trunked small tree. But it is, so to speak, 'self-coppicing' and, if its branches are broken off or debarked by animals, hazel will send up straight new shoots from the base. No doubt these were used by early people before deliberate

A coppiced hazel by the River Teign, near Dartmoor, with wild daffodils beneath.

coppicing was begun some 4,000 years ago.

However they are encouraged, hazel poles have two invaluable properties. They can be split lengthways, and twisted and bent at sharp angles without breaking. This enabled them to be woven, bent back on themselves and even tied in knots. (Thin strips of knotted hazel are used to bind up bundles – faggots – of cut hazel poles.) From Neolithic times the basic product of cut hazel was wattle – split canes woven into a simple warp-and-weft lattice-work. Wattle made hurdles, fencing and the foundation on which wattle-and-daub walls were built. Hazel is also still used to peg down thatch (in which the hazel broaches have to be bent through 180 degrees).

Recently the use of coppiced hazel wood has been going through something of a revival, encouraged by (and encouraging in its turn) the nationwide revival of coppicing itself. There have been some ingenious new uses for wattle, in, for example, motorway sound screens. And the National Rivers Authority has revived the traditional Dutch practice of sinking 'mattresses' of hazel faggots and reed to help fortify the banks of the River Ouse near the Wash. (The mattresses work by catching sediment from the natural tidal flow, which builds up and strengthens the river bed and banks.)

In the Isle of Man, 'above the Great Laxey Wheel, hazel was planted to provide shock-absorbing brushwood for the mine machinery. The woodland is now preserved by Manx National Heritage as part of the mines complex associated with the Wheel.'[9]

Small-scale use continues, too. Hazel rods are still widely used for pea and bean sticks,[10] and remain popular with the carvers and whittlers of decorative walking-sticks, particularly because of the contrast between the white wood and the naturally flecked, almost notched bark. One south-country walking-stick maker bends and pegs down young hazel shoots in hedges to 'grow' the curve in the handle (cf. ash, p. 110).[11]

A modern coppice-worker has noticed great variation in the rods from different bushes: 'The hazel rods from different stools seemed to have different splitting qualities and varying suppleness and toughness. Moreover these varying properties of the wood seemed to be associated with particular textures of the bark, so it became possible to predict how a rod would split or how brittle the split rod would be simply by looking at the bark. Much of the hazel at West Wood [North Bedfordshire] has a lovely golden, almost metallic sheen and a fine-grained flaky texture (which could perhaps be likened to an even scatter of tiny flakes of bran). This type of hazel has a strong grain which is easy to split evenly (except when it gets very big and old and tends to become stringy). Another type of hazel rod has a very smooth ground texture to the bark, almost like dark olive-green lacquer-work, and has large, conspicuous widely-spaced lenticels. These rods tend to be very brittle and relatively difficult to split because the split has a tendency to shoot off to the side almost like a conchoidal glossy fracture. "Like splitting a stick of rock", one thatcher described it. Genetic variation is the cause of much of this individuality: adjacent stools of same-age regrowth and in apparently identical conditions can have markedly different features and each rod on a stool has the characteristic of that stool. The individuality is not confined to bark and splitting qualities. On some stools the stems of the new regrowth are a deep maroon-purple, on others they are crimson, and yet others are a washed-out green colour. Some stools have leaves with a purple blotch. Some grow new shoots that are tall and erect, others grow shorter and more prostrate. Some stools have nuts that are long and bullet-shaped, others are nearly spherical or even snub-nosed.' [12]

Hazel-nuts are the other great harvest from the tree. They were one of the staples of pre-historic peoples, especially the Celts, and were highly esteemed: 'An early Irish topographical treatise describes a beautiful fountain called Connla's Well, near Tipperary, over which hung nine hazels of poetic art which produced flowers and fruit (Beauty and Wisdom) simultaneously. As the nuts fell into the well, salmon began feeding off them; whatever number of nuts any of these salmon swallowed, a corresponding number of bright spots appeared on their bodies ... In Celtic legend they [hazel-nuts] are always an emblem of concentrated wisdom, something sweet, compact and sustaining, enclosed in a small hard shell: in a nutshell, so to speak.' [13]

The selection and breeding of cultivated forms dates back to classical times. Tudor farmers and fruit-growers favoured a variety called the white filbert, very similar to the wild filbert, *Corylus maxima*, of Asia Minor. ('Filbert' is named from St Philibert's Day, 20 August, when the nuts are recorded as being ripe.) The name 'cobnut' was not applied to cultivated hazels until later. It derived from a game called 'cobnut' – 'cob' meant to throw gently – which involved pitching a large nut at a pile of smaller ones. Those knocked off the pile became the property of the thrower. [14]

(The heart of cobnut-growing in England is Kent, and in the village of Ightham there is a pub called 'The Cobtree'. Until 1995 the pub sign showed a Welsh cob horse standing under a big tree. But Meg Game, grower of and enthusiast for cobnuts, persuaded the brewery to repaint the sign showing the catkins, leaves and nuts of a real cob tree.) [15]

But even wild, native hazel-nuts (*C. avellana*) were regarded as worth collecting in quantity. In the late seventeenth century, John Aubrey (echoing the experience of the coppice-worker above) praised the harvest from the great hazel woods of Wiltshire:

'Wee have two sorts of them. In the south part, and particularly Cranbourn Chase, the hazells are white and tough; with which there are made the best hurdles of England. The nutts of the chase are of great note, and are sold yearly beyond sea. They sell them at Woodbery Hill Faire, &c.; and the price of them is the price of a buschell of wheate. The hazell-trees in North Wilts are red, and not so tough, more brittle.' [16]

In 1826 the owner of Hatfield Forest, Essex, complained that: 'as soon as the Nuts begin to get ripe ... the idle and disorderly Men and Women of bad Character from |Bishop's] Stortford ... come ... in large parties to gather the Nuts or under pretence of gathering Nuts to loiter about in Crowds ... and in the Evening ... take Beer and Spirits and Drink in the Forest which affords them an opportunity for all sorts of Debauchery.' [17]

It is a depressingly familiar complaint by landowners. All fruit harvests, wild or cultivated, are quite properly occasions for socialising and celebration.

Nutting also generated several ingenious devices, including gathering-bags looped over the wrist and hazel-nut-crackers fashioned from hazel-wood. I have seen a pair of these made by a

Sussex hurdle-maker in the 1930s, which he used to carry when working in the coppices in autumn. After shaping a piece of straight wood with his knife, he soaked it, doubled it over, and then bound it tightly with a strip of split hazel until it dried out.

In Great Houghton, Northamptonshire, a more rough-and-ready implement was used: 'In the village, until 20 years ago there was a lane with a hazel hedge boundary, leading to a farm gate. The gate was used to crack the hazel nuts, and the lane had been known for as long as anyone can remember as "Crack-nuts". Development swept away lane, hedge and name. One house built on the land was the new rectory, and the then rector's wife thought Crack-nuts to be an inappropriate address for a rector, so with great imagination the area was renamed Rectory Close.'[18]

Perhaps this was retribution by the clergy for the ancient indignities of 'Nutcrack Night'. This was the evening when nuts, stored away to ripen, were first opened. (In Cleveland it was 15 November.)[19] In some parishes there was a custom for the nuts to be taken into church the following Sunday and cracked noisily during the sermon.

In fact most venerable customs involving hazel are far from straightforward. In many, the use of hazel-wood seems neither here nor there; it is simply the most convenient wood for the job. But behind this there are sometimes hints of white magic (hazel was lucky as well as bountiful), sly humour, commonplace economic custom – echoes of the character of the shrub itself. In Abbots Ann, Hampshire, the parish still keeps up the medieval custom of awarding 'Virgin's Crowns' made of hazel. A plaque in the church explains:
'The ceremony of this ancient burial rite takes place at the funeral of an unmarried person who was born, baptised, confirmed and died in the Parish of Abbots Ann, and was a regular Communicant. Such persons must also be of unblemished reputation.

The Virgin's Crown is made of hazelwood and is ornamented with paper rosettes, with five

Illustrations of some of the cultivated varieties of cobnut and filbert, from Pomona Britannica, 1812. The more robust, oblong filberts are native to southeast Europe.

white gauntlets attached to it. The gauntlets represent a challenge thrown down to anyone to asperse the character of the deceased.

The Crown suspended from a rod is borne by two young girls habited in white with white hoods, at the head of the funeral procession. After the funeral the Crown is carried to the Church and is suspended from the gallery near the West Door, so that all who enter the Church on the following Sunday will pass under it. There it remains for three weeks. If during that time no one has challenged or disputed the right of the deceased to the Crown, it is hung in the roof of the Church with a small scutcheon bearing the name and age of the person concerned, and the date of the funeral, and there the Crown remains until it decays and falls with age.

Most of the Crowns are awarded to women, but men are not excluded, provided they fulfil the same conditions.

The present Church was built in 1716, and the oldest Virgin's Crown still in existence approaches that date.'[20]

Hazel is also used in the Corporation of London's Quit Rents Ceremony:

'The Ceremony … is said by distinguished antiquarians to be the oldest surviving Ceremony next to that of the Coronation itself [over 750 years]. It is feudal in origin and character, since it represents the rendering of rents and services in respect of tenure of two pieces of land, one being a piece of waste land called "The Moors" in Shropshire and the other being a Tenement called "The Forge" in the Parish of St Clement Dane in the County of Middlesex. The services being rendered by the original tenants of these pieces of land having been commuted in kind by the Sovereign, the rents are only a token payment in kind. This is why they are called Quit Rents and Services, since thereby the tenant goes "quit" and free of all other services.

In respect of "The Moors", the Quit rent consists in the presentation of a blunt knife and a sharp knife. The qualities of these instruments are demonstrated by the Senior Alderman or the Comptroller and Solicitor of the City of London, who will bend a hazel rod of a cubit's length [taken from Shropshire] over the blunt knife and break it over the blade of the sharp knife. Hazel rods of this length were used as tallies to record payments made to the Court of Exchequer by notches made with a sharp knife along their length and after the last payment split lengthways with a blunt and pliable bladed knife, one half being given to the payer and the other half being retained by the Court to vouch its written records. On behalf of the Corporation of London, he will then render them to the Queen's Remembrancer on behalf of Her Majesty.'[21]

(Hazel tally-sticks, incidentally, were used in one Chiltern pub into the 1980s as 'the slate' for a local joiner.)[22]

'Mrs Griffiths had a Welsh slate sink that she used for separating the milk, and there was a hole at the bottom that could be plugged and un-plugged. During the summer months when the milk had to be left for a whole day to separate, she rubbed hazel leaves on the slate bottom before she poured in the milk, and this helped stop the milk turning sour.'[23]

Crack-willow, *Salix fragilis* (VN for willow in general: Withy, Sallies, Wullies, Saugh, Sauchan). Crack-willow is well named. The trunk grows fast but is apt to split open under its own weight. Its tendency to collapse is encouraged by its favoured habitats, which are damp, flood-prone fens and river valleys. But by riversides (and roadsides, where the roads run above dykes and damp ground, as in east Norfolk), crack-willows are often planted to stabilise the banks and are usually pollarded to reduce the chances of splitting and allow light on to the water. These rows of tufted trees – sheaves of narrow leaves above a wizened, knobbly, leaning trunk, with half its

A memorial seat at Rougham, Norfolk, made out of living willow wands.

roots in the water – are a quintessential part of the landscape of lowland rivers, especially the Thames and Cam. At the beginning of the century they helped create the drowsy atmosphere of Kenneth Grahame's *The Wind in the Willows*, and inspired Arthur Rackham's illustrations, and no slow river seems right without them now. (The two unrelated Rackhams – Arthur and Oliver – have between them quite transformed the image of the pollard in the twentieth century.)

Crack-willows make the most contorted of all pollards. Adventitious roots creep earthwards from inside their hollow centres. The crowns are often so full of holes, crevices and rotting leaves that they nurture second-storey woodlets of their own: ash, holly, gooseberry, elder, ferns, honeysuckle and brambles. Anita Jo Dunn, who looked at 400 willow pollards on the banks of the Evenlode and Windrush in west Oxfordshire and elsewhere, found 74 species growing in their crowns.[24]

The wands that are cut from pollard willows, on a five- to ten-year rotation usually, will themselves root immediately to make new willow trees (as will a collapsed portion of crack-willow trunk – cf. black-poplar, p. 105).

In Middleton Cheney, Northamptonshire, 'about thirty years ago, some fencing needed to be erected, and the farmer charged with this task, Johnny Pollard [*sic*], hammered 36 willow stakes into the ground as fence posts. A line of crack-

Ancient pollard willows. Crack-willow can regenerate from the rooting of split and fallen branches.

willows has grown from the stakes – a distinctive landscape feature along this stretch of the Far-thinghoe brook. Mr Pollard's grandson still lives locally and the story is well known.'[25]

I have seen the same thing happen by gravel-pits, where anglers have cut V-shaped willow rod-rests and left them in the ground.

Crack-willow poles, if cut young and thin enough, can be woven, though this is usually done with osier (see below). Rough-and-ready open-air baskets for cattle food were made from pollard cuttings until a few years ago. In the Lake District they were known as 'swills': 'Swills are large woven baskets made of willow wood. The branches for the body of the swill and the thin hazel branches for the rims were soaked for some days in a dammed-up stream. These were widely in use for holding cattle food and washing, both wet and dry.'[26]

In the Severn valley they were 'cribs': 'Mr Riddle [Thornbury, Gloucestershire] is aged 65 and last made a crib in this way 10 years ago. He said it took about two days for a man to cut the branches off a pollarded crack willow tree and weave the crib. The crib was 7 feet in diameter and the uprights were willow branches, 2 to 3 inches in diameter, around which were woven branches around 2 inches in diameter up to a height of two and a half feet. Several of the local farmers and farmworkers used to make these kind of cribs which lasted outside for about three years.'[27]

White willow, *S. alba*, is a large and spreading tree, with grey bark and silver-felted leaves, which stream dramatically in the wind. Native by streams and ponds and in marshes, it is also frequently planted. **Cricket-bat willow**, a tall, straight-trunked form, grown for cricket-bats in damp ground, in Suffolk and Essex especially, is var. *caerulea*. **Golden willow**, var. *vitellina*, has a cultivar 'Britzensis', with bright orange twigs, which are cut for basketry. It is often grown as low pollards along the rhines in the Somerset Levels.

Osier, *S. viminalis*, is a fast-growing shrub, especially when coppiced, with long leaves and straight shoots, which turn a shiny yellow-

Osiers, cut and tied with osier 'rope', Somerset.

brown when mature. It grows in fens, ditches and damp places throughout lowland Britain, but has also been widely planted in osier-beds to be harvested for basket-making. More than 60 different osier species, hybrids and cultivated varieties are grown in Britain, with different strengths, growth rates and flexibility, and in colours ranging from pale yellow to deep purple. (There is a naturally purple-barked willow, *S. purpurea*.) They are traditionally used for bas-ket-making, but 'wicker-work', as stripped and woven willow is called, is going through a renaissance at present, and osiers are appearing in novel situations. Some are being woven whilst still alive, with their cut ends stuck into the ground, to form living fences or pergolas. The Department of Transport is using a variant of these for sound screens along the edges of motorways. Wicker 'mattresses', 10 feet high, are filled with earth, into which the willow roots are planted.

They are irrigated where necessary to prevent drying out, and other plants such as ivy and honeysuckle are added at intervals. And, using more conventionally dried willow, the sculptor Serena de la Hay makes life-size willow figures for gardens, the strips of willow seeming like sinews of muscle.

In Chediston, Suffolk, there has been a revival of a 'willow-stripping' ceremony at a willow-grower and basket-maker's farm: 'For several years we have held a willow stripping, usually at the first full moon in May. We construct a Green George figure which is dressed with the willow strippings, and at the end of the festivities he is

danced up to the pond and ceremoniously cast in.'[28]

Many fast-growing willow (and poplar) varieties are currently under trials for large-scale cultivation as fuel-wood: 'Over the next five years we shall plant another six hectares of land [by the River Blackwater, Essex] and the crop will be coppiced every three or four years for about thirty years. The willows absorb and sequester carbon dioxide from the atmosphere and require very little spraying or fertiliser, so that they are environmentally friendly. The crop is cut by machines, chopped and then burnt in specially designed boilers. In Sweden small towns are heated by this method and it is hoped that in time the same thing will happen here.'[29]

Heather, *Calluna vulgaris* (VN: Ling). In an entirely natural situation, heather is a less showy and gregarious plant than the one that colours whole areas of upland moor and southern heath in August. It straggles about the understorey of northern pine and birch woods, and some open beech and oak woods in the lowlands, but elsewhere flourishes only where there is no natural tree cover – on gale-blown western cliffs and sand-dunes, for example, and above the tree-line on Scottish mountains.[30]

The great sweeps that are called 'heaths' because of the abundance of heather species are almost always the result of human activity. Heathland develops when trees are cleared on poor, acidic soil and grazing animals (or fire) prevent them becoming re-established.

There are no precise historical figures for the amount of heather-clad land. At the end of the seventeenth century Gregory King estimated that there were 10 million acres of 'heaths, moors, mountains and barren land' – about a quarter of the land surface.[31] For those who shared its frugal habitats, heather was one of the basic raw materials of domestic life, like the bracken and gorse with which it often grows. It has been used as fuel, fodder and building material where wood was in short supply (sometimes standing in as the framework of wattle-and-daub), and its springy stems have been bundled up into thatch and brooms and woven into ropes. Its roots were carved into knife handles, particularly for the ceremonial Scottish dirk. The spikes of honey-scented lilac flowers make an orange

White willow, gleaming in autumn sunshine by the River Severn, near Welshpool, Powys.

dye, a sweet tisane and a spectacular beer. It is so softly supporting and fragrant that it was used for human as well as animal bedding, and Scottish settlers took it to America with them, naturalising one of their national symbols thousands of miles beyond its natural range.

The widespread abolition of common rights and subsequent loss of grazing meant that in the nineteenth century and early twentieth century a great deal of heath returned to woodland. More, trapped in its simplistic image of 'wasteland', has succumbed to development. Today, there are probably not much more than two million acres across all of mainland Britain, and most of this is in the uplands, where heather moorland is conserved for sheep and grouse. In England, heath now covers less than one-third of one per cent of the land area. The losses have been greatest on the southern heaths, with many areas such as south Dorset and the Breckland losing three-quarters of their heathland this century.[32]

But in the surviving heaths some of the traditional uses of heather have been kept up, albeit on a reduced scale. In the New Forest it has been used to repair potholes in the rides and tracks: 'The local estate sends a tractor round tipping gravel where needed, but our sage says, "T'aint no good unless they puts down 'eather first." He must be right, too – the holes are still there!'[33]

Like bracken, it was also used as a packing material, as in Clwyd: 'Bricks used to be taken from Buckley by tram-road to Connah's Quay, wrapped in straw to avoid breakages. When foot and mouth threatened exports to Ireland, because of a ban on straw, a trade was created for heather as a substitute. This was gathered from the hills around Buckley and heaped up at the brickyards ready for use. There are still patches of heather beside the former tram-road and on old coal banks around Knowl Hill.'[34]

On the Isle of Man, 'heather was wound into ropes called Gadd. This was strong enough to be used for mooring boats.'[35]

Around Ashdown Forest in Sussex: 'While it isn't permitted to take hives on the commonland of Ashdown, beekeepers still move their hives into the gardens and land adjacent to the Forest

Above: Ling flowers (Calluna vulgaris).
Left: Ling on the North Yorkshire moors.

to take advantage of the heather bloom.'[36]

On other Sussex heaths, dead growth is cut and used as firelighters.[37] In Scotland, people still sometimes put a sprig of heather under their beds,[38] echoing its old use as a mattress plant – or maybe just for luck: 'White heather is considered very lucky, especially in Scotland, and many if not all bridal bouquets have a sprig of it; also wedding, birthday and celebration cakes.'[39]

Heather ale holds a special place in the mythology of the Highlands. It is a brew of ancient legend, lost recipes and a recent dramatic revival. Enthusiasts for the beer believe it to have been first developed by the Picts 4,000 years ago and have as their evidence some drinking vessels which were found during the excavation of a Neolithic settlement on the island of Rhum, in 1985. A crust on the inside of the cups contained pollen spores of oats, barley, heather and mead-owsweet. The archaeologists believed this to be the remains of a fermented beverage and were able to produce a moderately acceptable ale using the same ingredients.

Heather ale was once one of the staple drinks of the Highlands. It was made by clan 'yill wives' and drunk from cattle horns. It is even possible that the first 'uisgebeatha' (Gaelic for whisky) was produced by condensing the alcohol from hot heather ale against stone walls.[40] But across the Highlands it went into decline during the wars with the English and the Highland Clear-ances, though the brewing tradition was kept up in the Hebrides and Orkneys. When Thomas Pennant visited Islay in 1774, he found that the islanders made ale from 'the tops of young heath, mixed with a third part of malt and a few hops', and in some isolated spots such brewing may have survived into the nineteenth century.

But its reintroduction on a commercial scale on the mainland had to wait until the 1990s and the enthusiasm of a Glasgow home-brewer, Bruce Williams. The story of his enterprise reads like a Scots legend in its own right. In 1993 a woman gave him a recipe in Gaelic, which had reputedly been handed down through ten gener-ations. After many false starts, Williams found a way of making the process work on a commer-cial scale, and in 1994 he launched his remark-able, honey-scented, bitter-sweet 'leann fraoch' (Gaelic for heather) ale. His heather comes chiefly from Argyllshire: 'It is picked by local pickers, July to August, in the Oban to Connel area. North Connel hills' south-facing crops are earliest. Only flowering tips are removed. In August, the majority is picked between Tyn-drum and Loch Awe, also on the "Rest and be Thankful" Glen (which many pickers did!), mostly pale purple and white ling heather. Heather is abundant in Argyll. It is a wasted resource. The sheep farmers burn it … The plants do not appear to be damaged by cropping; the previously cut plants in my own garden flowered again the next year.'[41]

The brewing process begins conventionally enough, with the heather flowers added as an aromatic flavouring to the malted barley, as if they were hops. (They also provide, through their nectar, a small amount of additional, fer-mentable sugar.) The hot brew is subsequently filtered through a bed of heather tips.

Bruce Williams's enterprise has given a boost to the revival of interest in herb beers, and ales bittered with wormwood, bog-myrtle, ginger, lemon and even the original 'ale-hoof' (ground-ivy) are increasingly appearing in commercial brewers' catalogues.

Gorse, *Ulex europaeus*; **western gorse**, *U. gallii*; **dwarf gorse**, *U. minor* (VN: Furze, Fuzz, Fuzzen, Vuzzen, Whin, Whinny luck). 'When gorse is in blossom, kissing's in season' is a saying known throughout Britain. Unromantic botanists are apt to explain it away by pointing out that, except in Scotland, most gorse colonies are a mixture of common gorse (in flower chiefly from January to June, though often sporadically through the year) and either western gorse (July to November) or, in the south and east of Eng-land, dwarf gorse (also July to November), so there is always likely to be one species in flower. But I suspect that there is also a 'where' implied in the 'when'. Gorse is one of the great signature plants of commonland and rough open space, places where lovers can meet, walk freely and lose themselves, if need be, in its dense thickets.

Being an abundant, fast-growing plant, it has also been pressed into a multitude of more func-tional roles: as fuel (especially in bakers' ovens), as cattle food, as a convenient anchor for wash-ing, as a chimney brush, and (in flower) as a source of colour for Easter eggs.

'Gorse and heather were bound together to make besom brooms, which were then tied with the same jute string used for binding straw bales.' (Whitby)[42]

'Some local gardeners place chopped gorse or "fuzz" over germinating or emerging peas to deter mice and pigeons.' (Plymouth; also Ashridge)[43]

The gorse and stone 'hedges' of central Dartmoor. The stones were gathered from the moor; the gorse either found its own way in or was deliberately planted.

Western gorse (Ulex gallii), Cornwall.

'Branches of gorse (and some other shrubs), known as "brobs", were used by fishermen to mark safe routes out into Morecambe Bay.'[44]

'In Wales many farmers remember gorse mills, and how important a food gorse was, especially for horses. Fields were devoted to growing gorse as a crop, and at least one smallholder in Anglesey made his living cutting gorse for other farmers, at five shillings an acre. I am told that in one corner of Anglesey, European and Western gorse were thought to be male and female of the same species. The female, Western gorse, was the much more desirable and softer source of food.'[45]

On commonland there were quite strict rules about when and how much gorse could be cut for fuel: 'In Cumnor, Oxfordshire, under the 1820 Enclosure Award, parishioners had the right to go to Cumnor Hurst to cut gorse and broom (for burning, often in bread ovens due to the fierce heat) but they were allowed only as much as they could carry on their backs.'[46]

'Furze was regularly gathered for firing in the last century from Harpenden Common [Hertfordshire]. To quote a 90-year-old man I interviewed: "We gathered it carefully, not haphazardly, remembering there was a tomorrow." '[47]

On Berkhamsted Common, a few miles south of Harpenden, there were regulations prohibiting the cutting of gorse for sale outside the parish and the digging-up of entire bushes. In 1725, to prevent over-exploitation, the Manor Court even specified the type and size of the cutting implements: 'Imprimis wee order that no person or persons shall cut any furze growing on the comon or heath or frith belonging to this Manor nor any of the Wast thereto adjoining with any other weapon or working tool than an one handed Bill with a stale helve or handle thereto affixed of the length of twelve inches & no longer upon pain and penalty for every person cutting any furze contrary to this order every time offending five shillings.'[48] (One year later, exceptions were made in favour of persons over sixty or under fourteen, and of the disabled, who might use 'Hows or handbills but not longbills'.)

Gorse is also an important ingredient of many turf- and hedge-banks in western Britain: 'Above the River Eden near Egremont, hedges of whin stand on the top of very considerable turf-stone banks (locally known as kests).'[49] In the New Forest: 'A family with a very small smallholding had a gorse hedge around it. Their ruse was to prune back the inside of the hedge and let the outside grow, gradually increasing their acreage.'[50] On the Isle of Man:

'The native gorse is *Ulex gallii*. It grows everywhere except on the Calf of Man. No gorse of any sort grows there, which gives rise to the catch question, "What colour is the gorse on the Calf of Man?" Large quantities of *U. europaeus* seed were imported and planted on top of the old sod hedges to make a more effective barrier to cattle, but the gorse was also planted on small patches of rough ground for use as fodder. Here and there on upland farms one can find the remains of gorse-mills which were used to bruise the new growth and make it palatable. The older and dead stems were used for fuel. Sticks like this are known as Bonns, and people still gather them on country walks.

There was even a special tool evolved for cutting down the bushes called a Hack. No doubt they would be made by the village blacksmith. Patches of old bushes were cleared and rejuvenated by burning and this practice was also sanctioned by the May Eve custom of setting fire to the bushes to drive out witches. The gunwales of boats are still sometimes singed with a blazing branch for the same purpose. The burning of gorse on the hills is controlled now to avoid disturbance to nesting birds.'[51]

In the village of West Torrington, Devon, a traditional match-making dance involving gorse was revived in 1994. 'The Vuz Dance of Flowers' centred around an elaborate display made by the male dancer, or 'talesman'. It consisted of a tight faggot of gorse branches, supporting a hazel branch (called a 'nit-al') which was topped with another 'bush' of gorse tied with coloured ribbons. This is an account of the dance given to us by a villager, who had learned of it from his great-grandfather:
'A man would put his trade object (loaf of bread, horseshoe, nails, etc) in under cover on the top of a faggot, which he had made. There would be one dancer at least for one stand, i.e. more stands than dancers. The dance would be done with whistle pipe and drum, tune unknown. Dancers would dance singly in the fashion of "in and out the windows". When the band stopped, the girl would go to the nearest stand and pick out the talesman from the men who were standing on the side. If he liked the look of the girl who had picked [him], this talesman would go forward and stand by the girl. When all of this had been done they would do the dance together. On leaving the square, the men would take the faggots home with them, and if marriage resulted, they would use the faggot to cook their first loaf of bread.'[52]

Wherever it grows in quantity, gorse is one of the great landscape plants, especially when the blaze of yellow is mottled with purple heather. The Swedish naturalist Linnaeus reputedly fell to his knees and thanked God when he first saw furze on an English common. (It was probably on Putney Heath, in 1736, but it is a measure of

gorse's popularity that half the commons in the Home Counties have claimed the honour for themselves.) It is one of the most sensual of plants – the flowers smelling of coconut and vanilla, and the seed-pods' cracking in hot sunshine hard to tell from the clacking calls of the stonechats which perch precariously on the topmost sprigs. George Meredith caught all this in the great gorse stanza in 'Juggling Jerry', where he described an old man relishing familiar scenes and scents:

Yonder came smell of the gorse, so nutty,
　Gold-like and warm: it's the prime of May.
Better than mortar, brick and putty,
　Is God's house on a blowing day.
Lean me more up on the mound; now I feel it;
　All the old heath-smells! Ain't it strange?
There's the world laughing, as if to conceal it,
　But he's by us, juggling the change.

WILD HERBS

We are becoming so accustomed to the constant stream of wild plants currently being taken into cooking and medicine that it is easy to forget that many of these represent rediscoveries. All cultivated plants had, of course, wild ancestors, and investigating the properties of these as potential food (or poison) marked the first cultural contact between humans and the plant world. A herb could be said to be any plant which passed the test. One traditional definition is that 'herb' is 'applied to plants of which the leaves, or stems and leaves, are used for food or medicine, or in some way for their scent or flavour' Looking at the immense range of useful plants today, this definition would have to be broadened to include flowers and roots as well as stems and leaves, plants used as detergents and dyes, and the raw material of people as far removed as historic gardeners and holistic healers.

At some time or another, most of the wild plants of Britain have been pressed into medicinal service. Couch grass has been used for urinary complaints, sanicle and bugle for ulcers and wounds, lesser celandine for piles, borage for depression. Often these are very personal remedies, and their effectiveness depends on the degree to which they are believed in. But there are a handful of herbs – comfrey, feverfew and hop, for example – which seem to work with most sufferers and which have been validated by conventional medicine.

'Wild foods'. Since the mid-1970s, foraging for wild plant foods has become almost as common in Britain as on the continent. Even mushroom-hunting has ceased to be regarded as an outlandish and dangerous eccentricity, and you must be out very early in British woods these days to be sure of getting your share of the first ceps and chanterelles. Fortunately the practice has lost most of its early and sometimes overhearty associations with survivalism and (though it can reduce your food bills) its more fantastical links with self-sufficiency. Foraging is now simply fun, indulged in for the pleasure of new taste experiences, for insights into the history of our cultivated foods, and for more intimate and sensuous encounters with growing things. It can

Marjoram, the oregano of Mediterranean countries and a common summer-flowering herb of chalk country.

Young stinging nettles – here growing by the old Roman Wall at Silchester, Hampshire – are used in soups in the spring.

even be rewarding done as little more than wayside sampling: a wild red currant here, a sweet cicely seed there – what the 1930s fruit gourmet Edward Bunyan described delightfully as 'ambulant consumption'.

Since the late 1980s wild plants have also begun to make a perceptible impact on the commercial food business. In France, which has rather more raw materials at its disposal, there is a distinct school known as *cuisine sauvage*. And in Britain it is now not uncommon to find samphire, nettles, dandelions, bitter-cress, borage, wild strawberries, bilberries and ramsons served in some form or other in both smart metropolitan restaurants and local pubs. Perhaps most encouraging is the fact that they are no longer regarded simply as rough peasant foods, but are being used as ingredients for modern *styles* of cooking: wild herbs and fruits flavouring oils and vinegars (and even Danish-style schnapps);

spring greens – garlic mustard, nettle, sorrel – stir-fried; flowers added to salads. A contribution from a Hampshire woman of American ancestry illustrates the inventiveness of the modern approach to wild foods:

'I take so many of these foods for granted that I often forget that many people don't eat such things as dandelion pasta, nettle gnocchi, wild garlic and cheese soup or dandelion and mozzarella pie! I guard any dandelion greens that spring up in my garden with as much enthusiasm as some look after their most prized tomato plants. My latest invention is to chop a load of assorted greens I've gathered, sauté them with garlic and onion, fold in ricotta cheese, some fine bread crumbs and an egg and use this as a stuffing for pasta shells or home-made ravioli ... My grandmother's cousin, Amber, had all her workmates gathered round the bench in the mill one day to sample her dandelion and mozzarella pie. She had layered cooked dandelion greens, cheese, sliced black olives and

Sweet chestnuts are sweetest after the first frosts.

a little tomato sauce made with garlic into flaky pastry and baked it into a pasty. It became her favourite lunch-box treat ... Have you ever had pickled greens? They are wonderful. Mustard greens, turnip greens, wild greens, the patient and persistent dandelion greens – all potted up in a spiced, slightly sweet vinegar. They make a cheese sandwich sing.'[53]

Windfall wilding apples, often still edible deep into winter.

Trees

TREES HAVE SIZE, longevity, economic usefulness and a profound impact on the landscape – which means that they have entered our culture more thoroughly than most smaller flowering plants. Some – oak, elm and willow especially – could have whole anthologies of poetry and paintings collected about them.

Yet to an extent their individual cultural histories have been overshadowed by the roles they have played in the general business of growing and harvesting wood. Although each has its own unique set of meanings and uses, they are treated more as trees than as individual species. They have all been cropped for fuel wood and used as rough timber. Their names are found as frequent components in place names, and most, in their maturity, have contributed to our considerable legacy of landmark trees. These subjects have been elegantly and exhaustively covered in Oliver Rackham's books (see Select Bibliography), which have transformed our understanding of the way that trees and woods 'work', socially and ecologically. *Flora Britannica* concentrates more on modern perceptions and meanings.

But there are common threads running through the social and cultural use of trees which are worth summarising at the outset. Traditionally, woodland trees were harvested by *coppicing*, which involves cutting them back to ground level once every 10 to 20 years. All our native deciduous trees (given enough light) will send up sheaves of straight new poles indefinitely when treated in this way. The cut poles were chiefly used as fuel-wood, but also as small-scale domestic or farm timber, often regardless of species.

Outside woods, in parks, pastureland and hedgerows, trees were usually managed by *pollarding*. This involves cropping the branches six to 15 feet above ground level, again on a regular

Field oaks near Wenlock Edge, Shropshire.

rotation. Pollarding produces less reliably straight poles than coppicing, but means that the trees can coexist with cattle or deer, as the new shoots appear above the browse level. Pollarding also prolongs the life of trees by reducing their top-heaviness and making them more wind-resistant, and over the centuries can produce exceptionally gnarled, characterful individuals. Uncut trees – grown for higher-quality timber – are often referred to as *maidens* or *standards*.

Pollards and, to a lesser extent, uncut trees can attain great ages and can become landmark trees, symbols of continuity in the landscape that can outlive whole dynasties of humans. There are still large numbers of landmark trees in parishes throughout Britain. Some are nationally famous, such as the Tortworth Chestnut, the Major Oak in Sherwood Forest, and the Tolpuddle Martyrs' Sycamore. There are lost trees, too, such as Gerard Manley Hopkins's Binsey Poplars, the Selborne Yew, and, most recently, the Aston on Clun Flag Tree. Many are more local trees which mark ancient boundaries and meeting places or where, according to legend, Queen Elizabeth picnicked or men were hanged. There are also increasing numbers of deliberately planted memorial trees, commemorating coronations, jubilees, centenaries and battles (some even planted out in the *formation* of battles). And there is an unrecorded host of privately loved neighbourhood trees – hidden in by children, watched as weather-vanes from kitchen windows, chatted under or just nodded at on the journey to work.

'There is a large oak in Quinta Drive, Barnet, and although not unusual, it is surely a landmark in this area. It is the place where if we have a coach to meet, it's always at the oak tree, [it] is used for directions in finding your way round our estate, it's the turn round for our Hopper bus.'[1]

Pedunculate oak or **English oak**, *Quercus robur* (VN: Sussex weed). The English have a loving but proprietorial relationship with the oak. Since at least 1662, when John Evelyn lamented to the Royal Society the 'notorious decay' of Britain's '*Wooden-walls*', as 'nothing which seems more fatally to threaten a Weakning, if not a Dissolution of the strength of this famous and flourishing *Nation*',[2] the qualities of the oak and the character of the nation have been linked. Edmund Burke described the aristocracy as 'the great oaks which shade a country' (and two centuries later, in 1995, the felling in Windsor Great Park of a number of 150-year-old oaks was compared by one pundit to 'chopping down the Queen Mother'). In the mid-eighteenth century David Garrick wrote a shanty, two of whose lines were to enter the national folk memory: 'Heart of oak are our ships/ Heart of oak are our men'. They in turn were plagiarised by Samuel James Arnold in his poem on the death of Nelson. The prolific botanical writer and arbiter of Victorian taste John Loudon pronounced the oak 'the emblem of grandeur, strength and duration; of force that resists, as the lion is of force that acts ...'

This is a fair précis of the oak's qualities, though we might be more diffident about claiming them for ourselves these days. But we can have legitimate pride in our legacy of ancient oaks, which vastly exceeds that of any other western European country. There are not many lowland parishes that don't have at least one oak over 250 years old – marking a cross-roads, commemorating an accession, sheltering a village seat, or just marooned out in the fields because no one has the heart to cut it down. Old oaks can live well over 500 years, especially when they are pollarded, and become recognisable as characters long before that. They age with more craggy and eccentric individuality than beeches, with dead branches drying to driftwood grey, the trunks developing burrs and dark rain-trickles and tufts of epiphytic fern, and often collapsing in places to a powdery red mass of rotting heartwood. The survival of trees which are so alien to orthodox forestry standards is a marvel, given the way we have treated so many of our other ancient natural monuments.

The following are accounts of some surviving landmark oaks, or their surviving fragments. Their image tends to be more homely, vernacular and even irreverent than that of some of the regal trees of the past. The archway oak in Sladden Wood, Kent, is typical, commemorating as it does the illegal flattening of this wood in one morning by Hughie Batchelor, a notorious 'agricultural improver' of the 1970s and 80s.

'Of the few mature oaks that were not felled before 1977, only one still survives. It is dubbed the Hughie Batchelor memorial tree. The felling of this oak had been so inexpert that it snapped at about four feet above the cut, and now forms an archway across a path. It still lives, though last year [1994] beefsteak fungus was found growing

Heart of oak: an ancient pollard, encrusted with lichens, moss and ferns, at Croft Castle, Herefordshire.

at its base, which may shorten its life.'[3]

'An ancient oak tree in the centre of Caton village [Lancashire] was believed to be becoming dangerous because of an overhanging branch. Villagers have over the years adopted the tree as a symbol of Caton. It is used as an emblem for the uniform of the local primary school, and of the Caton Sports Association. Tree surgeons, as usual, suggested felling it. But villagers thought otherwise and rallied round to protect the land-

mark. One parish councillor, Mick Jackson, and another villager volunteered to do the work, and made a metal post and prop to support the falling branch. Mr Jackson said, "The tree is the most important landmark in Caton and we should try and preserve it as long as there is any life in it at all." '[4]

'The vast oak at Eardisley near Hereford, described by Loudon in 1867 (34 feet in girth at three feet high), is still standing. It is said to be well over one thousand years of age and is very much alive. This tree is hollow and children used to use it as a play den. Some years ago the tree caught fire but it was saved, thank goodness. I have been inside this massive oak and looked right up into the sky with ease.'[5]

'I remember weekend jaunts to Epping Forest when living in Walthamstow as a child. Some time leading up to 1956 the Old Oak Tree in Epping was burnt down by vandals. This was a famous old tree and it served as monument and symbol to my family. My dad made a journey to Epping that weekend to say farewell to the tree. We brought home a small piece of charred wood and carved a paper-knife from it, which he still has to this day.'[6]

'The Wishing Tree of Isle Maree, Wester Ross, a long-dead oak, is perhaps the most celebrated in all Scotland. The tree stands on an island in Loch Maree ... The original significance of the site lay in a wishing well, long since dried out, where rag (cloutie) offerings were hung from nearby trees. At some stage the clouties were replaced by coins, hammered edgewise into the tree. After hammering in the coin, the visitor makes a silent wish. The oldest coins examined date from the 1870s, and the custom may have become engrained after Queen Victoria's visit in the 1880s. The oak, a slender tree, was already dead by 1927, studded with pennies, a victim of copper poisoning. The tree is now in three three-yard pieces stacked upright like a teepee. It still bears its coat of pennies, and more coins have been hammered into two nearby oaks; still others are strewn among the leaf litter ... The site is of ancient holiness: the tree lies within a circular stone dyke, interpreted as a Druid's circle ... A

'The Nine Brethren', a landmark coppiced oak in Nocton Wood, Lincolnshire.

curse lies on the person who removes anything from the isle. Local people still attach significance to these beliefs, and coin-wishing is obviously still current.'[7]

'When I went to Collyers School in Horsham, I used to cycle past the tree [the Sun Oak at Coolhurst] every day and it was amazing to look at in the summer. I imagine it got its name because of its enormous rounded crown.'[8]

'The Bound Oak is a hollow oak tree in Farley Hill, Berks. Its name refers to the fact that it marks the boundary between the parishes of Arborfield and Swallowfield. A fine wild cherry is growing very close to the oak, giving the impression that it is the oak that is in flower each March.'[9]

'The Milking Oak [Salcey Forest, Northamptonshire], in its heyday, had a spread so huge that the cows grazing on the "lawns" were milked under it in very hot or rainy weather.'[10]

'The Baginton Oak, on the southern edge of the village of Baginton, Warwickshire, sits at the southern tip of a triangular patch of grassland which may be the remnants of an old green … It is an old hollow pollard, last pollarded probably over a century ago. Concrete was poured into it at one time to prevent fires being lit but that was removed and now wire mesh stretched over the top of the bolling tries to do the same job … The pub opposite is named after it.'[11]

'Here at Great Barrington [Northamptonshire], we have an avenue of oak trees, planted by a previous Earl Spencer, which leads across an arable field, with crops through the middle.'[12]

Aristocratic oaks besieged by EC corn and folk oaks beseeched to death. Landmark trees seem to rise above class and politics:

'The village [Hartley Wintney, Hampshire] is well-known for its glades of English oak, and must be unique in the UK in having these trees planted in rows on the commons surrounding the centre of the village. For the villagers therefore, the Oak is king, and we cherish and are proud of our historic trees, planted by Lady Mildmay of Dogmersfield Park. They are known as the Mildmay or Trafalgar Oaks.'[13]

'Our most noteworthy tree is an oak (now much dwarfed by a massive electricity pylon), which has carved on its trunk a coffin and the letters SC, 1849 – which commemorates the death of Stan Crumpler (a Lytchett name) having been gored near the very same tree.'[14]

'Kett's Oak, Wymondham. Robert Kett led a rebellion against the enclosure of common land in 1549 and rallied support under the oak which now bears his name. He was subsequently hanged from Norwich Castle walls for his part in the revolt. Last year children from Hethersett Middle School planted 12 sapling oaks, grown from acorns from the original tree, and planted these alongside the old tree, which still flourishes, but is supported. Hitler's Oak. Chris Boardman, yachtsman and gold medallist in the 1936 Berlin Olympic Games, was presented with an oak tree by Hitler which was planted at How Hill.'[15]

The diversity which these trees show is echoed by oaks growing in hedgerows and woods. At Castle Malwood near the Rufus Stone in the New Forest is an ancient tree which produces new leaves by Christmas and a second crop in spring. It was first noticed by Dr William How in the 1650s.[16] At Staverton Park in Suffolk, a uniquely well-preserved medieval wood-pasture, there are some 4,000 oak pollards, between 200 and 500 years old.[17] They show every conceivable variation that can occur in natural self-sown oak populations. There are broad and tapering trees, barrel and fluted trunks, smooth barks and dense burrings, trees which hold their leaves all winter and others leafing all the way up the trunk. In Birklands, Sherwood Forest, there are 500-year-old oaks of a highly distinctive shape, and all with dead, stag-headed tops (though the rest of the crowns are thriving). In Wistman's Wood on Dartmoor, the oaks are elfinesque. John Fowles has written an incomparable portrait of them in the closing chapter of *The Tree*:

'The normal full-grown height of the common oak is 30 to 40 metres. Here the very largest, and even though they are centuries old, rarely top five metres. They are just coming into leaf, long after their lowland kin, in every shade from

A modern (1990) carving of an oak tree in oak wood, in the tower doorway of St Mary's, Ludgershall, Buckinghamshire.

yellow-green to bronze. Their dark branches grow to an extraordinary extent laterally; they are endlessly angled, twisted, raked, interlocked, and reach quite as much downward as upward. These trees are inconceivably different from the normal habit of their species, far more like specimens from a natural bonsai nursery. They seem, even though the day is windless, to be writhing, convulsed, each its own Laocoon, caught and frozen in some fantastically private struggle for existence.'[18]

Extraordinarily, despite world-wide agreement about the importance of maintaining biological diversity, recent European Union 'harmonising' legislation insists on all commercial sources of oak seed coming from a few approved sources, mostly in eastern Europe. An

earlier European grouping, the Celts, had a more respectful attitude towards the oak. Like many of the customs of early religions this was absorbed by (or perhaps, in this case, actively infiltrated) the Christian church in Britain. Carvings of oak leaves, acorns, and even galls are to be found in almost every English cathedral and a great number of the older parish churches. Sometimes they are openly displayed in the decorations of fonts and pew-ends, but often seemingly secreted away – under misericords or on the bosses high up in the roof.[19] In a few churches the most pagan symbol of all – the Green Man, wreathed by the oak leaves foaming from his mouth and ears – is found blatantly carved on Anglican capitals.

Ancient and venerated boundary oaks were also Christianised. The 'Gospel Oaks' that frequently occur as place names, with or without surviving trees, may refer to stopping points on the Beating of the Bounds or Perambulation – itself a sanctified version of early fertility rites. At some time during Rogationtide, just before Ascension Day in May, a procession would tour the bounds of the parish, memorising and passing on the knowledge of its course and extent. At many traditional points, often significant oaks, crops were blessed and passages from the gospels read.

In the village of Great Wishford in Wiltshire an elaborate Rogationtide ceremony is still held to affirm the villagers' ancient common rights to gather firewood in Grovely Forest. Its date has been shifted forward slightly, to 29 May (Oak Apple Day – see below), but it still echoes the mixture of Christian benediction, political demonstration and village party that has characterised Perambulations since as far back as the Middle Ages.

The modern ceremony begins in the early hours of 29 May, when the local youths march through the village banging dustbin lids and blowing trumpets and shouting 'Grovely, Grovely and all Grovely!' at the houses. They then go to Grovely Woods to cut vast oak boughs, up to 'the thickness of a man's arm', which are taken back down the hill to the village. Many are set in front of the doors of houses in the village. Others are carried in processions later in the day. One large branch is decorated with ribbons and hoisted to the top of the church tower. It is called the Marriage Bough and is supposed to bring good luck to all those married in the church in the coming year. Later in the morning, four women carrying sprigs of oak travel to Salisbury, accompanied by many villagers and a tremendous banner bearing the Grovely Shout and the commoners' motto 'Unity is Strength'. They dance for a while on the Cathedral Green. (Previously everybody danced the whole six miles to the city, but this was suppressed by the church in Victorian times, because it had degenerated into a revel.) The whole company then go into the Cathedral to make their claim by crying 'Grovely, Grovely and all Grovely!' The phrase 'all Grovely' is crucial. The only other village bordering the forest and having similar common rights was Barford St Martin. But their rights lapsed and Great Wishford now has 'all Grovely'.[20]

Oak Apple Day, 29 May, is the anniversary of the triumphant return of Charles II to London at the Restoration of 1660. Of his many adventures during exile, it is his concealment in the oak at Boscobel which seems to have left the most lasting impression, and Charles declared that the day should be set aside as a public holiday 'for the dressing of trees'. Hence the date of the festival, and the tree species associated with it – though why it is Oak Apple – the spongy, crab-apple-like galls formed on oak twigs by wasp larvae at the end of May – Day, rather than simply 'Oak Day' is not clear. In late Victorian times it was simply called 'Royal Oak Day', though there was a custom of covering any oak apples attached to sprigs with gold leaf in honour of the crown.[21] Oak Apple Day is still celebrated in many schools and military establishments by the wearing of sprays of oak, though nothing like as extensively as it once was, and has tended to absorb other May-time festivals (see Spring festivals, p. 43).

'As a celebration of the Royalist village [St Neot, Cornwall] saving its church from destruction by the Puritans, a fresh leafy oak branch is

Oak sprigs are worn by the Garland King's horse during the Oak Apple Day celebrations in Castleton, Derbyshire.

put up in the church tower each year and the old branch taken down. Villagers who take part in the ceremony wear a sprig of oak.'[22]

'The chant on Oak Apple Day was "29th May, Oak Apple Day, if you don't give us a holiday we'll all run away." '[23]

'A local name for oak apples [in this case clearly the spherical 'marble galls'] was "chick-chacks", from the sound they make when used as marbles. In Dolton [Devon] 29th May was Chick-chack Day and it coincided with the parade of the village Friendly Society.'[24]

Alongside this traditional mythology of strength and ancient lineage, there is another more modern group of scientific myths, which stress the oak's weaknesses and irregularities in reproducing itself. Despite the fact that it grows all over Britain in most kinds of soil, seedling oaks are rare inside oakwoods – though abundant on heathland, on railway embankments, and even, since set-aside, on fallow arable land. At the historic 1974 conference on the British Oak,[25] there were even foresters who dared to suggest that, though obviously native, the oak was not really at home in Britain. It was a continental tree on the northern edge of its range, and not suited to our late frosts and often cool summers.

But at the same conference the real reasons why oak was reluctant to regenerate in oak-woods also began to emerge. The acorns and oaklings are under siege at almost every stage in their life: eaten by small mammals; often not having sufficient light to germinate because of the end of coppicing in so many woods; and finally, if they do succeed in developing into seedling trees, they are likely to be defoliated by tortrix moth caterpillars parachuting down from their parent tree. Mature oaks can cope with losing almost all their leaves to caterpillars in the spring, simply by growing another set; but oaklings with tiny root systems cannot, and usually die. This is why oaks are so much more successful at regenerating in the open (where their acorns are planted by jays and squirrels), away from the shade and insect rain of their own kind.

Sessile oak, *Q. petraea*. The sessile oak, so called because its acorns (unlike *Q. robur*'s) are not carried on stalks (peduncles), but directly on the outer twigs, has an intriguing distribution. It is commonest in the north and west of Britain, but chiefly in semi-natural woodland, in which it also occurs more sparingly elsewhere in Britain. In hedgerows, plantations and scrub, even in its heartlands, it is largely replaced by the pedunculate oak. The two species seem in fact to regenerate in quite different patterns, the sessile growing well under its own shade and often forming quite dense single-species woodland, but not readily colonising land beyond woods; the pedunculate behaving in exactly the opposite way. Superimposed on this have been the effects of human preferences. Pedunculate oak usually produces a much greater crop of acorns, which were valued as food for pigs and cattle (the Domesday Book, 1086, actually measures the area of woodland in terms of the number of swine it can support), and its stocky trunks and naturally angled branches were prized as more desirable and adaptable timbers. As a consequence it has been widely planted throughout Britain, and has the look of an invasive species. Sessile oak, by contrast, seems largely confined to the areas it must have occupied in the wildwood, and has a relict distribution, analogous to that of small-leaved lime

(see p. 121).[26] In the north and west, sessile oak-woods were largely perpetuated by coppicing. The wood was used in iron-smelting, and the bark in the tanning industry.

The culture surrounding sessile oak echoes the tree's rather inferior economic role and is very sparse. Recognisable carvings of the leaves in churches are few. But they are clearly distinguishable on the shrine of St Frideswide in Christ Church Cathedral, Oxford, and carved on bosses at Claydon church, East Suffolk.[27]

The undersides of sessile oak's leaves are downy, which sometimes gives them a silvery sheen. A remarkable colony of such oaks (still thriving) is commemorated in the place name 'Whiteleaved Oak' near Bromsberrow in the southern Malverns.

Hybrids between the sessile and pedunculate oak are often commoner than either of the parents where both species are present, and occur throughout Britain.

Evergreen oak or **Holm oak**, *Q. ilex*, is an evergreen species from the Mediterranean which is widely planted. It is often killed (or defoliated) by severe frosts, but has self-seeded quite widely in southern and central England and Wales, especially on the Cotswold limestone.

A well-known grove are the Bale Oaks in north Norfolk, planted outside the church in about 1716 by Thomas Bullen. But the ancient English oak whose company they joined was a much more interesting tree. Its trailing leaves and acorns are represented in a fifteenth-century stained-glass window in the church, and in the early eighteenth century it was 'so large that ten or twelve men may stand within it. A cobbler had his shop and lodge there of late, and it is or was used for a swinestry.'

The former rector described its end and last rites:
'In 1795 the Bale Oak was severely pollarded, and the Hardys of the village of Letheringsett purchased the wood and the bark (for tanning). It never recovered from this drastic treatment, and a poem was written about the tree in this state, and learnt and passed down to villagers, who can even quote it to this day:

Here stand I all in disgrace,
Once the wonder of this place;
My head knocked off, my body dead
And all the virtues of my limbs is fled …

By 1860 the Oak had become dangerous, and as the Parish Officers would take no responsibility for anyone getting injured, the Lord of the Manor – Sir Willoughby Jones, Bart., had the tree taken down and carted off to Cranmer Hall, Fakenham. The waggons employed were decked with flags, and all Fakenham turned out to see them pass through.'[28]

Beech, *Fagus sylvatica*. The beech, alone among our large forest trees, has something of a feminine image. When I was a boy growing up in the Chilterns, the tree was always offered as an example of elegance and classicism, the foil to the rugged masculinity of the oak. Fine specimens were often called 'Queen beeches'. Even today, the gracious but solemn plantations of the Chilterns and Cotswolds are referred to reverently as 'nature's cathedrals'.

Yet there have always been other kinds of beech, rowdier, more accessible, less obscured by idealisation: the stumpy workhorse pollards of Burnham Beeches and the gnarled giants of the New Forest; scraps of bristling coppice in the Chilterns; wind-pruned hedges on Exmoor; and, increasingly, these days, wind-*thrown* beeches, with root-plates like small cliffs.

Contrasting kinds – and contrasting images –

One of Paul Nash's many paintings of Wittenham Clumps, a landmark beech grove on the site of an Iron Age fort near Wallingford, Oxfordshire. Nash drew the Clumps obsessively and saw them as a symbol of the repossession of human works by nature. But, as is so often the case with beeches, 'It was the look of them that told most. They were the Pyramids of my small world.'

of the beech have a long history. Even its arrival in this country has been a contentious matter, and it is often claimed to be a Roman introduction (another echo of its 'classical' aura). But beech pollen remains have been found in the Hampshire basin that date from 6000 BC – about 2,000 years after the oaks returned to post-glacial Britain and 500 years before the Channel opened. So the beech just passes the key test of botanical nativeness: it was here when Britain became an island. It advanced under its own steam up to a line between the Bristol Channel and the Wash, and, as a planted tree, much further. In parts of south-east England it became one of the commonest woodland trees. But early beeches would have been less gainly and upright than those we are familiar with today. In medieval woods, beech was rarely grown as timber and almost never used for buildings. Even in the Chilterns houses were framed in oak. The beech was valued historically as a more basic kind of workhorse. It was an energy source, providing firewood for humans and nuts ('mast') for grazing cattle. As far back as the late Roman period mixed beechwoods supplied fuel for ironworks. In the Weald, beech was the fuel of choice for the glass industry. In the Chilterns, wood cut from pollard (and coppiced) beeches was shipped up to London by barge, for the city's hearths and ovens.[29] Between cuts, on wood-pastures and commons throughout southern England, grazing animals would feed on the mast.

In the eighteenth century, the 'Age of Improvement', beech began to be valued for ornament and timber, and tall, smooth-barked, straight-trunked trees became more frequent both 'in woods and parkland. Gilbert White thought beech 'the most lovely of all forest trees, whether we consider its smooth rind or bark, its glossy foliage, or graceful pendulous boughs'.[30] William Gilpin, another late eighteenth-century Hampshire cleric and one of the arbiters of Picturesque taste, preferred the old vernacular

Beech high forest in winter sunlight, Chilterns.

beech, 'studded with bold knobs and projections', to the tall timber trees, whose branches ran 'often into long unvaried lines, without any of that strength and firmness, which we admire in the oak'.[31] But by the end of the century the timber beech had won the day. The rapid development of the Windsor chair industry (which used turned beech for chair legs) led to the conversion of vast areas of beech coppice and pollards to timber beech lots, especially in the Chilterns.

The situation remains much the same today. The beech's role in popular culture is almost exclusively as a landscape tree – elegant in mature plantations, gothically rugged on old commons, and spectacular in its autumn coloration wherever its grows.

Planted beech landmarks are typically avenues and groves on hilltops:

'At Elveden Hall near Thetford, there is a beech avenue running due south of the main house. Many of these trees have plaques commemorating the date and the planter. Most, if not all these trees were planted by members of various European Royal Families, including Queen Victoria, King Juan Carlos, and the Tsars of Russia.'[32]

'There are beech trees on the top of Howe Hill, just outside Ingleby Greenhow. They are used as a logo for the local primary school, and over 45 years ago my husband recalls going up there with the children of the local Sunday school where a service was held.'[33]

Famous hilltop groves include the Seven Sisters at Cothelstone Hill, which can be seen from much of Somerset and South Wales, and Wittenham Clumps on an Iron Age hill-fort in Oxfordshire, which was such an inspiration for Paul Nash's paintings. Wittenham also has the 'Poem Tree', now dead, alas, but still bearing the verse carved by Joseph Tubb in 1844 and celebrating the landscape around the hill-fort.

Graffiti are more usually associated with old pollards, the self-sown, 'vernacular' beeches. It is a venerable tradition, going back to the Romans, who had a proverb for it: *Crescunt illae; crescant amores* – 'As these letters grow, so may our love.'

(There is even a possibility that slabs of beech or *bok* wood or bark, etched with ancient Teutonic graffiti, were the first *books*.) In Frithsden Beeches, one of the finest surviving groups of ancient pollards, there are graffiti going back a hundred years, through messages carved by American airmen, to prim Victorian initials. Stretching as the trunks expand, they seem entirely in keeping with the other ways old beech trees register their lifetime's experiences: the lightning scars, woodpecker holes, fungal rots, squirrel-browsed elbows in branches and aerial ponds in crucks, as well as the rounded bosses that mark where the last branches were cropped,

Beech pollards acquire a remarkable individuality over the centuries.

a century and a half ago.

The Frithsden pollards also include several trees (known locally as 'the Praying Beeches') with fused branch-stumps, as if the last loppers had deliberately tied the young regrowing twigs together. Young beech shoots will graft very readily, even from close natural contact, as one of the most touching twentieth-century landmark trees demonstrates: 'My father lived in Garforth and Mother worked as a live-in dairy maid in Aberford, so he used to walk down the Fly-line [a disused railway track] to visit her. He found three beech saplings growing by the path and – as he was courting Nellie – he grafted the middle trunk across the left-hand sapling to form the letter N. He gave it the name Nellie's Tree. This would be about 1920, and the tree is still there.'[34]

Another beech oddity in the Chilterns are patches of relict coppice, one at Maidensgrove Scrubs, the other at Low Scrubs, near Ellesborough in Buckinghamshire, which was a parish fuel-allotment apparently last cut in the 1930s.[35] These are particulary intriguing, as the coppicing of beech, once a widespread and successful practice in the area, has proved notoriously tricky to reintroduce. Cut trees, even when protected from browsing, usually die after a few years. The wood at Low Scrubs may provide some clues as to how beech coppicing was carried out.

It is an extraordinary collection of hunched, low-growing trees, surrounded at their bases by masses of twiggy growth. These have the look of 'witches'-brooms', but in fact are the dense network of shoots that beeches throw out when they are cut or browsed, snagged up with fallen leaves and bits of branch. Behind this are two generations of poles, typically two or three stout trunks six to ten inches in diameter, surrounded by a number of thinner poles about two inches wide. Deer-browsing might explain this, but I wonder if the secret of beech coppicing was to leave a leading pole or two uncut, as was the practice sometimes with hazel. (This was the custom amongst older coppice-workers in nineteenth-century Sussex, where full coppicing was believed to 'bleed the spirit of the trees away'.)

Aside from the uses of its wood and its contribution to the landscape, beech has little in the way of associated custom or folklore. The three-sided nuts make a pleasant nibble in the years when they form, and during the two World Wars were collected in German villages for pressing into oil. The leaves have been made into a potent alcoholic drink – beech-leaf noyau. This is a recipe remembered by a 70-year-old man in the southern Chilterns: 'Wash and dry enough beech leaves to fill your stone jar – cover them with gin. Leave for a week, then strain off the liquid and measure. To each pint add a pound of sugar which is dissolved in half a pint of boiling water. Add a good quantity of brandy and stir together,

then leave to go cold before bottling.'[36]

Sweet chestnut, *Castanea sativa*. The sweet or Spanish chestnut was almost certainly one of the few species that was introduced to Britain by the Romans. Its nuts, roasted over winter braziers or ground more frugally into flour, are satisfying and savoury, and the trees may have been brought over to provide a home-grown supply of chestnut-flour for the legionaries.[37] But it is now an 'honorary native' and in south-east England behaves like a native tree. It is well-established in many ancient woods and propagates itself by seed – though not in the invasive manner of the more recently-arrived sycamore.

Frithsden Beeches, Hertfordshire, a beech wood-pasture now grazed by deer.

Sweet chestnut fruits, edible after the first frosts.

Ancient chestnuts are spectacular trees. They develop exceptionally broad trunks for their height, which with age become deeply fissured and covered with burrs and bosses. Quite often the fissures run in a left- or right-hand spiral round the tree. (Phil Gates has suggested, not too seriously, that this may be the origin of the name 'Spanish chestnut' for a tree which has no particular affinities with Spain: 'I favour an implausible theory that it is because the twist in the bark is like the swirl of a flamenco dancer's skirt.')[38]

Trees with girths of over 25 feet have been reported from Cranford, Middlesex; Holmbrook, Cumbria; Felbrigg Hall, Norfolk; Wiveliscombe, Somerset; between Bigsweir Bridge and Hudnalls in the Wye Valley; at Studley Royal near Ripon; and around the old observatory at Herstmonceux, Sussex.[39] There are even bigger specimens in Clwyd and Gloucestershire:

'In a field by the side of the Ruthin to Denbigh road, there were three enormous sweet chestnuts. One is quite dead and gone, one is still there as a pile of dead wood, and the third is still just holding its own. The locals say they are 2,000 years old – I doubt this, but they are marked on Ordnance Survey maps.'[40]

'Perhaps the oldest living individual in Longhope [Gloucestershire] is a chestnut tree. This tree stands in the field just east of the old railway line halfway between the Post Office and the Church. The circumference of the tree this October [1993] is 10.5 metres and 10.6 metres at two places ... It is a hollow tree with an inside "room" measuring roughly seven feet across with about one foot of living and dead tree making an outer ring.'[41]

But the biggest of all is the Tortworth Chestnut in Gloucestershire, which stands at one side of St Leonard's Church. It is unprepossessing at a distance and looks much like a grove of young chestnuts. But inside (it is surrounded by an iron fence) is something quite remarkable: an immense mass of contorted trunk and branch, like wooden lava or a wood-slip. The tree is still very much alive, though, and the collapsed side branches have all taken root and are sending up new shoots continuously. It is now virtually a wood itself, more than 30 yards across and with bluebells, dog's mercury and ramsons growing in its shade. It is impossible to date, but a plaque on the fence, dated 1800, reads:

THIS TREE SUPPOSED TO BE
Six Hundred Years Old 1st Jan
1800
May Man still Guard thy Venerable form
From the Rude Blasts and Tempestuous Storm.
Still mayest thou Flourish through
Succeeding time,
And Last, long Last, the Wonder of the Clime.

Elsewhere there are also ancient chestnut coppice stools, including one in Viceroy's Wood, Penshurst, Kent, which is known locally as 'The Seven Sisters' from its seven stems. These are reckoned to represent 250 years of regrowth, but the stool must be very much older, as its overall circumference is more than 50 feet.[42] Kent and Sussex are the major areas for chestnut coppice, and thousands of acres are managed commercially to produce chestnut fence-paling.

Many of these single-species Wealden cop-

The Tortworth Chestnut, probably not far short of 1,000 years old and now resembling a wooden cave-system more than a tree.

pices were planted in the mid-nineteenth century. Elsewhere, especially in deer parks, sweet chestnut was often planted for its nuts, which are popularly assumed to be attractive to deer. They grow inside rounded, spiny seed-cases, very similar to conkers, and are often blown from the trees early in October, before they are ripe. Perhaps this is why home-grown chestnuts have a poor reputation as winter nibbles beside the large nuts from Italy and the Balkans. In fact when they are ripe they are crisper and sweeter than imported varieties, and quite palatable raw. (I can remember three gardeners in a Chiltern pub debating the chestnuts of Ashridge Park as passionately as French countrymen discussing grapes. The best were along the Queen's Ride. No, they were in the woods below Lord Bridgewater's monument. The best of all, wherever they were, were those that hung on until they were brought down by frost.) Modern recipes for cooked wild chestnuts include soup, vanilla-flavoured spread and a stuffing which is then battered and fried as croquettes.[43]

One curious children's ritual with the nuts is 'Philippines': 'There was a custom originally associated with almonds but which became associated with any nut that had twins in one shell. You shared one of these nuts with someone present saying, "Here is a Philippine, share it with me." Next morning the first one to remember greeted the other with "Bon Jour Mon Philippine." The forgetful one had to find a present for the winner. I was astonished to find the next generation still keep up this custom. Perhaps it is a corruption of a German greeting "Vielliebchen", dear little one.'[44]

The long, jagged leaves are also used to make 'fishbones'. 'The soft leaf tissue would be removed between finger and thumb, great care being taken not to break the ribs of the leaf.'[45]

One final oddity. The long strings of yellow flowers, out in July, smell, as one contributor noticed, 'unmistakably of semen'.[46]

Elms, *Ulmus* species. In many parts of Britain, elm trees have already become a memory, and sometimes not even that. Only 25 years after the virulent new strain of Dutch elm disease

struck, it is proving increasingly hard to remember where big elms grew, what shape they were exactly, and what the English farming landscape looked like when it was still full of those heavy, fulsome, towering trees.

Elms have always been tinged with nostalgia and melancholy. In literature and popular mythology they are trees of drowsiness and brooding, dark reflections, it sometimes seems, of the piled cumulus clouds of late summer. At their most sombre, they have been constant reminders of mortality, dropping vast branches without warning and providing the wood in which human remains are finally laid to rest. 'Elm hateth Man and waiteth' is an old saying.

It is John Betjeman's poignant poems that best catch the tree's image (Tennyson's memorable 'The moan of doves in immemorial elms' excepted). Betjeman's elms are emblematic but always exactly placed. In Highgate he sees 'rich elms careering down the hill/ Full billows rolling into Holloway ...' In Hertfordshire, 'shadowy cliffs' with 'pale corn waves rippling to a shore'. In 'Dear Old Village', 'The elm leaves patter like a summer shower/ As *lin-lan-lone* pours through them from the tower.' His elm epithets themselves sound the complex depths of the tree's presence. They are 'guardian', 'waiting', 'shadowy' and 'whelming' – that extraordinary, perfect adjective from the funeral poem 'In Memory of Basil'. One of his oddest poetic images, at the start of one of his strangest poems ('The Heart of Thomas Hardy'), is also enacted before a gallery of elms:

> The heart of Thomas Hardy flew out of
> Stinsford churchyard
> A little thumping fig, it rocketed over the elm
> trees.[47]

All of these poems were written before the wave of Dutch elm disease that began in the late 1960s, whose impact is hauntingly documented in Gerald Wilkinson's book, *Epitaph for the Elm* (1978). The book's opening echoes the elegiac way elms were talked about in their prime: 'The elms are dying. Gaps appear in familiar lines of trees that we never bothered to think of as elms.

Half the tall trees, and many smaller ones, in the roadside hedges seem to have been elms, we notice, now they are so unhappily conspicuous … Rich corners of rustic England are one year a little yellowed, the next as bare as battlefields. Those dusty summer lanes in the heart of England that were half black shadow, half tattered sleepy sunlight among cobwebs, nettles and leafy elm shoots will soon be exposed to an unnatural glare.'[48]

Since then elm disease has fulminated, waned and returned again – the pattern you would expect from a virulent fungal disorder. The spores of Dutch elm disease are carried from tree to tree by bark-beetles, but the lethal agency itself is a fungus, *Ceratocystis ulmi*, which damages trees chiefly by blocking their water-conducting channels. Its effects may be mitigated in several ways. As more elms die, the distance to uninfected trees may be greater than the beetles can fly. And with time, even aggressive new strains of the fungus catch infections of their own, which make them less virulent, or able to grow only in sizeable elm branches. This was almost certainly one of the processes that was happening during the 1980s, when, throughout the country, shoots and suckers were reported growing from apparently dead elm stumps and often getting some way beyond the bush stage.[49] Many reached as high as 30 feet and began to flower again. Then, in the early 1990s, the disease struck again – a consequence of these now sizeable young trees being more attractive to both beetles and fungus, and the fungus having had

Dead elms at Dallinghoo, Suffolk, their almost identical profiles showing their common ancestry as suckers or cuttings from a single tree.

*'Elms in Old Hall Park', East Bergholt, Suffolk, a
pencil and wash drawing by John Constable.*

time to evolve strains less vulnerable to viral
attack. This see-saw is likely to continue, with
sometimes the fungus in the ascendency and
sometimes the virus (and young trees), until a
modus vivendi is reached.

But the single most important reason why the
elms have not been driven into extinction by the
current wave of disease (as many prophesied
they would be) lies in the nature of the elm family itself. Although four to six species are conventionally recognised, in the real world elms
refuse to be be confined to them. Over the past
millennia they have formed a bewildering range
of races and hybrids, so that there are now
almost as many kinds of elms as places in which
they grow. The elms' saving grace has been to
reproduce both by seed and by sucker. Seedling
elms, with all the variation that cross-breeding
brings, are common on the continent and probably were so in southern Britain when the climate
was warmer, six or seven thousand years ago (cf.
small-leaved lime, p. 121). With the exception of
the **wych elm**, *Ulmus glabra*, elms do not often
produce seedlings in Britain now. But the major-

ity of kinds produce suckers from their roots,
forming the genetically identical clusters of trees
known as clones. These differ in height and bark
texture, in their degree of uprightness and sym-
metry, in their vulnerability to disease, and in the
size and shape of their leaves. In Buff Wood, at
East Hatley in Cambridgeshire, Oliver Rackham
has identified at least 29 distinct elm clones in
just 40 acres.[50]

A similar diversity exists outside woods. Elms
have always been closely associated with human
settlements, and 'elm' is one of the commonest
components in Anglo-Saxon place names. The
foliage was cut for cattle and maybe even for
human food in prehistoric times, and later the
trees were widely planted, or encouraged to
spread sideways, as hedges and boundary markers. The suckers were an abundant and convenient source of young trees, and sometimes
whole parishes would be hedged from a single
clone, the character of the particular tree perpet-
uating itself through each new generation of
suckers. (And even after they were dead: the profiles of the stark skeletons in many East Anglian
hedges during the late 1970s matched up like
receding images in a mirror.)

Between 1955 and 1967 R. H. Richens con-
ducted an extensive survey of the village elms of
East Anglia.[51] He visited and took representative
leaf samples from trees growing in the ancient
boundary hedges of more than 500 parishes. He
found such a variation in leaf-shape (echoed by
differences in bark texture and the shape of the
whole tree) that it was possible to name types of
elm distinctive to small groups of settlements and
sometimes even to individual villages. (In Essex
alone he identified 27 village types, and the litany
of their names, from Frinton, Springfield and
Layer de la Haye, to West Hanningfield and
North Weald Bassett, is like something from a
Betjeman poem itself.)

Richens's explanation for this intensely local
distinctiveness was that prehistoric settlers in
different river valleys brought suckers of their
favourite or local elm type over from the continent. There is no evidence that this happened,
and it does seem an unlikely scenario, given the

highly forested nature of the countryside (which included plenty of wych elm then) when these early farmers were creating their settlements.

Rackham's alternative explanation is that these varieties of elm were naturally present in Britain, having migrated back with our other forest trees in the post-glacial era.[52] It has now been established by pollen analysis that the species which shows the most variation – the **small-leaved** or **East Anglian elm**, *U. minor* – was present in England before Neolithic settlers arrived. So was the wych elm, which is really a species apart, being both non-suckering and rarely growing naturally outside woods. The **English elm**, *U. procera*, the tall, billowing, traditional tree of the Midlands and southern England, and the most severely hit by Dutch elm disease, is possibly a human introduction. It may be a variety of *U. minor*, as is the narrow, erect-branched **Cornish elm** (*U. minor* ssp. *angustifolia* or *U. stricta*). The **Wheatley elm**, fashionable in the 1920s, is a variety of the Cornish, and the **Huntingdon elm** a variety of the hybrid between wych and smooth-leaved elm known (confusingly, in elm disease days) as **Dutch elm**, *U. × hollandica*. Mapping the elms' family tree is a Byzantine business …

But its complexity is the group's best hope of survival. Almost all the suckering types can survive the disease, albeit as bushes; and two – **Boxworth elm** (Cambridgeshire) and **Dengie elm** (Essex) – seem promisingly resistant even as adult trees. There are also many surviving trees in Brighton. This has long been a city with a huge variety of elms in streets and parks, and the local authority made great efforts to protect what was in effect an elm gene bank by burning dead trees promptly, before beetles had emerged, and inoculating living trees: 'Elms dominate so many streets in Brighton, including the London Road from Preston Circus, and indeed the Level, which were saved from the ravages of Dutch elm disease only to be decimated by the Great Storm [of 1987]. Plenty are left and the Council replanted the Level.'[53]

Most of the famous landmark elms – the Nine Elms in south London, the Tenor, Bass and Alto

Elms in Sigglesthorpe, Humberside, the Palmers Elm at Hewish in Somerset, the Watch Elm in Avon, for example – have gone.[54] So have the Dancing or Cross Elms of Devon round which May Day dances were performed. Sometimes these were planted close to churches – though one of the hazards associated with elms growing in churchyards was that they were liable to send suckers under the church, as at Ross on Wye in the late nineteenth century, where some sizeable trees grew *inside* the church. (Many of these his-

East Anglian village elms (near Little Wigborough, Essex) regenerating from suckers. They may reach 20 feet in height before succumbing to Dutch elm disease again.

toric elms are catalogued, along with elm paintings and literature, in R. H. Richens's *Elm*.)[55] But a few elm customs survive:

The Wicken Love Feast in Northamptonshire commemorates the union in 1587 of ' "Wikehamon and Wikedyve into one church and again called Wicken" … Ever since, on Holy Thursday (Ascension Day), after morning service in the church, the 100th Psalm is sung under an elm tree near the Parsonage, where the rector has given cake and ale to all in the parish that assembled or came to it. The elm was blown down some years ago, and a young one is growing in its place. On Ascension Day we still process to the spot after a service in the church and sing the Old Hundredth and pray for the village. Then we go to the Rectory for Holy Thursday cake and Ruddles Ale.'[56]

'In Lichfield, Staffordshire, there is an old custom of carrying twigs in procession round the Cathedral Close on Ascension Day. It happens during Rogationtide and the Beating of the Bounds, and, even the church acknowledges, has fertility overtones. (When there was a theological college in the close, it was "believed" that a student's wife observing the procession would conceive!) We end by throwing all the twigs in the font.'[57]

'This tradition has been taken over during the past few years by the younger choristers of the [Lichfield] Cathedral School, who place elm twigs and branches on the doorways round the Cathedral Close early on the morning of Ascension Day. The elm was cut from the nearest available tree, in the Palace gardens … The twigs carried in the procession later in the day by clergy and congregation are now usually lime – elm having vanished from the bulk of the close.'[58]

'Another nasty habit that we had was rubbing elm leaves between the hands and then rubbing the hands on the face of an unsuspecting victim. It was almost as if one had been stung by nettles – except that, fortunately, the effects did not last more than a few seconds. Hardly surprising since elm and nettle are closely related.'[59]

When elm timber was plentiful it was widely used where durability in wet conditions was needed – for instance in wooden pipes, floorboarding and coffins. The intricate and irregular grain pattern found in some trees (and especially in elm burrs) also made it popular for furniture. These days, the dwindling remains of dead elm trees, which bleach to the colour and texture of bone when dry, are chiefly used by sculptors in wood.

But there is every chance that mature elms may one day return to both commerce and the landscape. Although the current wave of Dutch elm disease may be the worst in historical times, the disease itself is nothing new, and the tree has always crept back. There was an epidemic in southern England between 1819 and 1864, another in Oxford in the 1780s. The dead elms common in Italian paintings between 1450 and 1530 are almost certainly stricken with it. And it may even be implicated in the phenomenon known as the Elm Decline (*c.* 3000 BC), when the pollen deposits from a tree which covered something like one-eighth of the British Isles fell dramatically to half their previous level. Commenting on these events (and echoing elm's morbid mythology) Oliver Rackham concludes, 'Why was it possible in the eighteenth century to insure one's elms against death? Elm was evidently well known to be the tree that specially shared man's fragile tenure of life, and it is difficult to suggest any other explanation than Elm Disease.'[60]

Black-poplar, *Populus nigra* (VN: Water poplar). On late afternoons in March, especially when there is a patchy sun glinting from the west, parts of the Vale of Aylesbury in Buckinghamshire are suffused with an exotic orange glow. All over the flood-plain, by dykes and lanes and thin streams, rows of craggy pollards begin to shine, as if they have been coated in amber. Closer to, the sprays of twigs seem kaleidoscopic. They have ochre bark, ginger-shellacked buds, and the germs of what will soon be voluptuous crimson catkins. This spectacular display is the largest concentration of our grandest native tree, the black-poplar, in all its spring finery, and there is not another treescape like it in Britain.

It is astonishing that such a conspicuous species should have passed so thoroughly out of common knowledge. But up till the mid-1970s, when the distinguished botanist Edgar Milne-Redhead began to study it, the black-poplar was overlooked by the public and regarded by most botanists as indistinguishable from nursery-bred hybrid poplars. Even the definitive 1962 *Atlas of the British Flora* lumped *P. nigra* var. *betulifolia*, as our native race is properly styled, along with all the various 'Italian blacks' so beloved of municipal authorities. In the early stages of Milne-Redhead's survey it looked as if there might be fewer than 1,000 trees surviving. Twenty years later some estimates put the national population at between 2,000 and 3,000.

But my own estimate would be double that figure, especially as the Aylesbury Vale population has never been properly censused and almost certainly exceeds that of all the rest of Britain put together. The tree's contribution to local landscapes is also beginning to be appreciated, as is what is proving to be a fascinatingly complicated social and ecological history.

Once you have an eye for them, it is hard to believe that mature black-poplars could ever have been mistaken for any of their characterless hybrids. They are distinctive, not just in their spring flush, but at all times of the year. They have thick fissured trunks, covered with massive bosses and burrs, grow to over 100 feet if uncut, and often develop a pronounced lean in middle

Black-poplars in March, Vale of Aylesbury, Buckinghamshire.

Native black-poplars develop pronounced burrs and bosses on their fissured trunks.

age. The branches turn downwards at their ends, often touching the ground, then sweep up again into sheaves of twigs, as if they have been caught by a gust of wind. The catkins are followed by masses of shiny, tremulous, beech-shaped leaves. Black-poplars appear in several of John Constable's landscapes of the Stour Valley (still a good place for the tree), though art historians have repeatedly misidentified them as willows or elms. One with a typically deep fork and a lost limb is in the several views that the painter made of the river by Flatford Mill; another vast tree lours in the background of *The Hay Wain* (1821) – which was itself probably planked with black-poplar wood. The lightweight, springy timber was used for brake-blocks, clogs, and even a

clutch of arrows which was discovered aboard the Elizabethan galleon, the *Mary Rose*. It is a very heat- and fire-resistant wood, and was consequently also popular for floor-boards, especially in oast-houses. The large forked trunks grow naturally into the shape required for cruck-framed buildings. In Frampton on Severn, Gloucestershire, what looks like a black-poplar cruck survives over the hearth of an Elizabethan house not far from an exceptionally tall and gracious tree on the village green.[61] A Shropshire family told Edgar Milne-Redhead that the top floor of their country house was made of black-poplar wood so that the staff who lived there would be less likely to set fire to the house with their candles and oil lamps!

The highly distinctive appearance of black-poplars meant that they were also employed as landmark trees. One ancient, weatherbeaten tree (*c.* 200 years old), in the Bourne Gutter near Berkhamsted, marks the intersection of parish, manor and county boundaries.

The decline of the black-poplar, both on the ground and in our culture, says much about changes in the landscape over the past few centuries. In prehistoric times, it was a tree of winter-flooded riverine woods (a virtually extinct habitat itself in Britain now), growing with willow, downy birch, alder, ash and elm. It would have survived the clearing of these forests as a tree of riversides and wet meadows, but not the wholesale drainage of the landscape. Like holly and yew, black-poplar is dioecious, and the red male and green female catkins grow on separate trees. To regenerate, male and female trees need to grow moderately close to each other, and the fertilised seed needs to fall on mud which is still damp in June, and which remains damp and bare during the seedlings' first critical months into the autumn. Such conditions virtually vanished once serious agricultural drainage works began in the seventeenth century. The surviving trees became marooned, ghosts of a wilder and wetter landscape, and from then on could regenerate only when they were deliberately struck from cuttings or 'truncheons' (which were mostly taken from male trees, because of the vast quantities of fluff produced by female catkins). The new trees were planted out as boundary markers on low-lying and often flooded grazing-land, and were usually pollarded to make them more stable and to provide a crop of wood for bean-sticks, thatching spars and fruit baskets. In the last hundred years many of the populations have become even more embattled. Increasingly they are being replaced by more upright and faster-growing hybrids. Elsewhere the policy of regenerating the tree by cuttings is producing increasingly vulnerable cloned colonies.

In the first 20 years of his still ongoing survey, Edgar Milne-Redhead discovered only one natural seedling, in a ditch in Gedgrave, Suffolk; and for a while only one place was known where male and female trees grew close enough together – and far enough away from hybrid trees – to ensure 'pure' pollination, at Hallwood Farm Marl Pit in Cheshire. In 1979, seedlings from these trees were planted out at Sturminster Newton in Dorset. 'They are well spaced on the banks of the River Stour and the mill stream and should grow into fine specimen trees. [Unlike in cloned colonies] considerable variation is already noticeable in the angle of branching ... the shape of the leaves and the colour of the leaf stalks, some being green and others red.'[62]

Since 1992 what look like relict wild populations have been discovered on an island in the Great Ouse at Fenlake near Bedford and at a site by the River Exe within the city bounds of Exeter.[63] And along the Fairham Brook at Widmerpool in Nottinghamshire there is a collection of unpollarded trees, including six large females, which 'have every appearance of being a native grouping'.[64]

In all these places – and others where there are no females, but the trees are unmanaged – the black-poplar is proving that it has more than one stratagem for reproduction. Fallen trunks will often strike roots, if they land on moist ground, and send up new vertical shoots. So, less certainly, will green boughs and twigs which are

A puzzle solved: this photograph found its way into Edgar Milne-Redhead's black-poplar files unlabelled. It has now been identified as standing in the grounds of Christ College School, Brecon, and is one of the largest in Wales.

broken off and washed into muddy river-banks. In Dorset 'there are two black poplars growing in my home village of Hazelbury Bryan, which started life as stakes for a chicken run and which accidentally grew'.[65] And in a few places (e.g. at Binham in Norfolk) I have seen new trees rising from what are in effect suckers, where a tree has been destroyed but its root system survives. These tangles of regenerating root plates and branches (plus occasional clumps of seedlings) must have been what young black-poplars looked like in their ancestral flood-plain forests.

The survey has also revealed the great variety that still exists in the species and in the range of places where it survives. One of the most northerly individuals, the Sunderland Point Tree in Lancashire, is said to have come from America on a ship trading with Lancaster and to have been planted by the skipper. (This may be an example of reintroduction, since European black-poplars were introduced to New England by early settlers and became so well established that American botanists described them as native early in the nineteenth century.) [66] The genuine North American black-poplars are known as 'cottonwoods' – a name that is echoed for black-poplars of an unspecified origin further inland in Lancashire: 'The black poplar is known locally as the Cottontree on account of the way its seed pods look like cotton seeds on the ground. The village is named Cottontree and the inn, which is much older than the village and stands on an old drove road by the tree, is called the Cottontree Inn.' [67]

Further south, the tree is frequent in river valleys all along the Wales–England border.[68] In Cheshire, near Alderley Edge, I have seen tall, narrow roadside trees whose bark, for once, merits the description 'black'. (No really adequate explanation of this epithet has yet been given.)

In Aston on Clun in Shropshire is probably the best-known black-poplar in Britain, which every 29 May is dressed with multicoloured flags

The Aston on Clun Flag Tree, before it was toppled by a gale in September 1995.

Black-poplars figure frequently in Constable's paintings, as in this study of the river near Flatford Mill. The Stour Valley in Suffolk is still a good area for the tree.

cutting taken from it some years before was quickly re-established on the same site.

On the Welsh side of the border there are several fine trees, including one 20 feet in girth and 80 feet high a mile north of Ruthin, Clwyd, and the landmark tree near the bridge in Newtown, Powys.[70] In Gloucestershire (one of the few counties where the tree was distinguished in an early Flora)[71] the trees were meticulously surveyed under the direction of Sonia Holland, and in 1992 numbered 355 (264 males and 91 females).[72] Herefordshire almost certainly has as many, including the remarkable cluster of 80 pollards on Castlemorton Common, which are still harvested for use in the village. There are also vast and majestic trees close to the churches at Blakemere and Hollybush.

Norfolk's trees were surveyed in 1992, and 54 mature specimens were found, mostly in river valleys and farm hedgerows, though there is a fine female on the village green at Old Buckenham.[73] Suffolk has some hundreds of surviving trees, and (perhaps because Edgar Milne-Redhead had his roots in the county) seems already to be taking the tree back into parish life:

'A female tree stands by the River Lark in "The Ebney Gardens", Bury St Edmunds. Another notable female grows in The Street at Dalham … A facet of the black poplar in Suffolk is its alleged ability to foretell approaching rain. It is possible that this originated from the highly mobile leaves rustling in the breeze and sounding very much like the downpour that might be on the way.'[74]

'We have several large old black poplars in the parish of Marlesford. There are two huge specimens by the Ford. We have successfully transplanted cuttings which now seem to be well established. The two trees just to the east of Milestone Farm have grown side by side from the fallen trunk of an earlier tree.'[75]

'There is one on the village green at Bardwell. It is growing on a slight mound at one end of the Green known locally as the Stocks. Cuttings have been taken of it, and one planted next to it, and one in the church-yard.'[76]

There is a hollow black-poplar outside Honeypot Hall, Wattisfield. ('When we lived there

and bunting. The flags remain on the tree until the following year, when they are taken down and replaced with new ones. The earliest records of the ceremony date from 1786, and it is believed to commemorate the wedding of squire John Marston to Mary Carter. Mary Carter is said to have so liked the flags that adorned the tree during her wedding that she gave a sum of money for the festivities to be repeated annually. (The wedding is now portrayed in a pageant which forms part of the ceremonials surrounding the replacement of the flags.)[69] But the date of the flag-dressing – Oak Apple Day, which in 1660 Charles II declared a public holiday 'for the dressing of trees' (see p. 89) – suggests that this 'Arbor Day' ceremony may have become attached to an already existing festival. Perhaps the wedding of John Marston and Mary Carter was deliberately arranged to coincide with the late May fertility rites – which long preceded King Charles's Restoration. The ancient tree was blown down in a gale in September 1995, but a our cat had four kittens in it.')[77] And a stately, unusually straight tree by Butley Church has become the archetypal black-poplar silhouette.

But the Vale of Aylesbury remains the tree's classic location. In the 2-km square (tetrad) containing the villages of Long Marston and Astrope there are more than 270 black-poplars visible from roads and footpaths alone. Amongst them there are specimens in just about every conceivable form: maidens, short and tall pollards, even a couple of two-storey pollards, cut once at about 10 feet, and then the leading shoot cropped again 10 feet above that. Trees are regenerating from fallen trunks and from the tips of low branches which have become buried in mud. I have even found one windthrown pollard sending out a new shoot from the *underside* of the root plate. The colour, fissuring and degree of burring on the trunks of the Vale's colonies are enormously varied, suggesting that they have originated from many sources. These days the trees are pollarded chiefly to ensure their stability. But historically the lopped wood was used for cattle food, and for making matches, bean-poles and fruit baskets,[78] and a peculiarly local form of wattle: 'The wood was used with willow to make sheep hurdles, for pens to confine sheep at night when they were brought down from the Chiltern downland. The wood was also used for

making rifle butts in the 1914 war.'[79]

Slowly the tree is coming back into visibility. A survey organised by the *Daily Telegraph* in 1994 located dozens of previously unknown trees. And the appearance of misnamings, deliberate or accidental ('dark popular' has been heard in Kent), is a sure sign that it is also winning back its place in popular imagination. Edgar Milne-Redhead's eightieth-birthday cake was decorated with black-poplar leaves and had a representation of the Butley tree on top. But the best tribute to his virtual rediscovery of the tree would be the re-establishment of at least one example of the flood-plain wildwood that was the black-poplar's aboriginal home. Plans have already been put to the Forest Authority.[80]

Field maple, *Acer campestre*. This is a handsome tree, common across much of England and Wales, but often curiously overlooked. A mature maple on a hedge-bank, with its pale, furrowed, bossy trunk and dense crown of delicate, lobed leaves, is a picture of elegance and compact strength. A contributor from Somerset regards it as the signature tree of the local limestone woods: 'The autumn tone in the woods and hedges here is painted with brilliant colours as the maples turn first golden yellow and then vivid orange brown – truly a landmark tree.'[81]

'This lady and friends who were in their 20s at

Field maple turns the brightest yellow in autumn of any native tree.

the time [1930s] often went to Whippendell Woods near Watford. One of the young lads found a lump of puddingstone [a local rock, like natural concrete] and lifted it up into the crook of a field maple for a lark. They often went back to look at it, but then must have forgotten. When this lady was much older, she and her husband showed me the tree, where the lump of puddingstone could still be seen, though the tree had done its best to grow round it. When I looked for it this year [1992] it was almost hidden.' [82]

Maple wood is tough and fine-grained and is used chiefly for high-quality carved or turned work, in musical instruments or ornamental bowls, especially the medieval drinking bowls called 'mazers'. Oliver Rackham's Cambridge college is proud of its 'Swan Mazer described in an inventory of *c.* 1380 as "one maser with lid ... with broad silver bindings on the circumference and base of the bowl ... and in the middle of the bowl there is a silver-gilt column on which sits a gilded swan ...". The wooden bowl measures about 5 x 1¼ inches, and was doubtless a rarity because maple-trees seldom have bosses with such a large solid core ... The word "mazer" was apparently first applied to the bosses of any kind of tree, including birch. The bosses were thought to be pathological; etymologists derive "measles" from the same root. Later the name was associated with the maple-tree.' [83]

Maple has been the favoured wood for harps. A maple harp has been excavated from a Saxon barrow at Taplow in Berkshire, and another maple harp-frame, wrapped in a sealskin bag, was part of the treasure unearthed from the Sutton Hoo ship burial in Suffolk.

Representations of field maple leaves, which have that fingered shape so beloved of medieval carvers, can be found in Southwell Minster and on the pew ends in the Lackham aisle of St Cyriac's Church, Lacock, Wiltshire. [84]

Ash, *Fraxinus excelsior* (VN: Esh, Hampshire weed, Widow-maker). In Scandinavian mythology, the ash was Yggdrasil, the tree of life, 'the greatest and best of all trees. Its branches spread all over the world.' In Britain, up until the end of the eighteenth century, it was regarded as a heal-

ing tree, and Gilbert White knew Hampshire villagers who, as children, had been through an ash ritual as a treatment for rupture or weak limbs. It was an extraordinary ceremony, a relic of pre-Christian sympathetic magic. A young ash was split and held open by wedges, while the afflicted child was passed, stark naked, through the gap. The split was then 'plastered with loam, and carefully swathed up. If the parts coalesced and soldered together ... the party was cured; but, where the cleft continued to gape, the operation, it was supposed, would prove ineffectual.' [85]

These days, its mystique has disappeared. It is regarded as a second-class timber tree, neither as gracious as the beech nor as sturdily useful as the oak. The speed with which its seedlings colonise open ground on damp and calcareous soils has given it a bad name with foresters, who call it a 'weed tree' and often treat it accordingly. In a sensible world we would be grateful for its hardiness and productivity, and see that it is, albeit in a new way, still a healing plant. It is young self-sown ash trees that have largely repaired the gashes in southern England's woods caused by the great storms of October 1987 and January 1990. It is ashes that fill gaps in hedges left by dead elms and turn abandoned arable fields on the clay into woods, sometimes growing six feet in a single season.

Its resilience and rapid growth made ash an invaluable tree in the economy of small farms and cottages. It is still the commonest tree in coppice woodland across much of lowland Britain and, up till the last war, the young poles, cut on a 10-year rotation, were probably the most versatile raw material in the countryside, used for everything from firewood to fork handles. It was a sustainable resource, too. The stools from which the poles were cut could go on producing straight, stout poles indefinitely. In Bradfield Woods, Suffolk, there is an ash stool eighteen and a half feet across and showing no signs of declining vigour. Oliver Rackham

What is reputedly the oldest ash tree in Europe, at Clapton, Somerset.

A Beadnell fisherman making a crab pot using ash sticks cut from a local plantation.

estimates that it is more than 1,000 years old.[86]

Ash is still the timber of choice wherever combined strength and elasticity are needed. No other wood can be bent so safely once seasoned, or is better at withstanding sudden shocks, and it is used, for instance, in many sporting goods – oars, billiard cues, hockey sticks. There is also a continuing small-scale trade in making walking-sticks from ash wood, which has a satisfying springiness when leaned against the ground. (The smoothness of the bark in the hand is a bonus.) The wood for the commercial manufacture of 'ashplants', as they are called, is sometimes cut from two- or three-year-old coppice growth, and the handles are formed by heating the sticks in damp sand and bending them in a curved vice.

In some areas of southern England sticks are still specially grown to have naturally curved handles. Nursery-raised ash seedlings are transplanted when they are one or two years old. But, instead of being set upright, they are planted at an angle in the ground with their end buds nipped off, so that the seedling has to use a side bud if it is to continue growing upwards. This new shoot – destined to become the shaft of the stick – rises almost at right angles to the original stem, which eventually becomes the handle.

Ash's adaptability is obvious in some of its other surviving uses:

'In Northumberland, crab and lobster pots, known locally as "creeves", are still made using traditional materials. Early this century, the bases of the pots were constructed from driftwood, which was then more plentiful than it is now. Today, all the wood for pot bottoms is bought in. The frames – the arched "bows" and straight "rails" – were traditionally made from ash and hazel sticks.'[87]

'It was well known that the best source for a catapult was a young ash where the terminal bud had failed and a natural fork had developed. We made lead slugs for the catapults somewhat in the shape of humbugs by pouring melted-down lead into a mould cut from a potato.'[88]

There was also a widespread game (known as 'mud yacks' in some places) in which a ball of clay was fixed to the end of a long, whippy ash pole. The pole was either stuck in the ground and bent back like a bow, or held in the hand and flicked. Either way, the intention was to hurl the mud-ball as high and far as possible, and perhaps get it to stick on a distant window. (Getting it *over* the house was the aim in my childhood.)[89]

'In the spring when the ash shoots were young and had a purple tinge, we cut them six or eight inches long, bound them with rushes, and boiled them in burn water till soft. We sucked them like asparagus tips.'[90]

There was probably an echo of ash's old magical power, as well as pure practicality, in many of these uses. In Wales, for example, ash was always used for making 'adder-sticks', which were carried by the lengthsmen when the verges were cut by hand.[91] Foresters in Wiltshire use ash for making handles for fire-beaters, despite the fact that it burns well even when green.[92] (And forest workers in north-east Essex still occasionally refer to the tree as 'the widow maker', because of its lethal habit of splitting as it is felled.)[93]

The opening of ash leaves is widely used for predicting summer weather. The conventional formula is given in a distinctively Scottish version from Roxburgh:

Ash before oak, the lady wears a cloak.
Oak before ash, the lady wears a sash.[94]

This is completely reversed in a rhyme from Surrey:

If the oak comes out before the ash,
'Twill be a year of mix and splash.
If the ash comes out before the oak,
'Twill be a year of fire and smoke
[i.e. drought].[95]

Something of the same uncertainty is reflected in an unusual children's ritual from the Weald of Kent. It was acted out on Ash Wednesday, the first day of Lent (which of course has nothing whatever to do with ash, the tree): 'On Ash Wednesday children arrived at school carrying a twig of ash (it must have at least one black bud) to avoid having their feet stamped on by the other children. But after noon this was reversed. Then any child still carrying a twig of ash had their feet stamped on by those children who had rid themselves of their ash twigs.'[96]

It is in fact almost unprecedented for ash leaves to emerge before the oak's, and, when they are finally fully open, they are something of an anticlimax after the gothic stages that have preceded them: the sooty, angular buds; the flowers like tufts of purple coral; and finally the green fish-bone fronds of the unfurled leaves. Ashes can become grand, spacious trees, letting through more sunlight than heavier-leaved species; and ash-woods, pale-trunked and feather-foliaged, have a special, invigorating luminosity about them, even in the heart of summer.

The ash tree is ubiquitous as well as useful, and it is the commonest tree as a place name element after the thorn.[97] But standard (uncoppiced) trees rarely live as long or develop such grainy character as oaks or beeches, and ashes have not often been landmark or boundary trees. They have tended instead to become more personal talismans, as perhaps befits a species that has been a congenial domestic workhorse as well as a refuge for ancient spirits:

'We had an ash tree where my sister, friends and I regularly played. We called it Anty's tree (but we don't know why!). It had numerous holes ideal for posting letters and hiding poems we had written. And of course these also pro-

The coral-like male flowers of ash, which emerge before the leaves. The more feathery female flowers sometimes occur on the same tree.

vided good hiding places for special pebbles. With quite a large hollow at the bottom that was twisted and gnarled, it was like a living doll's house ... Sometimes I would take a handful of grass and try to form a bird's nest.'[98]

'The weald and champion plain of West Sussex contain a considerable number of venerable ash stands and in former times most farming communities contained an ash wood. Some communities were named as such: Ashurst, Ashlington, East and West Ashling ... In many old Sussex communities the ash was regarded as a tree of magic and mystery. As a child, I was taught never to pass an ash without wishing it "good-day", and never must we harm an ash tree ... I still hold the ash as a tree to be respected, and find myself furtively dipping and bidding whenever I pass one.'[99]

Plants as Historic Landmarks

TREES, which so frequently outlive human beings, are the most notable and obvious botanical landmarks. But more modest plants can also be persistent and can sometimes give clues to the history of a place. Wood anemones, for instance, growing in a meadow or hedgebank, often indicate the site of a vanished woodland (the relict vegetation of which is evocatively referred to as a 'woodland ghost'). Herbs and economic plants can endure for centuries in the places in which they were first cultivated or conserved. Many southern European species (e.g. peony, birthwort and savory) were first introduced to this country in the physic gardens of monasteries and often hung on to become naturalised long after the buildings had crumbled. Soapwort, once used as a detergent, can suggest the site of old cloth mills, and clusters of asparagus and currant bushes on railway embankments land that was temporarily used as a kitchen garden, perhaps during wartime.

Just as some plants are characteristic of ancient woodland (poor colonisers such as woodruff and early-purple orchid) so there are plants that are associated with ancient churchyards (e.g. yew, snowdrop, stinking iris, cowslip and pink primrose) and that sketch in clues as to how the churchyard has been used (see p. 191). Unusual shrubs in hedges are also clues to the hedge's history. Numbers of fruit trees, such as damson, occur in the hedges around common land which was enclosed by squatters or smallholders, as along the Welsh borders. Laburnum hedges (parts of Wales and the Lake District) seem all to date from the mid-nineteenth century.

Gateway and old hedge and bank, Lower Kingcombe, Dorset. The species growing on banks can be vital clues to their age and history.

Scots pine, *Pinus sylvestris*. There are Scots pines all over Scotland, but barely a vestige of surviving folklore. They have the status of an endemic subspecies (ssp. *scotica*), a Scots speciality, but do not even have an indigenous name. In England, where the tree has not been native for probably 4,000 years, it nevertheless abounds with associations. It is an ironic twist of history, because it was exploitation by the English that led to the destruction of 'the Old Wood of Caledon' and the virtual elimination of the Scots pine from Scots culture.

In medieval times, the great forest of native pine and birch stretched across most of the Highlands, from Perth to Ullapool. But from the late seventeenth century, it began to be ransacked, first to provide charcoal for the lowland iron foundries, then to support the insatiable timber demands of the Napoleonic Wars. Any chance that the trees might regenerate was dashed by the notorious Highland Clearances in the eighteenth and nineteenth centuries and the blanketing of the denuded hills with sheep and later with deer. By the 1970s it was estimated that little more than 25,000 acres remained, much of it in small scattered clumps.[1]

But regeneration appears to be winning over the browsers, and the latest Forestry Commission surveys suggest an area of natural pinewood far in excess of this, though the figures are not strictly comparable as the 1994 survey includes woods self-sown from nineteenth-century plantations. In areas fenced off from deer, something approaching the conditions of the boreal pine forests can be glimpsed: rotten trunks still standing, young self-sown saplings, a dense understorey of bilberry and heathers, and the air tangy with the scent of pine resin and juniper.

In England and Wales, the warm period that set in about 5,000 years ago meant that pines were finally driven out by deciduous trees. Since then, all Scots pines have been planted or have self-seeded from planted trees. On many heaths in southern Britain they regenerate almost as vigorously as birch and are regarded as a menace. But many of the older specimens are of great historic interest. The conspicuousness of the tree in the lowlands – the fissured, ruddy-brown bark and rough shelves of evergreen needles amongst the deciduous oak and ash – made it invaluable as a landmark tree. In parts of the country crossed by drove-roads, Scots pines were planted in clumps to mark the way and signal where grazing and hospitality could be had for the night: 'Pines were planted in groups of three or four trees on high ground visible from the previous group ... When were they planted? By whom? Who organised this mass marking? The nearest group to my home [Lower Broadheath, Worcester] is almost directly opposite Sir Edward Elgar's birthplace on the road from Wales via Tenbury Wells, Clifton, Martley, Broadheath to Worcester.'[2]

There are no easy answers to these questions (except that Scots pines live to about 250 years of age), but there is no doubt that the drove-roads across the Welsh border carry one of the great concentrations of waymark pines, from the outstanding group on Bromlow Callow near Minsterley in Shropshire,[3] to the scatter along the roads joining Bewdley, Leominster and Weobley:

'Near Bewdley, many of the farms have two or three Scots pines near the buildings. These we have always believed were markers for drovers bringing cattle and sheep to this area from Wales.'[4]

'The old tale is that the firs were planted to let travelling folk know they would be welcome at the farms [Yatton, Herefordshire].'[5]

There are similar clumps at the entrances to the ridings in Salcey Forest, Northamptonshire, and around farms on the old Brownlow estates at Ashridge (now National Trust land).[6] In Yorkshire, pine-marked fields where cattle could be rested were known as 'Halfpenny Fields'.[7] In Oxfordshire: 'Many farms have plantations of Scots pines around them, or as an avenue leading to the house. There is a theory that these pines had been planted by Jacobite supporters who had moved south when times were hard for Scottish farmers, as a sign of a safe house for Jacobite farmers.'[8]

But the most extensive 'pine-ways' are to be

found on the southern chalk downs – rather surprisingly, given that this is not the tree's favourite soil. Kenneth Watts has made a detailed study of the droveways in Wiltshire, and some of the best examples of pine waymarking he has found include: Stock Lane from Aldbourne to Marlborough; Swayne's Firs on the Wiltshire–Dorset border, north-east of Martin Drove End; at Four Barrows on Sugar Hill, on the drove down into Aldbourne. There are also large enclosures surrounded by Scots pines ('drove closes') on, for example, Horse Down west of Tilshead, presumably associated with the Yarnbury Fair, which was held five miles to the south. A single sentinel pine marks Trowle Common Junction near Trowbridge. And there are pine-fringed drove ponds on Golden Ball Hill on the north scarp of

Pewsey Vale, associated with the droveway from Tan Hill to Marlborough, and on Pertwood Down on the drove between Monkton Deverill and Tytherington.

'Perhaps the best example is Limmer Pond beside the Chute Causeway in the extreme east of the county. This pond – which is surrounded by massive pines – stands near the line of a drove running south from near Scots Poor to Weyhill Fair site.'[9]

During the enclosure of the East Anglian Breckland in the nineteenth century, large numbers of pines were planted as hedges and shelterbelts. (They were known as 'Deal Rows' locally.) On the light and often windblown soils of this region, pines were felt to stand a better chance of surviving than the more usual hawthorns or

A massive dead pine, Glen Strathfarrar. One of the essential components of natural pine forest.

Native Scots pine on Beinn Eighe, and, in the background, scattered remnants of 'the Old Wood of Caledon' that once covered much of the Highlands.

hazels. But, remarkably, they were often managed as deciduous hedges – lopped off at the top and then trimmed to encourage denser, wind- and sand-proof foliage. When cutting and management ceased around the beginning of this century, the region's strong winds took over the trimming process. (The geographical location of fields in Breckland was jokingly regarded as dependent on the direction of the wind: 'Sometimes that's in Suffolk, sometimes that's in Norfolk.') As a result Breckland is characterised by miles of dwarfed, contorted Scots pine belts. One of the most extensive runs for several miles alongside the A11 near Elveden, Suffolk. On Barnham Cross Common, nearby, one pine has become so contorted that part of the trunk has looped round itself, forming a hole. It is called the 'Trysting Tree' locally, and lovers link hands through the hole.

In the Lake District, there are pockets of naturally twisted Scots pine, presumably naturalised but with a wild cast about them:

'Between Penrith and Appleby there is a low hill of infertile sandstone called Whinfell, planted mainly with Scots pine. Here and there, I think always self-sown, there used to be odd trees which were also Scots pine but clearly of a different race. The boles were short and stubby, coarsely and very heavily branched and the timber full of big knots. They were the sort of tree no forester would want to encourage and I called them "Whinfell Rogues". Though we are often told that Scots pine became extinct in England and Wales, I have often wondered whether pockets survived, of which the self-set Whinfell Rogues are one.'[10]

There are plenty of small-scale domestic uses for pines. The cones (sometimes known as 'dead apples') are used for weather-forecasting and as kindling. The resin (which seeps through and hardens on the outside of the trunk) is the source of an antiseptic oil and has occasionally been used as a rough-and-ready medicinal chewing-gum for throat infections. Steeped in white wine,

A lopped Scots pine windbreak, Breckland.

it also makes a passable imitation of Greek retsina. Pine shoots can add a resinous flavour to cooking oil and vinegars, and may have been the coniferous bittering agent used in the ancient Scots recipes for 'spruce beer' (cf. heather ale, p. 75) – though true spruce could have been imported from Scandinavia.[11]

London plane, *Platanus × hispanica*. The London plane is unquestionably the city's most dominant tree, but there is no evidence that it is a native Londoner, bred by metropolitan horticulturalists within the sound of Bow Bells. It has traditionally been regarded as a hybrid between the oriental plane, *P. orientalis*, a native of the eastern Mediterranean, and the American plane, *P. occidentalis*, which arose in Spain or southern France in the early seventeenth century, and was first planted in England in about 1680 (though, in 1919, a Dr Augustine Henry claimed that it had appeared at Oxford in 1670).[12] There is little hard evidence for theories about the tree's origins, however, and arguments still simmer about its

Plane leaves in autumn.

pedigree. Even its status as a hybrid has been challenged (it produces fertile seeds even in Britain). But it has never been found growing truly wild, so it is unlikely to be a separate species. And though there is a possibility that it is simply a vigorous sport of one of its suggested parents, it is now more usually consigned to that convenient category 'of unknown origin'.

But there is no doubt about its qualifications as a city tree. It is tough and resilient, rarely sheds branches, is indifferent to the most ruthless pruning, and will flourish even in compacted or paved-over soil. Its leathery leaves are easily washed clean of urban grime by rain (though its habit of regularly sloughing off large flakes of old bark, to leave a mottle of pale green, yellow and fawn underbark, is no longer reckoned to have a similar cleansing effect). As a result it has been planted along streets and in squares and parks throughout urban England, and, following the great success of John Nash's plantings in the early nineteenth century, across Europe and North America too.

In London, planes account for more than half the trees along streets and in public spaces, and shape the character of many districts – especially the squares in the West End, where some trees date from the early eighteenth century. But it must be said that, *en masse*, they have their drawbacks. They look marvellous in the sunshine – especially amongst the white buildings and fierce light of southern Europe. But in London on a grey day, against sombre municipal concrete, their heavy foliage can be oppressive. And planted in such numbers, often in close-packed rows, they have proved vulnerable to fungal disease in recent years.

Many of the London park and square planes were blown down in the great storm of October 1987, and this led to the rediscovery of the tree's exquisite pinkish and fine-textured timber, which was once valued as 'lacewood' veneer. Some more robust carpentry was also done with the fallen trees. In St James's Park, one of the rangers chain-sawed a whole tree where it lay into a kind of rustic children's climbing frame. But many large trees remain, not just in London (e.g. Berkeley Square), but in Oxford, where a specimen at Magdalen College, planted in 1801 (and described as a scion of one raised in the Botanic Garden in 1666), is 23 feet in girth, and at Woolverstone Park, Suffolk, where one has the same girth.[13]

The London plane has a very long flowering and fruiting season. The globular flower-heads – 'bobbles' – dangle on long stalks in May and June (male and female being separate but on the same tree), and develop into a spiky brown fruit-cluster resembling a small mace-head. These hang on the leafless trees throughout the winter, to break up early the next spring, releasing the individual seeds. Both flower-pollen and seed debris seem to be allergenic to many people – which may have encouraged children from a school in Beckenham, south London, to use the hairy seeds as an itching powder, an urban substitute for rosehip seeds.[14]

The seeds are fertile, and in hot summers will germinate in great numbers even in smidgens of dirt in inner-city gutters. These rarely survive long before they are squashed, swept up or weeded out. But in the outer suburbs, especially on walls by the Rivers Thames and Lea, the plane is now becoming at least a naturalised Londoner, with some of the self-sown saplings growing into tall trees.

Small-leaved lime, *Tilia cordata* (VN: Pry, Linden tree). The ubiquity of planted common lime (*Tilia × vulgaris* – see p. 126) on streets, avenues and village greens has obscured the fact that its two parents – small-leaved and large-leaved lime – live here in the wild and are amongst the most beautiful and historic of all British native trees.

Small-leaved lime is the more widespread of the two, but is strongly and mysteriously local. It grows in widely separated clusters, chiefly in the South Hams region of Devon, the Mendips and Wye Valley, north Essex around Earl's Colne, west Lincolnshire, the Derbyshire Dales and the Lake District. In most of these areas it survives as coppice – perhaps the most striking underwood there is, with straight, steel-grey poles and small, heart-shaped leaves.

The dappled shade of London plane trees in a London square. Berkeley Square, early spring.

But 6,000 years ago, in the warm 'Atlantic' period, it would have grown as an uncut, rugged, maiden tree, draped with fragrant flowers in July. And, to judge from pollen deposits from prehistoric lime-blossom, it was once the commonest tree throughout lowland England. But it is a southerly species and below a mean summer temperature of about 20°C ceases to produce fertile fruit. When the climate began to cool around 3000 BC, lime could no longer rely on seed to perpetuate itself and was more or less frozen in the sites it already occupied. As the wildwood was progressively cleared or grazed, lime retreated even further and survived only where soil conditions suited it and it was maintained by coppicing.

Yet it must still have been a comparatively well-known tree as late as the Anglo-Saxon period, to judge by the number of place names which feature it. 'Linde' was Anglo-Saxon for lime, and many parish and wood names preceded by lynd- or lin- refer to the presence, past or current, of *Tilia cordata*. At Lyndhurst and Linwood, both in the New Forest, lime has gone. But it survives in Linwood, Lincolnshire, and in individual woods, for instance, Linsty Hall Wood, Grizedale, and Lynderswood at Black Notley, Essex.[15]

Since then the number of lime woods has shrunk, but the territories of the 'lime province' have remained tenaciously constant. This has much to do with lime's longevity and its remarkable powers of regenerating from broken roots, toppled trees and buried branches. It will even layer itself, rooting along ground-level shoots much like a bramble. In the severe winters of the early 1980s, coppice shoots in Lady Park Wood in the Wye Valley were welded to the ground by

The fragrant flowers of small-leaved lime.

the ice, took root and sent up new stems. Lime sometimes survives in hedges which are the 'ghosts' of cleared woods. In the parish of Shelley in Suffolk, a hedge along 600 yards of lane consists almost entirely of overgrown small-leaved lime coppice. A search of early maps showed that the lime strip coincided exactly with the northern edge of Withers Wood, which was cleared in the early nineteenth century, leaving, it seems, just enough to form a hedge.[16]

Coppicing itself can prolong the life of small-leaved lime almost indefinitely. In Tiddesley Wood, Worcester, there is a still-living stool 'about 10 metres across. It is represented as a circle of ... 15-year-old stems, and I regularly take groups of people into it, when walking in the wood. It is rather like being in a small cathedral.'[17]

In Swanton Novers Great Wood, a similar hollow stool measures 27 feet across.[18] But by far the most impressive stool is at Silk Wood, next to the Westonbirt Arboretum in Gloucestershire. It consists of 60 sizeable trees growing in a circle 48 feet in diameter. It used to be assumed that they were unconnected individuals, planted or accidentally grown as a circular grove. But DNA 'fingerprinting' of the trees has shown that they are part of a genetically identical clone, whose parent tree – originally at the centre of the circle – no longer exists. Oliver Rackham and Donald Pigott, one of the world's leading authorities on limes, have estimated the clone's age as at least 2,000 years, by assuming that coppice growth was harvested at 25-year intervals as it grew outwards from the mother tree. But there is now private speculation that it may be more than 6,000 years old – which, if it were to be regarded as a 'single' organism, would make it probably the oldest living thing in Britain, born in the summertime of the limes and outstripping any of the ancient yews.

There are younger but no less remarkable landmark limes in the Lake District. In a scatter of woods – for instance, Linsty Hall Wood, Wash Dub Wood and Hartsop Low Wood – there are huge small-leaved lime trees that look as if they are ancient pollards. They also have something of the look of massive wooden stalagmites, and Dr Pigott, who has investigated them, realised that they were old coppice stools whose roots had been exposed by soil erosion. At some of the sites, pieces of rock more than eight inches in diameter are embedded in the exposed roots up to four feet above present ground level. Comparisons with coppiced limes of known age and calculations of the average rate of soil erosion around the roots has led Dr Pigott to estimate that the limes are probably 1,000 years old and possibly much older.[19]

Lime coppice was used in much the same way as other coppice-wood, as fuel, hop-poles, etc. (An unusual modern use for part of the crop from Collyweston Great Woods National Nature Reserve in Lincolnshire has been to make sticks for the Rutland morris men. Lime wood is well suited for morris-stick thwacking, having a tight grain and not splintering even when hit hard.)

Larger poles (and timber trunks) were stripped for what is called 'bast' – the fibrous layer between bark and greenwood, which was twisted into ropes (and generated another group of lime place names, e.g. Bastwick in Norfolk).

Lime wood itself is pale, soft and cuts very cleanly. It has been a favourite with woodcarvers since at least the Middle Ages and was the wood used by Grinling Gibbons (1648–1721) in his elaborate decorative work. The effects that can be achieved with it can be seen, for example, in a Gibbons frieze in St Paul's Church, Covent

The distinctive grey-tinged, straight poles of lime coppice.

Grinling Gibbons's exuberant carving in lime wood: a detail from the fireplace in the state dining-room at Chatsworth.

Garden, where there is a wreath of flowers and fruit – some with stalks only a fraction of an inch wide. They have both a breathtaking intricacy and a kind of Shaker simplicity, with the still-visible chisel marks giving a freshness and depth to the carvings. Horace Walpole, fifty years after Gibbons's death, wrote that 'there is no instance of a man before Gibbons who gave to wood the loose and airy lightness of flowers, and chained together the productions of the elements with a free disorder natural to each species'.

David Esterley, who restored the Gibbons carvings damaged in the 1986 fire at Hampton Court Palace, echoes Walpole and says: 'Fresh limewood foliage carving seems to float, with leaves and petals as light as air.' He also discovered that the carvings were not left exactly as they had been carved by Gibbons, but were roughly finished-off with Dutch rush: 'The moment I rubbed a dried section of this tubular stalk against a piece of limewood it became clear that the key to Gibbons's long-lost technique had been found. The rush left behind on the wood exactly those curious striations which are discernible on Gibbons's carvings.'[20]

In Hallwood Green, Gloucestershire, there are two ancient pollard small-leaved limes that mark the boundary between Dymock and Much Marcle and which were the site of open-air church services up to the 1920s: 'The services were held every Sunday afternoon during the summer months. The vicar … gave his sermon while standing on an old pair of blacksmith's bellows which at that time stood under the trees on the green.'[21]

Another remarkable group of landmark limes is the avenue at Turville Heath in Buckinghamshire. There are many eighteenth- and nineteenth-century avenues, but these almost invariably consist of common limes. The trees at Turville are unique in being small-leaved limes. They were planted in the 1740s, by William Perry, along what was then the coach road to his house at Turville Park. He had been Lord Lieutenant of Radnorshire, and Donald Pigott believes he may have brought the trees from local woods in Wales. Despite losses to gales, there are still 35 statuesque trees with massive gnarled trunks and sheaves of small leaves. Alas, the gaps have been filled partly with common limes, and more recently with nursery grown *Tilia*, rather than by cuttings from the original trees, which would have kept intact the unique character of this avenue.[22]

Large-leaved lime, *T. platyphyllos*, is a tall and elegant tree, and one of our rarest native hardwoods. Up till a few years ago it was known in any quantities only from a few woods in the Pennines, Wye Valley and Cotswolds (though widely planted elsewhere). Then, in the early 1990s, Francis Rose and colleagues discovered a string of some 16 new sites along the foot of the South Downs, between Hampshire and East Sussex. Most of the trees are in ancient copses or on boundary banks.

The most impressive site, Rook Clift near Reyford, is a remarkable place and one where it is hard to believe that the trees could have gone unnoticed for so long. Even from a lane a quarter of a mile away, the limes look stupendous, their

Statuesque small-leaved limes in an avenue at Turville Heath, Buckinghamshire.

'Preaching limes' at Hallwood Green, Gloucestershire.

domed, billowing crowns standing clear of all the other trees. There are more than 50 in the wood, a mixture of huge coppice stools, some maybe 1,000 years old with poles that have something of the sinewy grey sheen of tropical hardwoods, a few pollards and some handsome maiden trees, sprung from seed or old stools and now maybe a century or so old, and all bearing bright, large, viridian leaves.

T. platyphyllos is now cropping up in other, similar sites (I have found coppiced stools at the foot of a Chiltern escarpment at Fawley Bottom, Buckinghamshire) and it looks as if large-leaved lime was a component of the original wildwood on the lower levels of the chalk, just as it was on limestone.

Lime or **Common lime**, *T. × vulgaris*, is the fertile hybrid between the two native species above and occurs naturally in the wild where both parents grow together, as in woods in the Wye Valley and Derbyshire Dales. But these trees tend to differ slightly from the variety that has been so abundantly planted in town streets,

parks and churchyards throughout Britain, which almost certainly originated with stock imported from the continent in the mid-seventeenth century. It is hard to see why this latter form became so popular, apart from its fast growth and tolerance of grotesque lopping and mutilation at the hands of municipal authorities. It sprouts great nests of side shoots at the base and around burrs on the trunk, and the leaves are notorious for the aphid honeydew which in summer rains down on anything beneath them. It has its friends, nonetheless:

'A lime tree was planted to replace a willow tree in the centre of Stratton St Margaret, near Swindon. It was a lucky tree and survived a Second World War aeroplane crash which exploded near the site.' [23]

'Five lime trees were planted on the slope of Corton Denham Hill [Somerset] behind the church when the five bells were rehung after the church was rebuilt in 1869–1870.' [24]

'In Ewell village, Surrey, the "Grove" consists of lime trees planted to commemorate the accession of William III to the throne in 1689, and originally contained 38 trees – one for each year of William's age. There are still some of the originals remaining.'[25]

'We have two lime trees outside our old house in Enfield, side by side, only three yards apart. In 1981 we took a holiday in Sweden, to an old country rectory in Gotland. In the garden our cousin showed us two large lime trees growing side by side and close together and in full view of the windows of the house. When his parents took up residence there (in the early twentieth century), they were newly married, and following an old Swedish custom, they planted two lime trees close together to symbolise their marriage, and gave the trees the same names as themselves – Gustav and Lydia. Does the same tradition exist here, or were the earlier occupants of our house Swedish?'[26]

Perhaps the most romantic lime avenue is at Kentwell Hall in Long Melford, Suffolk, which is recorded as having been planted in the late 1670s. The limes are hybrids, but combine the features of their parents in a more attractive way than usual, and Oliver Rackham believes they may be of English and perhaps even local origin.[27] They seem originally to have been pleached (that is, had their lower side branches joined) as a formal avenue, but they have now grown exceptionally tall and wide-spreading. They also have curious crooks and swellings in their upper branches produced by generations of mistletoe (see p. 211).

All groups of lime trees, of whatever species,

The billowing crowns of large-leaved lime at a recently discovered site: Rook Clift, West Sussex.

are wonderfully fragrant when in full blossom in July. They are also the noisiest of trees at this time, and the roar of bees in them can often be heard 50 yards away. The blossom makes a rich tea, *tilleul*, which was recommended as a mild sedative during the last war. Other bits of lime are used domestically, too: 'We rolled the inner bark or bast of common lime into a tightly packed cigarillo, perhaps two to three mm thick, and smoked it in the ordinary way. The effect was rapid and heady.'[28]

The young leaves make refreshing sandwich

Woad, the ancient dye plant, is undergoing a revival. It is also becoming popular with flower arrangers.

fillings. After the aphids have been at work they have been described as tasting like 'honey-coated lettuce leaves'.[29] Even the small round fruits are just about edible and have a curious cocoa-like taste. In the late nineteenth century the French chemist Missa tried to patent a chocolate substitute made from a mixture of ground-up lime flowers and fruit.

Woad, *Isatis tinctoria*, may or may not have been the dark blue dye with which the Ancient Britons daubed their skins. This is one of the stories from Caesar's *De Bello Gallico*, which is notoriously prone to generalisations based on Caesar's one short visit to Britain. But there is no doubt that it is a dye plant of great antiquity, probably brought to Britain by Celtic immigrants from western and southern Europe. Glastonbury, in Somerset, derives its name from the Old Celtic *glasto*, and means 'a place where woad grows'. Names from the Anglo-Saxon 'wad' are more frequent: e.g. Wadborough in Worcestershire ('woad hills'), Wadden Hall, Kent ('nook where woad grows'), Waddicar, Lancashire ('newly cultivated land where woad grows'), Waddon, Dorset and Surrey ('woad hill').[30] In a sparkling essay on the plant written in the early 1950s, Geoffrey Grigson describes a farm close to his home in Wiltshire 'called Woodhill Park. Woodhill did not mean the "hill near the wood". In 1086, in the Domesday Book, the farm was called "Wadhille", the hill where the "wad" or woad was cultivated.'[31] Wiltshire, Dorset, Somerset and Gloucestershire seem to have been the main centres of woad cultivation, though there were others in East Anglia. It was cultivated in the Fens up until the beginning of this century, and reputedly last used in the dyeing of policemen's uniforms. In Essex a 'Blueman Farm' is believed to be named from woad-growing.[32]

The process of manufacturing the dye was quite elaborate. The woad leaves were crushed to a pulp in a mill, and then moulded into balls, which were allowed to dry in the sun (but protected from the rain) until the pulp began to ferment. A crust formed over the balls, and care was taken to ensure that this did not split. When fermentation was complete the balls were pulped again in the mill and again formed into cakes. The whole cycle was repeated a third time before the fully-fermented balls were thoroughly dried and sent off to the dyer. It took a hundredweight of leaves to produce 10 lb of the final dye, and the ammoniacal stench of the fermentation process was so notoriously disgusting that Elizabeth I issued a proclamation that woad production had to cease in any town through which she was passing.[33]

Woad was made virtually obsolete by the growing popularity of indigo, which gave a stronger, faster blue, and was cheaper, even though it had to be imported from the tropics. But woad has become naturalised on a precipitous cliff close to one of the ancient cultivation areas in Gloucestershire, and in 1818, when the colony was first discovered, 'the cliff was quite golden with it about the end of May'.[34] It has proved remarkably persistent in spite of – or perhaps because of – repeated disturbances to the site:

'On the red marl cliff called the Mythe Tute, north of Tewkesbury, woad grows in a small colony. Early writers on botany considered it to be indigenous in this area in the nineteenth century, but in the nineteenth century it was cultivated around Wotton-under-Edge. We have watched the colony since the mid-1960s, and the number of plants show great variation, from the twenties down to two plants in the early 1970s. Then cliff-falls and the removal of dead elms provided open soil and the biennial woad again flourished, so that in the late 1970s there were over a hundred flowering stems. The colony is again declining as the surface becomes overgrown. In the mid-1980s we were surprised to see three plants growing on the verge of the M5 nearby.'[35]

With the growth of interest in natural dyes, woad is experiencing something of a revival. It is, for example, being grown by craftspeople in Essex, Somerset, and in West Sussex, where the seed stock has been bulked up at the reconstruction of an Iron Age farm at Butser.[36]

But woad is an unusually attractive plant, not simply what Ruskin would have scorned as a 'chemical factory'; and its aesthetic virtues have also been rediscovered – or perhaps noticed for the first time. Its yard-high stems, its long, almost succulent leaves, which seem to shine like stained glass with an inner, immanent blue, and its foamy clusters of brilliant yellow flowers – all put together, as Grigson wrote, rather like a 'wireless mast' – have made it a grail for flower-arrangers, who have also begun to grow it, providing another source of seed. In one Suffolk churchyard, woad's new role and ancient resilience came fortuitously together in the summer of 1992:

'Earlier this year, I thought I had found something special in Framsden churchyard. Woad has only two established colonies in England ... From its position I guessed that the seed had been dropped by a bird sitting on the church gutter. But where had the bird got the seed? Surely not from the nearest wild colony, in Surrey [a chalk-pit near Guildford]. Perhaps somebody had been experimenting with growing it for its dye? I soon met two or three people who had done just that in years gone by. Then, on a return visit to Framsden, I met a lady in the churchyard who told me that somebody in the village grew a variety of plants for their natural dyes, and that she had passed woad to several of her friends. It looked well in flower arrangements, and was often used in the church. The position where the plant was growing was not only under the church gutter, it was also outside the door where the flower ladies removed their dead flowers.'[37]

Wild service-tree, *Sorbus torminalis* (VN: Chequer tree, Maple cherry; (for fruit) Chequers, Chokers). The wild service is one of the most local and least known of our native trees, yet it has a fascinating ecological and social history, revolving chiefly around its small but exotically flavoured fruits. The story of its rise, decline and subsequent rediscovery is something of a parable of the fortunes of our scarcer domestic plants. The fruits were a Neolithic staple, gained enough popularity at one time for houses, farms and pubs to be named after them, and then passed into obscurity, as the tree's ancient wood-

Wild service, or 'chequer-tree', in autumn foliage. The leaves are often blotched with scarlet and copper.

Clare. His poem, written about 1830, is entitled 'The Surry Tree', which was a nineteenth-century Northamptonshire name, echoing the Old English root of service, *syfre*.

Tree of tawny berry rich though wild
When mellowed to a pulp yet little known
Though shepherds by its dainty taste beguiled
Swarm with clasped leg the smooth trunk timber
    grown
& pulls the very topmost branches down
Tis beautiful when all the woods tan brown
To see thee thronged with berrys ripe & fine
For daintier palates fitting then the clown
Where hermits of a day may rove & dine
Luxuriantly amid thy crimson leaves ...[38]

In Bernwood Forest, Oxfordshire, where wild services have been left to grow on amongst newly planted conifers, the splashes of scarlet among the dark evergreens are dramatic.

The unravelling of the history and distribution of this secretive tree owes much to the efforts of Patrick Roper, who lives in the tree's heartland in the Weald. The survey he organised through the Botanical Society of the British Isles, beginning in 1974, showed it to be more widespread than had been believed, but largely confined to ancient woods and hedgerows on clays in eastern and southern England and limestone in the west. Its northernmost station is the southern Lake District.[39]

The loyalty of wild service to ancient woods is probably due to the fact that, in our climate, the tree spreads almost exclusively by suckers. Seedlings are rarely found, and I have only once seen them developing into young trees, in Roydon Wood in the extreme south of Hampshire. Suckering, on the other hand, can be prolific. In Longmans Grove Wood, near Rockhampton, Gloucestershire, there is a patch of close on a thousand wild service-trees, probably all suckers from a single parent and covering an acre of ground. From the air in autumn they show up as a large, irregular crimson circle.[40]

The main concentrations include the Severn and Wye Valleys and much of the Welsh Marches; Bardney Forest in Lincolnshire; many

land habitats were destroyed and more glamorous fruits became cheaply available.

For much of the year a mature service-tree is an inconspicuous tree, a little like a maple in habit and leaf-shape, and with a dark, red-tinged bark that is sometimes cracked, like mud baked in the sun. But for two brief spells it can be spectacular. In May it is covered with white blossom, almost as thickly as a hawthorn. And from late October, after the brown fruits have set, the leaves on many of the trees turn a brilliant red tinged with copper and ochre. The best description of service-trees in autumn, and of the one-time popularity of their fruit, is given by John ancient woods and hedges in Essex, Suffolk, and east Hertfordshire; wind-pruned woods on cliffs and in river valleys in Cornwall and Pembrokeshire (where the trees still have the unique local name of 'maple cherry'); a curious suburban cluster south and east of Birmingham, especially round Solihull and Tanworth, perhaps relics of the Forest of Arden[41] (they even occur in hedges in urban parks in the Bournville area); and the old Rockingham Forest area in Northamptonshire, John Clare's countryside, where service boughs used to be carried in May Day processions and Beatings of the Bounds.[42]

But the tree's main stronghold is the clays of the southern Weald, from Kent to Hampshire. Wild service often occurs in parks and pastureland here, and reaches a much greater size. What may be the biggest tree in the country, at Parsonage Farm, Udimore, in East Sussex, has a 13-foot girth and in a good year bears two tons of berries. At Brooks Green in West Sussex, there is a hedgerow that may possibly have originated from seedlings (though it is more likely a woodland 'ghost' – see Hedges, p. 142): 'We have about 25 wild service-trees, mostly in a long line down an old field boundary. We have always assumed that they spread by means of bird droppings from birds which sit on the fence. There is a very large tree in a small wood some 300 yards away. Mistle thrushes love the berries.'[43]

These southern counties are the area where the tradition of eating the fruits persisted longest. The brown berries, which may be round or pear-shaped, are hard and bitter at first, but as the autumn progresses (or once they are picked and taken indoors) they begin to 'blet' and turn soft and very sweet. The taste is not quite like anything else that grows wild in this country, with hints of apricot, sultana, overripe damson and tamarind, and a lightly gritty texture. They were a boon when other sources of sugar were in short supply, and were enjoyed as a kind of natural sweet by children. W. A. Bromfield described how they were sold in markets in the 1850s: 'The fruit is well known in Sussex by the name of Chequers, from its speckled appearance, and is sold both there and in this island [Isle of Wight],

in the shops and public markets, tied up in bunches, principally to children.'[44]

The custom was to hang the chequers up in strings in the kitchen or over the hearth: 'I was born in St Michaels near Tenterden, Kent, and well remember gathering the berries from the tree which grew in the hedge bordering our garden. They were picked in clusters and threaded on lengths on string, layer upon layer, which were then hung in the larder to ripen. We were then allowed to pick them singly, as they ripened, leaving the strings.'[45] (Some modern children seem to enjoy service berries nibbled like this just as much as their predecessors.)[46]

The Weald, and Kent especially, is also the site of a still unresolved connection between Chequers pubs and chequer trees which may be the source of this local name for the wild service. There is an unusually high proportion of Chequers Inns in the area (12 in the Canterbury, Kent, Yellow Pages alone),[47] and too many have chequer trees growing in their gardens or close

The berries of the wild service-tree are edible once they have been softened, or 'bletted', by frost. Their taste has hints of dried apricot, tamarind and sultana.

by to be explained away as a coincidence. There are trees, for instance, at Chequers Inns at Rowhook, West Sussex, Smarden, Kent, and (at one stage removed) Four Elms, Kent: 'The wild service-tree grows by our village pond in Four Elms, which coincidentally has a "Chequers Garage" near one corner of it, although the name came with the garage from a "parent" garage of that name in the neighbouring village of Bough Beech. This Chequers Garage originated from a Chequers Inn which gave up as a pub about 30 years ago.'[48]

Patrick Roper believes that the link may lie in an alcoholic drink made from chequer berries and that the tree and its fruit derived their local name from being served in Chequers Inns. (A chequer-board was often hung outside public houses, as brass balls are outside a pawnbrokers.)[49] But it is doubtful if the drink was a beer, and there is certainly no etymological connection, as has sometimes been suggested, between the Latin *cervisia* (or Spanish *cerveza*) and 'service'. (Its root is the OE *syfre*.) Most probably the drink was a ratafia, like sloe gin and cherry brandy, and made by steeping the service berries in spirit.

A modern version from Essex uses whisky and fruit from Halstead Wood: 'Cover ripe service with cheap whisky, and add sugar at about 1 lb per pint. Leave to infuse for a couple of months. Give a good shake every week and then strain. Ours has a lovely golden colour and a very distinctive and agreeable taste.'[50]

The Chequers Inn at Smarden has an undated house recipe for a kind of wild-service wine: 'Pick off bunches in October – Hang on strings like onions (looks like swarms of bees) – hang till ripe. Cut off with scissors close to checkers [*sic*] – do not pull out – Put in stone or glass jars – Put sugar on – 1 lb to 5 lb of checkers – Shake up well. Keep airtight until juice comes to top. The longer kept the better – Can add brandy.'

Service-trees also haunt non-Chequers inns. A gnarled specimen grows out of a Barnack stone wall opposite the Hare and Hounds in Greatford, Lincolnshire.[51] Another is in the garden of the Snooty Fox, Lowick, Northampton-

shire.[52] The tree at the Chequers, Gedney Dyke, Lincolnshire, was planted in 1992, and is a practical example of renewed interest in the tree and its fruit.[53] A somewhat improbable wild service memorial tree was planted on the campus at Welwyn Garden City to celebrate Nick Faldo's golfing achievements (as he was brought up in the town).[54] Even the pale, tough, close-grained wood is coming back into use now that more trees are being discovered. (In France, even though it is much commoner, it is the most expensive native wood.) A musical-instrument-maker from Billingshurst, West Sussex, uses it for making the jacks which pluck the strings of harpsichords.[55]

Service-tree, *S. domestica*. What is sometimes called the true service-tree is a native of central and southern Europe, with rowan-like leaves and large pear- or apple-shaped fruits, which is occasionally grown in botanic gardens and parks in Britain. But for more than three centuries there has been a cryptic specimen in the depths of Wyre Forest, Worcestershire, that seemed, from its situation, as if it might have a genuinely wild ancestry.

The Wyre 'Whitty Pear' was first recorded in the Forest in 1678 by Alderman Edmund Pitts, who wrote about it in *Philosophical Transactions* for that year in a note entitled 'An account of the *Sorbus pyriformis*'. He plainly regarded it even then as a very ancient tree. He described the fruit 'in September, so rough as to be ready to strangle one. But being then gathered, and kept till October, they eat as well as any medlar.' The names 'whitty', 'whitty-tree' and 'wicken' were widely used in the region for the rowan and were no doubt borrowed for this rowan-like tree. In 1842 it was burned down, reputedly by a poacher to spite a local magistrate who was fond of it. Fortunately, two grafts had been taken from the tree some years before by the Earl of Mountmorris and grown on in the grounds of nearby Arley Castle. One of these – already a mature tree – was planted out in 1913 at the whitty pear's ancestral site in Wyre Forest, where it continues to thrive.[56] Subsequent grafts were planted elsewhere in the vicinity of the Forest, and the fine specimen in the Oxford Botanic Garden is believed to have originated from Wyre stock (possibly seed – though the fruits are rarely fertile in our climate).

And that might have been the end of the story of *S. domestica*'s presence in Britain, had it not been for the remarkable discovery between 1983 and 1991 of two indisputably wild populations of the species on cliffs in South Glamorgan. It was an extraordinary find, not least because this area has for centuries been one of the most intensively botanised in Britain.

There are 13 or 14 separate trees, stunted by the wind and growing on inaccessible ledges on crumbling limestone, so that they rarely or never fruit – all reasons, perhaps, why they were not noticed for so long, or mistakenly assumed to be rowans. They are multi-trunked, and microscopic counts of the very narrow rings in dead branches suggest an age of up to 400 years for the individual living trunks, and possibly of over a thousand years (cf. small-leaved lime, p. 123) for each whole tree.

More recently, biochemical tests have verified that these are indeed true service-trees, and more closely related to the Wyre Forest whitty pear (and its Oxford descendant) than to cultivated trees from continental stock – which suggests that there may once have been a more widespread native population of *S. domestica* in Wales, the South-West and the Midlands. (There are very old records from Cornwall, for example, which Patrick Roper suggests should be re-examined, along with any stunted 'rowans' on Cornish cliffs.)[57]

Dr Quentin Kay, of the University College of Swansea, who has co-ordinated much of the research, comments: 'We have not found any records of medieval (or indeed modern) cultivation of *S. domestica* in South Wales, and deliberate introduction in the past seems most unlikely for these inaccessible cliff sites; in fact the most likely explanation is that the Glamorgan populations are fully native and have survived in their cliff refuge sites since their arrival during the spread of the deciduous trees in the early Postglacial!'[58]

Medlars, like service berries, are edible once they have softened. The taste is a little like baked apple.

Medlar, *Mespilus germanica*, was, with quince, mulberry and walnut, one of the quartet of trees often planted at the corners of herb gardens and orchards. But, unlike its old partners, medlar's fruits have gone out of fashion, and the tree has become one of those intriguing species (along with, for example, asarabacca and true service-tree) whose provenance – and distribution, for that matter – are shadowy issues, prone to throwing up myths.

It is hard to mistake, with its dark, contorted trunk (spiny in the wild forms) and solitary white flowers sitting on the branches like camellias, and most of the vaguely wild specimens are obviously relics of plantings in orchards or parks. It is, strictly, a native of south-east Europe and south-west Asia, anciently introduced and barely ripening its fruit unaided in this country.

So what is one to make of the individuals which have been found in much wilder situations in woods and hedgerows in the extreme south-east? Gerard reported that it could be found 'oftentimes in hedges among briars and brambles'.[59] In 1831 John Stuart Mill found a spiny specimen in a hedge on Redstone Hill, near Reigate, Surrey (still there in the 1980s),[60] and there are others in apparently semi-natural woods in Surrey and Sussex. Were they bird-sown, or examples of the once widespread peasant practice of planting orchard trees in the wild? Or was the eminent botanist A. H. Wolley-Dod right to believe that medlar might be native in the extreme south-east?[61]

The fruits are like large, brown rose-hips, and in our climate become edible only when they are 'bletted' – made soft and half-rotten by frost, like service-berries (see p. 131). In the Mediterranean region they can be eaten straight off the tree. The flesh tastes a little like baked apple, but with the consistency of chestnut purée. The slightly 'high' flavour and granular texture made them popular for serving with whisky. They also made jellies, preserves and fillings for pies or were baked and eaten directly out of their skins with a spoon.

Laburnum, *Laburnum anagyroides* and *L. alpinum*. Popular garden trees from the mountains of southern central Europe, quite often self-sown on rail- and roadsides. They are the most frequent cause of plant-poisoning amongst children, who eat the seeds in mistake for peas.[62] Animals are also occasionally poisoned by eating the fallen pods, yet there are miles of planted laburnum hedges in the upland pasture countryside of western Britain. The choice of this toxic (and far from stockproof) tree as a hedging plant in what are almost exclusively stock-raising areas remains an intriguing mystery. One of the concentrations is around the squatters' and smallholders' settlements on the commons of south and west Shropshire: 'There are many examples of laburnum hedges in the old mining areas immediately to the west of the Stiperstones, in particular around Shelve, Pennerley and Stiperstones villages. Due to neglect over many years they are in fact rows of laburnum trees rather than hedges, and they are a wonderful sight in early summer.'[63] They also crop up in the vicinity of Brown Clee Hill, ten miles to the south-east.[64] Some way further north, there is another nucleus in Cumbria (where Coleridge wanted to plant laburnum in the woods around Grasmere):

Laburnum – or 'golden rain' – well known in gardens but also widely planted in upland hedges, despite its poisonous seeds.

'In various West Cumberland parishes, Arlecdon, Haile, and the township of Ennerdale and Kinniside, for instance, there are considerable stretches of laburnum in the "dykes", as the hedges and banks are called here. I farmed at Simon Keld on Kinniside Common close to the 900-feet contour, where there were numbers of laburnums in the garth around the farmhouse. I have no idea why they were there; it seemed odd to have a poisonous tree in a place where there were so many sheep.

Were they grown to feed bees or for their wood? In Arlecdon there is a tree with a girth of five to six feet. The parish was enclosed in 1823 – was laburnum planted in the dyke at the time of enclosure?'[65]

That laburnums were grown for their timber is a distinct possibility in these communities of self-sufficient farmers and craftsmen. Laburnum has a unique grain pattern, with a purple-choco-late heartwood core inside pale yellow outer-wood. It is hard enough to be cut thinly and has been used in ornamental furniture work, espe-cially for inlays and veneers. But this is unlikely to have been the reason for the much more exten-sive hedgerow plantings in west Wales, between Carmarthen and Llandysil, for instance.[66] James Robertson believes that, given their age, these farm laburnum hedges were more likely a ver-nacular echo of the ornamental plantings in the big Welsh landscape gardens of the time: 'There are many miles of laburnum hedging in Cardiganshire, predominantly *L. anagyroides*, but also *L. alpinum*. These occur both as pure hedges and as old trees in hedgerows, throughout the county. They are normally planted on banks and coppiced periodically, stools measuring up to a metre in diameter. Occasionally they are layered or pleached. Estate records may provide more information about the reasons for planting laburnum, but the trees are now valued as an amenity, and more than tolerated by farmers, despite the danger that they could poison stock. Most were planted about 150 years ago, and aesthetic considerations are likely to have been as important then as now.'[67]

Wild teasel, *Dipsacus fullonum* (VN: Brushes and combs, Venus's basin). Teasel is named from the use of its spiny heads to 'tease' out the sepa-rate fibres of wool before spinning (a process known as carding) or to raise the pile or 'nap' of finished cloth: 'At Otterburn Mill [Northum-berland], a local tweed mill, there are still many old looms and tools remaining, and some frames containing teasels for raising the nap on the cloth. These were split with all the prickles going the same way, and placed in frames which were

Wild teasel – a statuesque plant related to fuller's teasel, formerly used for carding wool.

fastened onto rotating drums.'[68]

In most mills, teasels were replaced by steel brushes in the nineteenth century. But they have proved themselves unsurpassable in the finishing of cloth that needs an exceptionally fine and evenly raised pile – as in some hats and, espe-cially, the baize covering used for billiard tables. The reason for teasel's superiority lies in the small hooked spikes which cover the conical flower-heads. They have a 'give', as if they were mounted in rubber, and if they meet a snag or irregularity in the cloth they bend and skate gently over it, unlike steel brushes, which are apt to tear through it indiscriminately.

The teasel used most commonly in the cloth industry has been **fuller's teasel** (*D. sativus*, formerly *D. fullonum* ssp. *sativus*), a species or subspecies of uncertain origins, possibly in southern Europe, in which the stiff, spiny bracts curve down at their tips. Fuller's teasel (fullers were the craftsmen who cleaned and finished cloth) is still cultivated on the Somerset Levels and was once grown much more widely, including in damp areas of Gloucestershire. It lives on in the form of occasional naturalised specimens in ditches and waste ground, and in field names, pub signs (e.g. the Clothiers' Arms at Stroud, and the one-time inn of the same name at Nailsworth) and church kneelers (as at Witney, Oxfordshire, in the heart of the Cotswold wool country).[69]

But the wild teasel, whose spines are longer and weaker and grow straight upwards, was doubtless also used for carding wool at one time (though its spines are too weak for it to be of any use in nap-raising). It is still found adequate for small-scale carding by the Oakfield Ladies' Circle in Liverpool, and probably other hand-spinners.[70] Being a tall and statuesque plant, common on waysides and rough ground and by streams throughout much of the British Isles, it is also widely picked for flower arrangements. Children use the heads to make toy hedgehogs, and occasionally makeshift hairbrushes.[71]

Richard Jefferies caught the architectural elegance and detail of the plant wonderfully in an essay written in the 1870s:
'The large leaves of this plant grow in pairs, one on each side of the stem, and while the plant is young are connected in a curious manner by a green membrane, or continuation of the lower part of the leaf round the stem, so as to form a cup. The stalk rises in the centre of the cup, and of these vessels there are three or four above each other in storeys. When it rains, the drops, instead of falling off as from other leaves, run down these and are collected in the cups, which thus form so many natural rain-gauges. If it is a large plant, the cup nearest the ground – the biggest – will hold as much as two or three wine glasses. This water remains there for a considerable time, for several days after a shower, and it is fatal to numbers of insects which climb up the stalk or alight on the leaves and fall in. While the grass and the earth of the bank are quite dry, therefore, the teazle often has a supply of water; and when it dries up, the drowned insects remain at the bottom like the dregs of a draught the plant has drained. Round the prickly dome-shaped head, as the summer advances, two circles of violet-hued flowers push out from cells defended by the spines, so that, seen protruding above the hedge, it resembles a tiara – a green circle at the bottom of the dome, and two circles of gems above.'[72]

Water or 'dew', held or gathered by plants, has always been thought to have rejuvenating powers. In the eighteenth century, teasel-water was believed to remove freckles.[73] Two hundred and fifty years later it is still being used as a soothing cosmetic: 'Every year I get hay fever and my eyes itch. I relieve this by bathing them in teasel water collected from their deep leaves.'[74]

Snowdrop, *Galanthus nivalis* (VN: Candlemas bells, Mary's taper, Snow piercer, February fairmaids, Dingle-dangle). The snowdrop has always seemed an ambiguous, paradoxical flower. It is a species of winter as much as spring, and the eighteenth-century poet Thomas Tickell called it 'vegetable snow'. We look on it as a wild flower, yet most of its colonies probably began as garden escapes. It may not even be a British native, despite its seemingly ancient pedigree.

The whole of the snowdrop's history is fascinatingly contrary, and it is quite possibly both native and naturalised in Britain. It grows in wild habitats on the continent, in damp woods and meadows up to 1,600 metres. (Though, despite its alpine aura and leaf-tips specially hardened for breaking through frozen ground, it does not occur at all in Scandinavia or the colder northern reaches of Europe.) It is regarded as a native in northern Brittany, not that far from the most persuasively wild colonies in south-west

Damerham churchyard, Hampshire.

England. And where it turns the ground white, as in 'Snowdrop Valley' near Timberscombe in Somerset or along the shelving banks of the Coundmoor Brook in Shropshire, it is difficult to believe that the plant is not anciently native here too.[75]

Yet snowdrops were not recorded as growing wild in Britain until the 1770s, when they were found in Gloucestershire and Worcestershire. Even as garden plants they seemed slow to attract attention. The first mentions of the name which *The Oxford English Dictionary* can trace are in 1664, when it is listed in John Evelyn's *Kalendar of Horticulture*, and Robert Boyle referred to 'Those purely White Flowers that appear about the end of winter, and are commonly call'd Snow drops'. But thirty years previously, in his revised edition of Gerard's *Herball*, Thomas Johnson adds a footnote to the entry on the 'Timely flouring bulbous Violet': 'Some call them also Snowdrops.' There is no doubt that this is the snowdrop, and, as in Gerard's original edition of 1597, there is an unmistakable drawing and description.[76]

Yet 'Timely flouring bulbous Violet' is too mannered a name for a plant which was already loose and familiar in the countryside, and Gerard and Johnson make it plain that they knew it only from London gardens. The manner in which snowdrops spread also suggests that they may have been originally introduced from an area with warmer winters. Most colonies in Britain, whether in gardens or the wild, reproduce almost exclusively by division of the bulbs rather than by seed. This is partly because cultivated populations (and those naturalised from them) usually come from the same genetic stock, and are sterile; and partly because there is rarely enough insect activity in February to cross-pollinate them. But where different species or varieties grow close together, and there is mild weather at flowering time, seedlings appear.

Despite the lateness of both garden and wild records, it is likely that snowdrops were growing in this country much earlier than the eighteenth century, albeit rather locally. Their pure white blooms have long been accepted by the Catholic Church as a symbol of Candlemas (2 February), the Feast of the Purification of the Virgin Mary, and the link with monastic sites is striking right across Britain:

'I spent six months at the Benedictine Priory of our Lady at Burford, and remember that on the Feast of Candlemas great bunches were picked to decorate the chapel for the day.'[77]

'When I retired to the Dorset–Wilts border I was charmed by the sheets of snowdrops round the village of Donhead. At first I thought of them as garden escapes, but came to realise that the reverse might be the case, and that those in the gardens had come from the hedgerows and wooded areas from a considerable distance around. There are some areas in this county where the snowdrops do appear to be native, but a remark by a villager prompted me to think of Shaftesbury Abbey, founded by Alfred the Great for the Benedictine Nuns with his daughter the Lady Aethelgiva as abbess. This was on a scale of some importance and its wealth increased with subsequent monarchs, with the abbey gaining vast areas of land as far as Tisbury [three miles north of Donhead] ... This seems to support the theory that snowdrops, symbols of purity, were originally planted by the nuns.'[78]

'There is a wonderful display near the remains of Ankerwyke Priory, Middlesex. This is a vast area of Crown Lands, and surrounds the priory where Henry VIII courted Anne Boleyn under the yew tree [this tree, which still survives, is one of the oldest in Britain].'[79]

'In Newbury, there is a church called St Mary's of Speen. It is in a beautiful setting, and very old. The churchyard, and a lot of the surrounding wood, is full of snowdrops; they are so thick they look like a bluebell wood. They lie in woods that belong to a Dominican monastery right by the churchyard.'[80]

Snowdrops thrive amongst the ruins of St Rachunds Abbey Farm in Kent. The present owner thinned the bulbs and sold them for the Methodist Church restoration fund: 'I probably sold over £150 worth in two years. We were pleased that from the ruins of the old abbey money was made and used to enlarge a twentieth-century church. I think the old monks would have been pleased.'[81]

There are also large surviving colonies at the site of the twelfth-century Cistercian Roche Abbey, near Maltby in Yorkshire; within the skirting walls that are all that remain of the Grey Friars priory in Dunwich, Suffolk; in the ruins of Walsingham Priory, Norfolk; in a cemetery in Abbotskerwell in Devon, which was created by the Augustines in the nineteenth century; at the twelfth-century priory at Brinkburn near Rothbury, Northumberland; and around a farm at Copdock, Suffolk, built 400 years ago on the site of a monastery.[82]

The likelihood that many colonies of feral snowdrops originated with ecclesiastical plantings is supported by records from more workaday church grounds:

'The whole village [Reighton, North Yorkshire] is teeming with snowdrops. The churchyard is scattered with them. There are several small wooded areas in which they are massed, and a large tumulus and a very long drive leading to Reighton Hall are white at this time of year [February]. They are scattered along all the old hedgerows and tumbling out of most gardens.'[83]

In Hampshire, there is a celebrated colony in St Wilfrid's Church at Warnford, which seems to have been quite indiscriminate in its spread: 'The churchyard is full of them, they grow alongside the park boundary railings ... There is also a small clump growing by the side of a footpath leading to an area called Betty Munday's Bottom. Apparently Betty Munday was a lady of the night many years ago.'[84]

There is a Snowdrop Open Day at Castle Hedingham, Essex, and in Kirk Bramwith, South Yorkshire, an annual 'Snowdrop festival' with a brass band concert in the churchyard.[85] Colonies are also cherished by local inhabitants at churches, for instance, at Lamberhurst in Kent, Lower Bourne in Surrey, Burton in South Wirral, Falkenham near Ipswich, Wherwell in Hampshire, Newchurch on the Isle of Wight, Damerham in Hampshire, at the tenth-century Church of Merthyr Issui, Gwent, and at an old people's home in Bocking, Essex, which is on the site of a

Snowdrops – 'February fairmaids' – are used to celebrate the Feast of Candlemas (2 February) and are often found associated with churches and monastic foundations.

monastic foundation dating back to AD 995. One of the most northerly sites is in an old graveyard outside Cromarty on the Black Isle, Easter Ross.[86]

In Monkton in Wiltshire the churchyard colony is a living memorial to the Revd J. Brinsdon, an eighteenth-century incumbent: 'Among other things he tried his best to teach the children to read and write. To make them more eager to learn the alphabet, he planted snowdrops in the churchyard in the shape of letters. After his death the snowdrops spread all over the churchyard.'[87]

The churchyard of St Mary the Virgin at Drayton Beauchamp in Buckinghamshire has more earthy associations. Between 1860 and 1883, the incumbent was Henry Harpur Crewe, a distinguished botanist and plantsman, with a penchant for snowdrops, after whom a green cultivar was named earlier this century. There is no trace of this in the churchyard (or of an improbable pink variety some villagers claim to have seen), but it is full of more common varieties of single and double snowdrops, set amongst aconites and ground-ivy. They cluster around the grave of Harpur Crewe himself, which is marked by a simple Victorian cross wreathed with carved ivy leaves.

Snowdrops will linger wherever there have been gardens and cottages. Isolated roadside colonies often mark the sites of demolished cottages:

'One of my favourite walks at Wern-y-wil was along a cart track between a field hedge and an area of scrubland. It was only when I went one February and found flourishing patches of snowdrops, that I thought to scrabble amongst the winter-thin brambles. I found the remains of two cottages – stone-built but less durable than the snowdrops in their gardens.'[88]

'My grandsons have a den which occupies a table-sized clearing in a vicious thicket of blackthorn scrub. In February they bring me a token snowdrop that I cannot reach.'[89]

'Snowdrops occur on Salisbury Plain Army Ranges, on sites of old or destroyed cottages, e.g. Framstead on the Larkhill Artillery Ranges, and in what were the gardens of the now vanished village of Imber (taken over by the Army in the Second World War).'[90]

'Another memory from childhood is that of making regular winter trips to a burnt-down cottage at Shadwell, near Thetford, Norfolk, to pick snowdrops. This place seemed mysterious to me as a child and I always wondered if the occupants had died in the fire. The derelict garden was white with snowdrops growing from the surrounding undergrowth into the charred remains of the cottage's timbers and foundations.'[91]

At Bourne End, Hertfordshire, I have found them lining the leats of what was once a mill (also burnt down) where they were first recorded in 1849.[92] The Oxfordshire writer Mollie Harris has noted that they were sometimes planted to mark the line to outside privies, for a few weeks in winter anyway.[93]

Yet the bulbs clearly travel further and faster than can be explained by vegetative spread alone, and being ferried by water is one plausible explanation: 'A large colony extends for about half a mile through the entire length of a wood facing onto the River Mole, Surrey, and reaches up to 100 yards back from the river. Interestingly most of the plants are submerged when the river floods, and if a flood coincides with flowering, it rather spoils the plants. However I think that on balance the flooding is beneficial. There are several large houses in the area with grounds bordering the river, and there are clumps of snowdrops in the grounds, some along the banks. I am inclined to think that the river may spread the plants from one area to another.'[94]

In Wiltshire, which could well claim to be the top snowdrop county in England, the pattern of snowdrop spread is clearly visible. In the valleys of rivers such as the Nadder and Ebble, which thread their way between the chalk downs, snowdrops grow profusely on streamsides, village greens and road-verges. They seep perceptibly into lower or damper patches and runnels, so that even the most subtle contours of the low ground seem to be marked out with white tracery.

Despite its sanctification for Candlemas, the snowdrop is one of the white blossoms that are still regarded as being unlucky if brought into a house. In parts of Northumberland, Westmorland and Hampshire, for instance, single flowers especially are still viewed as 'death-tokens'. (One Victorian explanation for this was that the flower 'looked for all the world like a corpse in its shroud'[95] – though the belief may have anti-Catholic roots, as with the similar fear of bringing may blossom indoors.) Yet the diary of a young girl from Harpenden, Hertfordshire, for February 1901 notes: 'Our February Fair-Maids were up very early this year to grace the mourning for our Queen, and we have had them on our table every day since the first Sunday after she died.'[96]

A more secular Victorian role (though echoing the ancient associations with religious purity) was as an emblem for virginity in the 'language of flowers'. A few blooms in an envelope were often used to warn off over-ardent wooers. In Yorkshire 'there was an old custom, celebrated on February 2nd, for village maidens to gather bunches of snowdrops and wear them as symbols of purity … In some parts here they are known as "snow-piercers", like the French "perce-neige".'[97]

Yet this history of deliberate introduction and cultivation does not mean that snowdrops are not authentic wild natives in some parts of the west and south. And even where their origins are doubtful, they always have a wild cast about them. Perhaps more than any other garden bulb they are planted haphazardly, in untended corners of lawns and shrubberies, dared almost to break bounds – and loved most of all when they do, edging in scattered clumps away into the shade, as one walker saw them in Durham: 'No white sheets billowing in the breeze here, as often seen in well-manicured churchyards, or secluded corners of equally secluded country houses; these were in *their* element, sharing their habitat with fallen branches, curled-up brown leaves, rotting vegetation and the sounds from the beck below. Some were even growing in the water's edge and on miniature islands, heads nodding the way towards the Greta half a mile away. They accompanied me for about 300 yards, by which time the beck had reached open fields, and there were no more. Looking at the map I now notice that there is the remains of an

Probable native snowdrops in woods at Timberscombe, Somerset.

ancient church only 100 yards from where the beck enters the river; also a site of the medieval village of Brignorth close by.'[98]

'Hedges'. Hedges are widely regarded as being uniquely British landscape features, deliberately created by farmers during the last two or three centuries. Not a single part of this assumption is true. There are recognisable hedges in northern France, in the Austrian Alps, across much of the United States, and even in the Peruvian Andes. In Britain there is documentary proof that many are over a thousand years old, and biological and archaeological evidence puts the origins of some back in the Bronze Age. Even hedges that consist of tidy lines of trees and bushes are not always the result of planting. Something very close to what we call a hedge can be an entirely spontaneous feature, forming for example in the debris at the edges of rivers prone to flooding and by the side of strips of scree and landslip. (I have seen similar, if more ephemeral, wisps of self-sown scrub colonising the bulldozed earthbanks during the building of new roads.) More permanent hedges arise when shrubs colonise an already established human boundary. All across the Texas prairies, nineteenth-century barbed-wire fences have been turned into dense hedges by seedling trees and bushes taking root at the base of the fences and being protected by them from browsing animals.[99] Precisely the same process can be seen along any temporarily neglected British fence or ditch – though it is rarely permitted to proceed beyond the bramble, scrub willow and ashling phase.

Natural, unplanted hedges were also created when fields were cleared directly out of the wild-wood, leaving a row of wild trees as a boundary. This process has been continuous since the early Middle Ages, and many rich hedges (evocatively christened 'woodland ghosts') are all that remain of woods destroyed comparatively recently. A celebrated example is at Shelley in Suffolk (see p. 122); another is 'the very outgrown hedge, with its 40-yard wall of small-leaved lime stools' which backs onto the Massey Ferguson factory in industrial Coventry, whose origins David Morfitt has traced to a wood grubbed out in the eighteenth century.[100]

Yet even planted hedges continually aspire to the condition of linear woodland. Max Hooper's well-known formula, that the number of woody species in a 30-yard stretch equals the age of the hedge in centuries, is a rule-of-thumb, not an exact equation.[101] But it does make the general point that with age hedges become progressively more complicated and richer in species. What generally happens is that bird-ferried or wind-blown seeds of new species take root in the shelter of the hedge and in their early years are helped to compete against the established shrubs by the process of hedge-cutting. And the average rate of establishment seems remarkably constant: one species per century per 30-yard stretch.

But the exceptions are as interesting as the ones that follow the rule. 'Reed hedges' in Fenland ditches, for example; the tall, moss-clad beech windbreaks on the Blackdown Hills in Somerset; the stone and turf banks of Devon and Cornwall, which are always called 'hedges' locally, though they barely carry any shrubs, and which, near Land's End, are sometimes as much as 3,000 years old.

There are modern exceptions, too, which, if Hooper's rule were applied too literally, would also appear to be prehistoric. Round the Stiperstones in Shropshire, eighteenth- and nineteenth-century squatters and free miners planted hedges around their smallholdings that were full of domestically useful shrubs, such as damson, gooseberry, laburnum, spindle and blackthorn. In some hedges the 30-yard count is in excess of 20 species.[102] Near Hargate, Lincolnshire, there are farm-hedges which echo the similarly resourceful medieval practice of planting orchard trees in hedgerows and headlands: 'There is a beautiful hedgerow of apples, plums, pears and rhubarb here, all the more beautiful for being one of the hedges left by greedy farmers. Nearer home along the same stretch are plums on one side and almonds and walnuts on the other.' In other parts of the country, often in deep country-side, there are hedges of laburnum, spiraea, fuchsia and flowering currant.

Alas, hedgerows of all kinds have continued to be destroyed at a rate that has scarcely diminished since the black days of the 1960s and 70s. Figures released by the Institute of Terrestrial Ecology in 1994 showed that total hedgerow length fell from 341,000 miles in 1984 to 266,000 in 1990, accounting in six years for a third of the entire post-war loss. Between 1990 and 1993, a further 6,750 miles disappeared. These figures are even more graphically confirmed at a local level. Vikki Forbes's survey of hedge loss in the parish of Ardleigh, Essex, shows that the period between 1980 and 1990 was the worst since records began. Between 1960 and 1980, 19 miles of hedgerow were destroyed; in the ten years between 1980 and 1990, 10 miles.[103]

The finding that many surviving hedges have in the same period become 'derelict' (i.e. tall, gappy and unmanaged) is more contentious. Although regular cutting and layering is appropriate where stock containment is required and is a good way of encouraging farmers to retain hedges, hedgerow management is now being zealously advocated almost for its own sake. As a result, even the tall Exmoor beech windbreaks are being hacked down to the level of Midland quicksets.[104] So-called derelict hedges – the wide, meandering rows of shrubs allowed to flower and fruit, studded with old pollards, festooned with creepers and supporting a vast range of ferns and flowers in their shade – are what most of us understand by ancient hedges and are the locations of many of the plant stories featured in this book.

Hedges along an old green lane, showing the rich mixture of habitats that results from not being too over-tidy: standard trees, pollards, bushy thickets and dense hedgerow bottom vegetation.

Immigrant Plants

SINCE THE BEGINNINGS of cultivation there has been two-way traffic over the garden wall. Attractive wildings have been taken into the garden and given sanctuary, whilst hardy imports from all over the world have begun to escape and spread out along the waysides. The number of immigrants (*c.* 3000 species) that are now successfully naturalised in the wild thanks to the Trojan Horse of the nation's gardens now exceeds the number of native species by two to one. Some of these were pure opportunists and found their own way out; others, too ambitious or just plain unfashionable, were given a helping hand with the shovel. Both contribute to those marvellous jostlings of colour at the edge of towns and villages, with the foreigner as likely to advance steadfastly through the lanes as the home-grown weed is to nip back into the vegetable patch.

Some of the most widely established plants, such as horse-radish, soapwort and feverfew, came straight from the herb garden. Others were brought over by the Romans as medicinal or food plants, for example fennel, ground-elder and wormwood, which were intended to deal, respectively, with wind, gout and intestinal worms.

Many of the most persistent and decorative garden escapes are also from southern Europe: alkanet, dame's violet, dusty miller, everlasting-pea, honesty, purple toadflax, opium poppy, rose-of-Sharon and half a dozen crane's-bills. Yet some of the most solidly rooted colonists have come from halfway across the world: Michaelmas-daisy and goldenrod from North America and Japanese knotweed from the Far East.

The curious thing is that, even thousands of miles beyond their natural range, so many of these species look thoroughly at home. It is hard

Drifts of rosebay willowherb on a Dumfries hillside.

to credit that winter heliotrope, whose heart-shaped leaves blanket many damp waysides as unaffectedly as those of its larger cousin butter-bur, did not even arrive in our gardens until 1806. At about the same time rock stonecrop (*Sedum forsteranum*) was beginning to creep out of rock-eries in East Anglia. By 1901 a local botanist noted that it had 'taken possession of a tract of land some miles square in north-east Norfolk'. It is still there.

The colonisers will invade almost any habitat. Stationmaster's lupins advance along railway embankments; Indian balsams fringe the edges of rivers; rhododendrons invade ancient wood-land. The delicate purple-fringed daisy *Erigeron karvinskianus*, which was introduced to this country from Mexico in the nineteenth century, has found its way to the venerable walls of thir-teenth-century Merton College, Oxford.

The aggressiveness and adaptability of natu-ralised plants have given them a bad name in some quarters. Many – especially large colonial species such as Japanese knotweed and giant hogweed – stand accused by nature conserva-tionists of invading sensitive habitats and crowd-ing out scarce native plants. Their supporters, conversely, point to the fact that they are resilient, colourful and most commonly haunt wasteland, where native plants are scarce and where these aliens constitute the true, sponta-neous, 'natural' flora. Both sides of this argument are thoroughly rehearsed by contributors in the pages that follow.

Fig, *Ficus carica*. The fig, though it came to Europe from south-west Asia and, like the olive, is irrevocably associated with the languid warmth of the Mediterranean, will fruit perfectly well in windswept Britain. The sweetest and most succulent fig I have ever eaten was grown outdoors on the very top of Harrow on the Hill in Middlesex.[1]

But setting seeds in the wild that will grow successfully into mature trees is another matter; and most wilding figs are isolated specimens which have had some fairly obvious head start, from warmth or inadvertent composting: one

close to a lime-kiln near Abergavenny; others on railway embankments, resulting perhaps from discarded food – on top of a tunnel in Oakleigh Park, Hertfordshire, for instance, and 'the sub-stantial population on the embankment between Castleford and Leeds'.[2] The tree which sprang from a grave in Watford in 1913 probably also originated in a snack taken by the unfortunate occupant; but there is a local legend (still well known) that it sprang from the tomb of an athe-ist, who asked for a fig to be placed in his or her hand in the coffin and who said that if there was life beyond the grave the fig would sprout.

There have also been car park figs, addition-ally nurtured by the warmth of car exhausts. A famous tree in the NCP park on Ludgate Hill in London was, at 35 feet, one of the tallest in Britain before the site was developed. There is also 'a large fig tree growing on waste land (at present a car park) in the centre of the one way system in Colliers Wood, south-west London'.[3]

But the most interesting and most plentiful colonies of fig trees are on the banks of urban rivers. Perhaps the specimen spotted by a sharp-eyed fan of the TV series *Last of the Summer Wine* growing on the banks of the Holme 'prac-tically opposite Nora Batty's cottage' is not quite in this category.[4] But most of the individuals or small groups of fig trees found on the banks of the Avon in Bristol, where one is rooted in verti-cal stonework near Temple Meads Station, the Thames in London, and a number of northern waterways (including a canal in Liverpool close to Tate and Lyle's sugar refinery) do fit into some kind of pattern, with nearby industry and sewage being the usual common factors.

'Figs occur on the banks of the Huddersfield Narrow Canal. The species is thought to have come from the unloading of canal barges carry-ing groceries. One specimen found by the side of a tiny stream is said to have come from a batch of rotten figs thrown out by my communicator's

Fig trees by the River Don, in the old steelworks quarter of Sheffield: 'as much a part of its industrial heritage as Bessemer converters'.

aunt! Two trees on the banks of the River Colne possibly came from sewage works formerly situated higher up the valley, and a third fig on the banks of the Calder came from a biscuit factory which used to be there.'[5]

'There is a large specimen growing out of the canal side at Brookfoot Mills, Brighouse, Yorkshire. The fig is growing opposite an outfall from the dyehouse which discharged hot water into the canal. A name painted on the wall of the building indicates that a sweet factory was there at one time. I have a fig tree in my front garden grown from a cutting from the Brookfoot plant, now about 10 feet tall.'[6]

Glasgow has a celebrated riverside specimen known as the Dalmarnock Fig. It has many thin

Figs in the fencing, Petworth House, West Sussex.

trunks about 10 feet tall and sprouts from the vertical stonework of the south-facing bank of the Clyde just downstream from Dalmarnock Bridge and close to the local sewage works.[7]

But the most substantial population so far discovered in Britain grows along the banks of the River Don in Sheffield. Isolated fig trees have been known there for some time, but it was not until there was a thorough survey of the riverbank vegetation, organised by Dr Oliver Gilbert of Sheffield University in the early 1990s, that it became clear that there was a healthy colony beside the Don. Some 35 specimens were found during the survey itself; more have been uncovered since, and in at least one place they form a small riverine wood.

Most of the figs grow in the base of retaining walls in the derelict industrial quarter, amongst a dense scrub of Indian balsam and Japanese knotweed. (See p. 151 for an account of the remarkable ecology of this and the other herbaceous plants of this urban river.) The trees are all well-grown specimens, up to 25 feet high and with multiple stems. Like all figs they fruit twice a year, once in May – pear-shaped fruits which swell and soften until mid-July – and again in September, harder fruits which fall off unripe in October. The wild fruits are rarely fit to eat.

There is a curiosity about these Sheffield figtrees. Why do they all seem to be of much the same age, roughly 70 years? And why are there so many more of them than along other urban rivers? There is no reason to think that Sheffield was a city of obsessive fig-eaters, flushing exceptional quantities of well-manured seeds into the river (though it had good numbers of pickle and cake factories). Dr Gilbert believes that the answer lies with the steel industry. The trees are concentrated in the steelworks area, and the period during which the trees seemingly became established, in the early 1920s, was when the Sheffield steel industry was at its height. The river water was used as a coolant in the factories, and as a result the Don ran at a fairly constant temperature of 20°C – warm enough for fig seeds washed into the river from sewage outfalls to germinate and thrive. When the steel industry began to decline in the city, river temperatures returned to normal, and though established trees were able to survive no new seedlings were able to sprout. As Dr Gilbert says, this 'means that the Wild Figs of Sheffield are as much a part of its industrial heritage as Bessemer converters, steam hammer and crucible steel'.[8]

This isn't just a botanist's view. There is a real interest in the trees developing in Sheffield, and Tree Preservation Orders have been placed on some of them. When I visited the Don in the autumn of 1992, I called into a riverside pub amongst the decaying warehouses and empty foundries and found it had a splendid, spreading fig-tree on its own stretch of bank. The landlord knew the figs' story (as did most of the regulars present) and told me how they had dug in their heels to save their tree when the brewery had threatened to grub it out in a modernisation programme. And if any proof of the 'rightness' of these trees were needed, whilst we were on the bank admiring the pub's specimen a kingfisher came and perched on one of the lower branches.

Japanese knotweed, *Fallopia japonica* (VN: Japweed, Sally rhubarb, German sausage). Japweed is now officially regarded as the most pernicious weed in Britain, and it is illegal to plant it deliberately in the wild. Its rampaging spread across Britain in the late 1970s and 80s is regarded as a parable of the dangers of casually introducing alien plants into the countryside – which goes to show how quickly perceptions of plants can change when their behaviour, or gardening fashion, begins to shift.

Japanese knotweed was introduced to Britain from Japan sometime between 1825 and the 1840s, and was an immediate hit with gardeners. Its dense sheaves of canes (up to six feet tall), heavy, heart-shaped leaves and spires of tiny white flowers suited the Victorians' austere taste. It was recommended for naturalising in the shrubbery by none other than the nineteenth-

Japanese knotweed, which the Victorian gardening writer William Robinson thought 'most effective in flower in the autumn'.

century pioneer of 'wild gardening', William Robinson, who described it as 'most effective in flower in the autumn' and advocated planting in groups of two or three – though he did warn that neither it nor its larger cousin, giant knotweed, can 'be put in the garden without fear of their overrunning other things, while outside in the pleasure ground or plantation, or by the water-side where there is enough soil, they may be very handsome indeed'.[9]

But even the pleasure ground and plantation proved too restricting for them, and when their formidable powers of colonisation were realised they were thrown over the garden wall onto rail-way embankments and rubbish-tips. From these

The other face of Japanese knotweed: dense and almost ineradicable thickets.

strongholds they advanced even further, able to sprout from the smallest fragments of root as well as by the remorseless extension of their whole root systems.

In the footnotes of local naturalists' societies' newsletters and county floras, it is possible to map Japanese knotweed's inexorable spread across Britain. It was first noticed in the wild in London in 1900. It had reached a rubbish-tip in Langley, Middlesex, two years later, and was in the smart adjacent village of Denham by 1918. The sharp-eyed botanist George Claridge Druce found it near Exeter in 1908. It was in Suffolk by 1924, West Yorkshire in the 1940s and Northum-berland in the 1950s. By the early 1960s its colonies stretched across Britain from Land's End to the northern tip of the Isle of Lewis. In many places they seemed so dense as to exclude all other species, and to be virtually ineradicable.

A species advancing as aggressively as this was bound to generate myths in its wake. In part of south Hampshire the arrival of the Japanese weed was blamed on the military: 'Our garden suffers from the invasion of knotweed from the adjoining Telecom exchange ... I have seen a photograph taken by the previous occupant, which seems to show an old army hut approxi-mately where the infestation is now centred. Maybe freshly billeted troops from overseas brushed some seeds from the seams of their uni-forms or corners of kit bags?'[10]

In one corner of Cornwall in the 1930s, it earned the nickname of Hancock's curse, having spread from the garden of someone with that name; and there is a story that a house in the same area was reduced in price by £100 because its garden was overrun by knotweed. These days it is regarded as a serious nuisance across much of the West Country: 'The Devon Community Council is embarked upon an eradication cam-paign beginning with the parish of Buckland Monachorum, with the aim of making the parish a knotweed-free zone.'[11]

Not everyone in Devon is so hostile though. In Chulmleigh, a father makes crude pan-pipes for his children by using dry knotweed stems of different lengths and diameters.[12] It has been successfully used as cattle fodder at the Cardiff City Farm (a practice once widespread in central Europe); [13] and it produces moderate-quality hand-made paper.[14]

Most encouragingly, the habit of eating the young shoots (which are used as a vegetable in Japan) has begun to spread. The knotweed is well naturalised along the eastern states of Canada and the United States, and is reportedly eaten by Japanese immigrants there. It was first introduced to a wider public by the pioneer writer on American wild foods, Euell Gibbons, in the 1960s. In his classic *Stalking the Wild Asparagus*, he calls it 'a combination fruit-vegetable' and stresses that, although it may *look* like an asparagus when it first appears, it has a tart taste more like sorrel or rhubarb (members of the same family), and recommends making jam or pies from the shoots when they are no more than a foot tall.[15]

Quite independently, people in Wales have been discovering knotweed's culinary potential. In parts of Dyfed, the young shoots and leaves are cooked like spinach. In Swansea children 'suck the sharp-tasting juicy stems during high summer' and know the plant as 'Sally rhubarb'. (It is an exact and evocative name, 'sally' being an old variety of 'sallow', traditionally used to describe low scrubby willows – of which a thicket of knotweeds can be reminiscent.) In Clwyd, the plant is known as 'German sausage' – though I suspect this is because of the speckled-brown appearance of the cylindrical stems, rather than anything to do with their taste.[16]

In Bristol in the 1960s it was precisely the jungle-like profusion of knotweed thickets that attracted one group of youngsters: 'The area "our gang" played in would now be regarded as inner-city dereliction; a few acres of waste land, partly the result of Hitler's bombs, and partly due to the demolition of houses, the occupants of which were removed to the city's periphery … Its crowning glory was the Japanese knotweed, which covered at least half of this wilderness of ours. Not knowing its name we christened it "Bambarb", because it showed characteristics of both bamboo and

rhubarb. The Bambarb grew much taller than the average fourteen-year-old, so consequently became a great hiding place from rival gangs and the local Bobby … and for enacting boyish fantasies of jungle warfare and tales of exploration. When the land was finally redeveloped in the early 70s, our beloved wilderness was taken from us for ever.'[17]

It is worth adding that, where Japanese knotweed grows under some constraint and one can put aside the prejudices and real worries that have come to focus on it, William Robinson's admiration is well justified. One such site is the industrial area of Sheffield. Here the River Don throws a corridor of wildness right through the heart of the city, wreathing distant views of the cathedral in an almost Amazonian luxuriance (see p. 148). Crack-willows sprout from the rootings of broken water-borne branches and in places grow into fantastic multi-stemmed shapes, like mangrove clumps. The banks and riverine islands are thick with showy immigrant flowers, Himalayan balsam, Michaelmas-daisy, soapwort – and Japanese knotweed. Every so often the river floods, with water pouring in from Pennine feeder streams, and it is consequently banked with high stone walls on either side. This has several consequences for the Japanese knotweed. It cannot spread outwards, for a start. And whenever the river floods, the accumulation of dead stems that usually carpets the ground is swept away, and in its place comes silt full of seeds and bulbs from plants in the high Pennine woods – bluebells, wood anemones, ramsons and celandine. They readily root in the rich mud underneath the knotweed stands, and come into flower as the new season's shoots begin to grow. And so in late April, before the Japweed leaves are fully open and the canopy closed, the banks of the Don look like nothing so much as some strange urban hazel coppice.

Giant knotweed, *F. sachalinensis*, similar to *F. japonica* but often taller, is also spreading, though as yet it is a much scarcer plant. Hybrids between the two species are also cropping up.

Russian-vine, *F. baldschuanica* (VN: Mile-a-minute-plant). A vigorous white-flowered

Russian-vine, a rampant climber from the Far East that is sometimes known as 'mile-a-minute-plant'.

scrambler from China that can cover walls, hedges and sometimes whole abandoned buildings in urban areas. It grows at a prodigious rate – hence its modern nickname, mile-a-minute-plant – and has been known to extend 50 yards from its roots along a hedge or fence.[18] It is always a garden escape originally, and, never setting seed in this country, can spring only from stray pieces of root or stem, though it is increasingly found some distance from houses. A pink-flowered variety has been found on a rubbish-tip in Dartford.[19]

An interesting hybrid between Japanese knotweed and Russian-vine (*F. japonica* × *F. baldschuanica*) appeared in 1987 in a nature reserve on one-time railway waste ground in Harringay, London. It is more elegant and less aggressive than either of its parents and has leaves shapely enough to make it a serious contender as a garden scrambler or ground-cover plant in the future. In the warm summer of 1993 it was being visited by many different species of native insect.[20]

Fuchsia, *Fuchsia magellanica* (VN: Drop tree). Introduced from South America as an ornamental shrub, and widely planted as hedging (even on farms) in western Britain, fuchsia persists where planted and can become naturalised as a throw-out, but rarely self-seeds. It is one of the best-loved plants on the Isle of Man: 'Within ten years of arriving in the British Isles in 1823, fuchsia was widespread in the Isle of Man. It grows freely up to the 750-feet level and beyond. I have a friend who has a cottage on the slopes of South Barrule at about this height which had an avenue of fuchsia meeting overhead in an arch some 20 feet high. It is widely used for hedging and scarcely a cottage garden is without it. "Beneath the fuchsia tree" is a poetic metaphor for rural life in the recent past. Many Manx people would like to see it adopted as the national flower.'[21]

In North Yorkshire one child found an ingenious way of turning the flowers into dolls: 'I used to remove all the stamens except two from fuchsia flowers and use them as puppet ballet dancers.'[22] A use which is echoed in one Cambridge family's coining, 'dancing ladies'.[23]

Horse-chestnut, *Aesculus hippocastanum* (VN for fruits: Conkers, Cheggies, Obblyonkers). For a tree which is still a greenhorn in this country (it was introduced in the late sixteenth century), the horse-chestnut has made a huge contribution to popular culture. It produces 'sticky buds' (or 'cackey monkeys')[24] for vases in February and exquisite candelabras of blossom in May. The 'spreading chestnut tree' has been a symbol of village peacefulness, as well as the theme of music-hall songs and a 1930s dance craze. ('On the word "spreading" you spread your arms, on the words "chest" you put your hand on your chest …')[25] Chestnut is one of the commonest components of street names (56 in the London *A to Z* alone). Its autumn fruits, conkers, are the raw material for what is still the most widely played children's game with plants. And these glossy red-brown nuts have added their own tally of words and metaphors to our vocabulary: 'chestnut' (shared with *Castanea sativa*) as a colour – especially for horses and hair; 'conk', slang for bash and also for head, which, in a neat conkery circle, is also called your 'nut'. And past-their-prime, over-played conkers are, of course, 'old chestnuts'.

The horse-chestnut is native to the Balkans and was first raised in northern Europe by the botanist Charles de l'Écluse in 1576, from seeds brought from Constantinople. John Gerard describes the tree well in his *Herball* of 1597 (though he is unlikely to have seen a live specimen and was relying on Lyte's description of 1578).[26] 'The Horse Chestnut groweth … to be a very great tree, spreading his great and large armes or branches far abroad, by which meanes it maketh a very good coole shadow. These branches are garnished with many beautifull leaues, cut or diuided into fiue, sixe or seuen sections or diuisions, like to the Cinkfoile, or rather like the leaues of *Ricinus* [castor-oil-plant], but bigger. The flowers growe at the top of the stalkes, consisting of fower small leaues like the Cherrie blossom, which turne into round, rough and prickley heads.'[27]

Thirty-six years later a note by Thomas Johnson, in his edition of Gerard, indicated that the tree was now growing in the South Lambeth garden of the plant collector John Tradescant.[28] It was already called horse-chestnut in English, and the modern interpretation of the name is that it is analogous to horse-radish, cow parsley and dog's mercury, and signifies that this chestnut (and its fruits) are an inferior version of the sweet or Spanish chestnut. But it is called horse-chestnut in its native Turkey, too, and given to horses for

A fuchsia hedge in south Devon, where the South American shrub is hardy and occasionally naturalises.

food and medicine. So perhaps the name is a functional one, analogous to 'motherwort'. At the very least the trees are appreciated as shelter by horses and cattle. On the common pastures of Boxmoor, Hemel Hempstead, horse-chestnuts grow in groups of four, like wooden horses themselves. (There is also a horse 'sign' in the tree, spotted by adherents of sympathetic magic: when the leaves fall, the stalk makes a horseshoe-shaped scar on the branch, which carries small nail-like marks.)

Although horse-chestnuts now naturalise freely in woods and hedgerows and on waste ground, they were slow to escape from cultivation and were originally regarded as mysteriously romantic and powerful trees. An early planting is recorded in a local legend from Herefordshire: 'On the Kidderminster side of Bewdley near the site of the old Wribbenhall church, there are three horse-chestnut trees (now in an electricity sub-station) which are reputed to be planted on the site where the black plague [c. 1660s] victims were buried.'[29]

The majority of early plantings were in parks and the grounds of big houses. Capability Brown arranged 4,800 in the Tottenham Park estate in Wiltshire. Oxford colleges have been planting them for at least 200 years. The spectacular mile-long Chestnut Avenue at Bushy Park, north of Hampton Court, was designed by none other than Sir Christopher Wren and planted in 1699. It was originally intended as a carriage drive for William III from Teddington to the palace. But in 1838 Queen Victoria opened Hampton Court to the public, and the Park rapidly became one of the most popular spring playgrounds in London. Not long afterwards the tradition of 'Chestnut Sunday' began, and vast numbers of people, from all classes, would gather on a Sunday in mid-May, parade up and down the Avenue and picnic under the trees. The trees were nearly two centuries old by the end of Victoria's reign and

Horse-chestnuts were introduced from Turkey in the sixteenth century and are often planted as shade trees for stock.

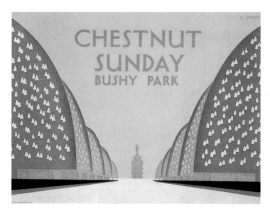

'Chestnut Sunday', a 1930 poster by C. Burton for London Transport, advertising the annual celebrations in Bushy Park.

deeply impressed one participant: 'the sight is certainly remarkable and worth seeing – a wide mile of lofty walls of foliage, bespangled with countless white spires – like tapering candles – and the boughs laden and almost sweeping the ground.'[30]

The custom flagged in the 1920s and died altogether with the onset of the Second World War. But it was revived again in 1977, the year of Queen Elizabeth's Jubilee, and has been formally observed by a group of enthusiasts ever since: 'Chestnut Sunday is [now held on] the nearest Sunday to 11th May, when the trees should be at their best. At 12.30 p.m. anyone who wishes to join in meets at the Teddington gate, says "The candles are alight", and walks down the avenue to the Diana Fountain where a picnic is held.'[31]

Despite the great fashionability of horse-chestnuts in the eighteenth and nineteenth centuries, and the numbers planted on big estates, the first record of the nuts being used in the game of conkers is from the Isle of Wight in 1848. There is an oddity about the lateness of this date, given that almost identical games had been played with objects on strings for centuries. There are descriptions from the seventeenth century of cobnut-fights, in which each player had hazel-nuts strung 'like the beads of a rosary' and exchanged strikes with his opponent.[32] In the eighteenth century boys played a game called

'conquerors' (which was even called 'conkers' in some places) with snail shells, sometimes with the unfortunate snails still inside. The shells were pressed against each other until one was smashed. The survivor was 'the Conqueror' and a tally was kept. The poet John Clare kept his shells threaded on a string and called the game 'cock-fighting' (cf. ribwort plantain, p. 48).[33]

Given the obvious suitability of horse-chestnuts for the game, why did it take children a century and a half to discover them? Jeff Cloves, author of *The Official Conker Book*, believes that the reason lies in the pattern and date of the early chestnut plantings. Most trees were nurtured on private estates, during a period of massive landscape rearrangement and draconian gamekeeping, and few children got the chance to gather the nuts with impunity. But, from the beginning of the nineteenth century, horse-chestnuts began to adorn the streets of spa towns such as Bath and Cheltenham and, from 1835, the public parks that were being created in big industrial cities. By the middle of the century the horse-chestnut had become a public tree, as common in urban open spaces, suburban streets and village greens as it was in big private estates.

Since then conkers played with horse-chestnuts has flourished, amongst girls and adults as well as boys. And, despite some regional variation in the jargon, the rules and rites, as the archivists of children's games, Iona and Peter Opie, discovered, are pretty standard throughout the country.[34] Gathering the nuts is the be-

'Obbly obbly onker, my first conker.'

ginning. Some are just collected from the ground, but the best are believed to be at the top of the tree and are invariably helped down by barrages of sticks and stones. Prising the shiny mahogany fruits from their prickly cases is also part of the fun and is usually done with the help of some light pressure from a shoe. Flat conkers, which often grow in pairs, are widely known as 'cheesers' or 'cheese-cutters'; under-ripe ones (in Yorkshire at least) as 'water-babies'.[35] The most promising fruits are often artificially hardened, by baking in the oven or soaking in vinegar. (Though one Putney boy rinsed his in water afterwards: 'If you did not put them in water the smell would keep on the conker and then people would not play you because they would think it was harder than theirs.')[36] These days deep-

freezing and microwaving have been added to the battery of favourite hardening tricks. But more patient children simply put a few conkers into a dark cupboard until the following autumn, by which time they are shrivelled and tough, and known as 'yearsies'.

To prepare a conker for combat, a hole is made through it with a skewer, and it is threaded onto a knotted string or shoe-lace. There are elaborate rituals, shouts and rhymes to determine who has first swing, but in essence the game proceeds by the two players having alternate strikes at each other's conker, or up to three shots in a row if the first two miss. The winner is the one who finally breaks his or her opponent's nut so that no pieces remain on the string. The triumphant nut becomes a 'one-er'. If it then breaks

The spreading chestnut tree – a symbol of village peacefulness.

another first-time nut, it becomes a 'two-er', and so on. But if a two-er breaks, say, a tenner, it absorbs the other's score and becomes a twelver. (In a contest staged by BBC TV in 1952, the winner emerged as a 7,351-er.) [37]

Since 1965, a World Conker Championship has been held at the village of Ashton in Northamptonshire on the second Sunday in October. It is an apt site, as Ashton is a 'model' village created by Charles de Rothschild in 1900, with a horse-chestnut avenue a mile long up to the mansion and a fully grown tree transplanted to shelter the new smithy. From small beginnings

the championship has grown into a major event, attracting crowds of over 4,000 and participants from all over the world. In 1976, it was won by a Mexican, R. Ramirez – the only time the title has left the country and a remarkable achievement at an occasion which is about as eccentrically English as it is possible to get.

Given the lively activity around roadside conker trees in autumn, it was predictable that some killjoy local authority (Lowestoft) would eventually plant a commemorative avenue of a horse-chestnut variety that bears no fruits. Less misanthropic kinds include very early leafers in,

for instance, Calverton, Nottinghamshire, and Ilkley, Yorkshire,[38] and the red-flowered hybrid, *A. × carnea*.

Conkers also have less strenuous uses in children's play. Model-making is widespread: 'For me, as a child, the conker season meant collecting the glossiest and then making a suite of furniture for my dolls' house. This involved sticking four straight pins in the underside of the conker to make legs and an arc of pins around the top. With a length of coloured wool my mother showed me how to weave in and out of these pins to make the back of the chair.'[39]

Conkers are also still used to deter moths, and the soap-like chemicals (saponins) they contain are added to enhance the 'natural' image of proprietary shampoos and shower-gels. Conkers are mildly poisonous in excess (though most children nibble the hard, bitter flesh without ill effects), but in Victorian England there were recipes for making a 'strictly agreeable and edible flour', by grinding them and then leaching out the bitterness with hot water. During the two World Wars conkers were gathered for their starch, which was converted to acetone by a process invented by Chaim Weizmann. More recently, German scientists have discovered that aescin, extracted from the nuts, is a powerfully effective remedy for sprains and bruising – precisely the ailments in horses that the Turks have used conkers to treat. The British Forestry Commission expect eventually to be helping to establish 10,000 acres of plantation horse-chestnuts to supply the needs of the pharmaceutical firms – a strange twist of fortune for a homely tree of village greens and schoolboy games.

Sycamore, *Acer pseudoplatanus*, was probably introduced to this country from central Europe some time during the fifteenth or sixteenth century and has been squabbled over ever since. Even in the late seventeenth century, when the tree was still comparatively scarce, John Evelyn was making the kind of complaints that have become familiar throughout Britain in the past few decades: 'The *Sycomor* ... is much more in reputation for its *shade* than it deserves; for the *Hony-dew* leaves, which fall early (like those of the *Ash*) turn to a *Mucilage* and noxious *insects*, and putrifie with the first moisture of the season; so as they contaminate and marr our *Walks*; and are therefore by my consent, to be banish'd from all curious *Gardens* and *Avenues*.'[40]

Since then it has spread rampantly across southern and western Britain, especially after extensive planting at the end of the eighteenth century. Sycamore 'Mucilage' is almost certainly 'the wrong sort of leaves' which has caused

Sycamores, sheltering an isolated Pennine farm.

159

Sycamore blossom, one of the brightest flowers of April.

British Rail's trains to skid to a halt every autumn. And the 'Hony-dew' (produced by aphids) makes tacky coats on the windscreens and bonnets of parked cars. Sycamore's newest antagonists are the nature conservationists, who see this exotic tree invading sacrosanct habitats – medieval churchyards, green lanes, even the ancient English greenwood – and shading out native species. As one Home Counties contributor (something of an admirer himself) reflects: 'The sycamore is often called a weed species. It certainly has one weed quality; it is a prolific seeder when mature. The winged, aerodynamic fruits are known as "locks-and-keys". If you would like a wood in your garden, then a nearby sycamore will oblige, without your lifting a finger … Rattling into London along the suburban rail lines here it is again, defying the diesel fumes on trackside embankments and urban wasteland. The adaptability of the tree in Britain is so com-

plete it is almost comic. Here is a Johnny-come-lately out-nativing the natives in almost every situation.'[41] In consequence many local conservation groups spend many working days pulling seedling sycamores by the thousand from their woodland nature reserves.

Yet the tree has an alternative and less disreputable history in Britain. There is an unmistakable carving of the leaves on the shrine to St Frideswide in Oxford Cathedral (carved in 1282), alongside native species such as maple, hawthorn and oak. Perhaps the carver knew the tree from elsewhere in Europe. But it is possible that a few individuals were brought here two or three centuries earlier than is usually assumed. It may have been a case of mistaken identity at first. 'Sycamore' is properly a Middle Eastern species of fig, *Ficus sycomorus*, celebrated as a shade-tree in the Bible, and *A. pseudoplatanus*, no mean shader itself, may have been popularly believed to be the same species. Gerard, who knew the difference, described 'The great Maple' as 'a stranger in England, only it groweth in the walkes and places of pleasure of noble men, where it especially is planted for the shadowe sake, and vnder the name of Sycomore tree'.[42]

And planted as individual shade-trees, on village greens and parkland and close to isolated farms in the hilly areas of Wales and the Pennines, sycamores lose their 'weedy' aura and take on something of the grandeur they show in their native mountain habitat.

There are many surviving landmark sycamores. The comparatively young tree that breaks up the long curve of Oxford High Street between All Souls and Queen's Colleges was called by the planner Thomas Sharp 'one of the most important in the world'.[43] Another lone tree, featured by Sir Peter Scott in his painting *The Sycamore at Eastpark* (1974), still stands at the edge of the wet and windswept pastures of Caerlaverock, Dumfries, where barnacle geese winter.[44] And two sycamores at Haworth in Yorkshire 'are a worldwide landmark for the thousands of visitors to the moorland above the Brontës' village … The trees are at the location written about by Emily Brontë in *Wuthering Heights*.'[45]

Less exalted, but no less valued locally, are the Posy Tree at Mapperton in Dorset (a village named after field maples, incidentally), on which a plaque reads: 'It was past this tree that the local victims of the great plague were carried to a common grave by the surviving villagers';[46] the Poo Hill Tree, used as a landmark on the pack-horse way between Lower Denby and Clayton West near Huddersfield;[47] and the Wishing Tree on Helm Common, Kendal. The tree grows by a bridle-path, and the custom amongst children when they walk under its branches is to make a wish, pick up a stone from the path, spit on it, and then add it to the adjacent drystone wall.[48]

'A well-known local tree … grows alone on the top of Oker Hill [near Matlock, Derbyshire]. The story goes that years ago two local brothers each planted a sycamore on top of the hill when they were young, and hoped to see the trees grow to maturity. Unfortunately only one tree survived and now is a fine specimen (two people can only just touch fingers round the trunk) whilst the other withered and died. This apparently reflected the brothers' futures – one flourished in business whilst the other was unsuccessful. Some versions say the second brother died just as his tree had done.'[49]

'At Dulverton, Somerset, there is a sycamore of enormous girth and a great age for the species. Called the Belfry Tree, it stands beside the Church Tower. It was struck by lightning during a hurricane in 1845, and lost the top of its crown. But the branches were braced, and recently they have been again strengthened with steel wires, while a drainpipe has been inserted by a tree surgeon to let excess moisture escape from inside the trunk.'[50]

The most celebrated sycamore of all is the Martyrs' Tree on the Green at Tolpuddle, Dorset. In the 1830s Tolpuddle was the birthplace of what was probably the first agricultural trade union, and it was under the village sycamore that the local farm labourers used to meet and talk – an illicit practice then that ended in the transportation of six of them to Australia. There is a story that their leader, George Loveless, took a leaf from the tree with him to Australia, pressed

Sycamore, in William Inchbold's painting 'In Early Spring', 1854–5.

between the pages of his Bible. By the 1960s (when it was well over two centuries old) the tree had become a rather sorry specimen, seemingly dying of heart-rot, and it was adopted by the Trades Union Congress. They had the hollow trunk filled with vermiculite and bound with iron hoops and it now looks in vigorous health again. In 1984, on the 150th anniversary of the deportation, Len Murray, then General Secretary of the TUC, planted out one of its seedlings a few yards away on the Green.

(A more modern 'moot' sycamore is in Sheriff Hutton in Yorkshire, where 'a speculative builder was anxious to buy the Glebe Field and develop it as a building site. The villagers were determined that this should not happen, so called a meeting on the mound under the tree – and bought the field.'[51] It is now established as a parish conservation area in perpetuity.)

Hostility towards the tree because of its alien

origins and aggressive habits meant that its positive contributions to indigenous wildlife were rather slow to be acknowledged. But it is now known, for instance, that, despite the initial sliminess of its fallen leaves, they decay very quickly and boost earthworm populations. Flower species characteristic of ancient woodland such as woodruff and wood anemone also thrive perfectly well on soils under sycamore. It is not particularly rich in insect species, but it makes up for this by having the highest insect productivity by weight (chiefly of aphids) of any widespread tree – 35.8 grams per square metre, as compared with 27.76 for oak and 11.15 for ash.[52] This is especially important in urban areas, where sycamore may be the only significant source of food for airborne insect-feeders such as house martins. But, because they are so frequently destroyed before they mature, very little is known about what would happen to a pure sycamore wood if it were given free rein. The seedlings are very vulnerable to fungal attack when growing under

a sycamore canopy, and it seems likely that at a certain point a pure sycamore wood would begin to break down and admit other species.

At present sycamore is better managed by coppicing than by attempted eradication. The regrowth is very fast, and it can be cut on a cycle as short as eight years. The wood is clean and pale, and liked by turners and makers of kitchen furniture: 'Sycamore is the best wood for kitchen tables. It has no odour to taint food processed on it, and a fine grain so that it can be easily cleaned. Rolling pins and baking boards also used to be made from it, and the best bread boards and wooden spoons still are.'[53] In Wales sycamore is carved into clogs, and is still the favourite wood for 'love-spoons'. These betrothal gifts, with their symbolically linked rings, were traditionally whittled out of a single piece of wood. (Today they have become part of a thriving if small-scale souvenir industry.)[54]

In the West Country sycamore leaves were used as bases on which to bake small cakes, either

The Martyrs' Tree at Tolpuddle, Dorset, the sycamore under which the local farmworkers held their union meetings in the 1830s, a practice for which they were later deported.

for Easter ('Revel Buns') or at harvest-time. The thick veins on the leaves make a distinct pattern on the underside of the buns.

'I do not know why they must be baked on sycamore leaves, but as a child I should not have thought them right if they had not had the imprint of the leaf under them.'[55]

'Years ago, my friend's grandmother [in Cornwall] used to send the children out to collect large sycamore leaves on which she baked the harvest cakes which were taken out to the fields for the harvesters.'[56]

Children have, as usual, been ingenious in their uses of all parts of the plant: 'In spring, when the sap was rising, we would take short lengths of sycamore twigs, about the thickness of one's little finger, and make whistles out of them. They would only last for a day before they dried out and became useless, so we used to make them more or less continuously until the bark became firmly attached to the underlying tissues.'[57]

The winged seeds – known as 'helicopters' in England, and 'backies' in Scotland, from their resemblance to small bats[58] – are used in flying competitions and model-making.

'Three generations of my family have made miniature water-wheels by impaling four single seeds of sycamore on a long blackthorn spike and resting them across two Y-shaped twigs over a stream.'[59]

'Edinburgh children play a game called "noses" in which you stick one of the wishbone-shaped seeds of sycamore on the end of your nose. The winner is the one who manages to keep it on longest.'[60] A similar game in England is called 'sticky noses'. The seeds are split and plastered down each side of the nose with the stalk pointing outwards, Pinocchio-style.

The 'Corstorphine Plane' is a sycamore sport with initially bright yellow leaves. The original tree, of unknown origin and planted out *c.* 1600, is preserved by the Corstorphine Trust in Edinburgh.[61]

Stag's-horn sumach, *Rhus hirta*, is a colour-

The vivid autumn foliage of stag's-horn sumach, a North American shrub naturalised on many railway embankments.

ful shrub from North America, much planted in parks and on urban road-verges. It spreads freely by suckers and can build up quite large thickets, especially along railway lines. Its autumn colours are spectacular. The drooping leaves turn a fiery orange-crimson and the fruits, like unopened cones, a deeper red. ('Stag's-horn' refers to the texture of the shoots in spring, which are similar to a stag's horn 'in velvet'.)

Tree-of-heaven, *Ailanthus altissima*, is a handsome tree, with ash-like leaves and panicles of strong-smelling creamish flowers, introduced to Europe from China in the mid-eighteenth century. The first British specimens were grown in about 1751 from seed sent to Philip Miller, of the Chelsea Physic Garden, by Père Nicholas d'Incarville. (Though until the tree fruited Miller obstinately maintained it was one of the Chinese lacquer trees.) [62] In parts of southern Europe it naturalises so freely that it has become a common part of open woodland and *maquis*. In Britain it is a much more restrained coloniser, but in south-east England increasing numbers of self-sown seedlings are appearing – and surviving – on waste ground and railway embankments. In London the oldest known wilding (on a river wall at Kew) dates from 1936. An opportunist sapling was even seen rising from a lidless bin left uncleared during one of the dustmen's strikes of the 1970s. [63]

It is especially numerous around Kensington, where planted trees are frequent in the nearby Royal Parks. And, though the flowers' nectar is regarded as acrid-smelling by many humans, it is relished by bees, and believed to be responsible for the muscat-flavoured honey that is occasionally found in west London beehives.

Indian balsam, *Impatiens glandulifera* (VN: Policeman's helmet, Stinky pops, Jumping Jacks, Bee-bums, Poor-man's orchid). Indian, or Himalayan, balsam is the most recently arrived of the family but already the most widespread and conspicuous. It was introduced to gardens from the Himalayas in 1839, and by the end of the nineteenth century had become widely naturalised, especially along rivers in the West Country. A. O. Hume found it in the Looe Valley in Corn-

Tree-of-heaven. London specimens are a favourite source of nectar for urban honey-bees.

wall, when it was still something of a novelty in the wild, and wrote the classic description: 'Growing in the soft warm south-west, with the base of the stem in the clear running stream, it is a magnificent plant, 5 to 7 feet or more in height, stalwart, with a stem from 1 to 2 inches in diameter just above the surface of the water, erect, symmetrical in shape, with numerous aggregations of blossom, the central mass as big as a man's head ... masses of bloom varying on different plants through a dozen lovely shades of colour from the very palest pink imaginable to the deepest claret, and with a profusion of large, elegant, dark green, lanceolate leaves, some of them fully 15 inches in length. Stunted specimens of this Balsam are common in Cornwall in orchard and cottage gardens; but in the Upper Looe the plant has become thoroughly naturalised, and I have never seen it quite as fine even in its native habitats.'[64]

Aggressive, colonial and frequently growing up to 10 feet tall in a year, it now dominates areas of river-bank throughout Britain, especially close to towns, sometimes to the point of swamping other summer-flowering species. The reason for its rampaging spread is the same as for other balsams: its seeds are fired off explosively and carried along by water. But, for all its territorial ambitions, many people still have a soft spot for Indian balsam, and it has been given a deliberate helping hand in some places, for instance in Somerset: 'My favourite plant. I am not quite sure if it is indigenous to this area, as I was given mine from somebody's garden. I have thrown the seeds in various hedges and ditches while walking the dog, so it soon will be! ... I was told that it was known locally as bee-bums and having noticed that bumblebees are attracted to it, and that their bums are all that is seen of them while they are on it owing to the shape of the flower, I thought it was an extremely good name.'[65]

'A great friend of mine married a Nobel prizewinner who was also a botanist. He took seeds from our Himalayan Balsams and would scatter them around – some on the banks of the Sheal where it flows through Sheffield, and some along the river banks in Derbyshire where he took his family for country walks. He *may* have been the one to introduce them to the Derwent Valley, c. 1946.'[66]

'When my sister dropped a rattle in the garden it split open and what looked like black seeds fell out. They were obviously old, but we planted them and they grew into large balsam plants. Ever since, the garden has been full of them, and this has been going on for almost 33 years.'[67]

It is, like many expansive foreign plants, viewed with mixed feelings, as in Worcestershire:

'Himalayan balsam has become a conservationists' nightmare in Worcestershire – the local Wildlife Trust regularly organises "balsam bashing" parties at our marshland reserves. However, in the Black Country, around Dudley and Stourbridge, it is a welcome addition to many industrial streamsides, where its gaudy pink flowers clash with the seepage of iron oxide from the factories. In the late 1960s my grandmother used to call it "poor man's orchid" [see lady's-slipper orchid, p. 238] – a name also used by people in the Halesowen and Stourbridge area.'[68]

Even the scent is debatable. In the Calder Valley in Yorkshire, for instance, where the Countryside Service also runs 'balsam bashes', one walker enjoys the 'heavy scent' of the mass of plants in the woods.[69] But in Cheshire, 'the River Mersey and its banks are infested with "Mersey Weed". This seems to be completely impervious to occasional industrial pollution, and has a pervasive evening scent reminiscent of Jeyes fluid.'[70]

Despite its comparatively recent arrival, children have rapidly learnt to exploit the potential of 'popping' the seed-pods, and at least one of the modern vernacular names ('stinky pops', Hertfordshire) was coined by schoolchildren. The secret of spectacular explosions is to choose a pod that is on the point of bursting spontaneously under its own tension. In the Lake District some children achieved what must be a record 12-yard throw with the seeds from one pod.[71] But more sophisticated, and sensuous, games have been invented, too: 'If a bunch of these seed-pods are held in the hand before they explode, and the hand is clenched, squeezing the seeds, there is a horrible "squirming" effect felt in the hand, like a lot of wriggling insects.'[72]

As for adults, if they feel above such things, they can always munch the pods: 'We always eat the seed-pods and ripe and unripe seed which have a pleasant nutty taste (but first catch your pod!). We first learned of this plant from an old friend who had undertaken an exploration of the Himalayas for the RGS. They had nothing but tinned food, except that he and his porters picked and nibbled balsam seeds. His wife, who would not eat them, became more and more ill and on

Indian or Himalayan balsam. It can hurl its seeds up to 12 yards.

reaching civilisation was found to be in an advanced state of scurvy.'[73]

Giant hogweed, *Heracleum mantegazzianum* (VN: Giant cow parsnip, Cartwheel plant, The Hog). Giant hogweed was a long while coming into its nefarious reputation. It had been growing in Britain for more than 150 years, an awesome but apparently well-mannered curiosity of Victorian shrubberies and ornamental lakesides, with no more than a hint of troll-like mischief in its huge, looming umbels. It seemed exactly what it was – a giant cow parsnip. Then, in 1970, it

broke cover. That summer large numbers of children began arriving in hospital casualty departments with unusual, circular blisters on their lips, hands and eyes, and it was not long before they were traced to a common cause – the sap from giant hogweed stems which had been used as blowpipes and 'telescopes'.[74] Overnight a plant from Asia that even botanists seem scarcely to have noticed in the wild (it is mentioned in very few Floras prior to 1940) was transformed into an aggressive and invasive public menace. The popular press immediately dubbed it 'The Triffid' after John Wyndham's science-fiction monster, and published pin-up-sized photographs of its speckled 15-foot stems and cartwheel-sized flower-heads. There were endless suggestions about how to eradicate the aliens: scythes, poison, flame-throwers, even excavators. One neighbour of mine dug out a plant to a depth of three feet, and then filled the root-hole with turpentine. None of these assaults had much effect. Except when it is young, giant hogweed is not very susceptible to weed-killers. Each plant produces up to 5,000 seeds, and, growing by rivers as it often does, is able to disperse them by water over long distances. So the expansion which had been quietly under way for nearly a century continued – though now under much more vigilant eyes.

It had seemed such an exciting and promising introduction when it was first brought to this country from the Caucasus mountains in the early nineteenth century, perhaps the temperate zone's answer to some of the titanic plants that were being discovered in the tropics. The great arbiter of gardening taste, John Loudon, certainly thought so, and praised '*Heracleum asperum* ... the Siberian Cow Parsnep' in *The Gardener's Magazine*:

'The magnificent umbelliferous plant, when grown in good soil, will attain the height of upwards of 12 ft. Even in our crowded garden in Bayswater, it last year (1835) was 12 ft when it came into flower ... Its seeds are now (July 29) ripe; and we intend to distribute them to our friends: not because the plant is useful, for we do not know any use to which it can be applied; but because it is extremely interesting from the rapidity of its growth, and the great size which it attains in five months … We do not know a more suitable plant for the retired corner of a churchyard, or for a glade in a wood; and we have, accordingly, given one friend, who is making a tour in the north of England and Ireland, and another, who is gone to Norway, seeds for depositing in proper places.'[75]

Whether this was one of the origins of rapidly expanding Norwegian populations is a moot point. But giant hogweed – known in the north of Norway as 'Tromso palm' – is regarded with much more affection than it is in Britain, and even appears as a feature on local tourist postcards.[76]

By 1849 its seeds were being offered commercially by Hardy and Sons of Maldon, Essex, as 'Heracleum giganteum, One of the most magnificent Plants in the World'.[77] And in 1870 William Robinson recommended them as 'very suitable for rough places on the banks of rivers or artificial water, islands, or any place where bold foliage may be desired', but added, prophetically, that 'when established they often sow themselves, so that seedling plants in abundance may be picked up around them; but it is important not to allow them to become giant weeds'.[78] Some large garden populations (e.g. a long-established colony in a 100-year-old garden in Hampton-in-Arden)[79] may date back to plantings made at this time.

By the early 1900s what was now called, with a more appropriately sinister buzz, H. mantegazzianum (after its Italian discoverer) was beginning to make its first sporadic break-outs. The collection in Buckingham Palace Gardens (which includes other closely related species and hybrids) edged into the Royal Parks and thence into the west London canal system.

In Colinsburgh, Fife, a large local concentration spread from an ornamental pond on an Edwardian housing estate which had used giant hogweed as a decorative plant: 'Since its introduction … the hogweed has escaped into the outfall stream, and this meanders about two miles to the burn, which is the main watercourse. A further two miles and the burn meets the sea. The banks of stream and burn are both covered in hogweed, almost to the exclusion of anything else.'[80] Further west in Scotland, its spread along the River Ayr has been traced to two identifiable country houses with large riverside gardens created c. 1939–45.[81]

What is remarkable is that it took so long for the plant's dermatitic effects to be noticed. It is hard to believe that gardeners had remained immune to the sap for more than a century. Yet a mother from Lancashire describes the confusion following her children's first clashes with the plant at the start of the 1970s: 'We had a holiday at a camp site where there was an awful lot of giant hogweed on the roadside and no one seemed to have done anything about it. We had four small children and they and some school friends were all going to the doctors who said they had been fire-burned and all various things. They were covered with burn-weals at the time. No one knew the reason. Till a doctor in Preston said the giant hogweed seeds had carried down the stream where they picnicked. At the time we had them growing close by us in a private garden. They are now gone, the lady got rid of them when *she* had children.'[82]

The irritant chemicals in the sap and bristles of giant hogweed are known as furocoumarins. They make the skin hypersensitive to bright sunlight and liable to blister and redden, often for long periods. The plant's aggressive spread – especially along river systems, where it can sometimes choke out native vegetation – has added to its bad reputation, and under the Wildlife and Countryside Act of 1981 it is now an offence to 'plant or otherwise cause [it] to grow in the wild'. Agencies such as the National Rivers Authority and local countryside management services have mounted campaigns against it. Needless to say it is generating its own myths: 'We have that awful giant hogweed here in Overstrand … It is so tall it is quite disturbing. I am told it is poison to children so should not something be done about it? I'm wondering what effect its pollen has on us.'[83]

In Richmond, Yorkshire, the story has grown

that the plant originally arrived as a stowaway on Russian ships, stealing up the Tees from Yarm, when it was still a port.[84]

But even those who have suffered from the plant are not unanimous in condemning it: 'We have a giant hogweed growing in our front garden and I discovered its dangers to my peril last year when I cut it down after it had flowered. We were aware of the danger of the plant, as the previous occupant had warned us, but I was quite unprepared for the burns I received on my arms and legs. It was while I was sitting in the casualty department of the hospital that I started to wish I had left it well alone. It is so unusual and spectacular, despite its hazards. We do not want to get rid of it; we just know now to treat it with a bit of love and respect.'[85]

Many contributors feel that the onus of responsibility is on us, not to 'tamper' with the plant; and that caution and respect are fairer responses than extermination[86] – an approach which has been taken to heart by an Australian musical instrument maker: 'My husband has recently purchased a Digeridoo made from a giant hogweed stem. The stem had been varnished and the mouthpiece heavily waxed (presumably to protect the lips from the irritants). P.S. It works.'[87]

'The giant hogweed has a long history here [Chester] ... Our Drive was built on the site of the famous Dicksons Nurseries Company who existed here for about a century, closing down in the 1925–30 period. The boundary of our garden, and the west boundary of the Nursery, was Newton Brook, and the Dicksons used this for growing all sorts of exotic waterside plants - the giant hogweed being one of them. Since the demise of the Nursery, survivors have existed roughly, growing along the brook route and even spread to the Bache area. Even more interesting is a local botanist's discovery that some had colonised the nearby railway track as far as Birkenhead! Locally, most have succumbed to

Giant hogweed, Hampshire. It is the tallest herbaceous plant growing in Britain.

over-zealous Council cutting-back – ostensibly to avoid youngsters being afflicted by the corrosive sap ... For all this, I and two family generations have survived to value these remarkably handsome plants. We now keep a couple of specimens each year in the garden. I should hate to see them vanish in this over-protective age.'[88]

'I have got two growing in different parts of my garden. Last year the main one had one flower head. This year it had three, probably because of my liking for this plant. I feed it on Growmore.'[89]

'To me the giant hogweed ... is one of our finest natural sculptures outside the world of trees and comparable to the smaller thistles and teasels as a "thing of beauty" ... The simple answer is to keep your distance, or wear gloves.'[90]

'It yomps determinedly along the banks of the River Kent at Jevens Bridge. Occasionally it escapes onto the roadside verge and causes a frisson of anxiety in the local newspapers which describe the dangers of handling it ... When gas pipes were being laid across the A6 nearby, a warning notice, "Danger, Heavy Plant Crossing", was displayed at the foot of one of these escapees.'[91]

For aficionados, there are hogweed landmarks all across Britain: in a fen above sweeps of marsh-orchid on the coast at Aldeburgh, Suffolk; by the side of the Art-Deco Hoover factory west of London; around the marina at Ilfracombe, Devon, and the Launceston Recycling Centre in Cornwall; by the sides of the Toll Bridge on the outskirts of Nottingham; and a large riverside sweep along the River Usk near Abergavenny.[92]

But Scotland has the most majestic – or insidious – colonies, depending on how you view them. In Glasgow, there are huge drifts on the banks of the Clyde, especially downstream of Kelvinbridge. Jim Dickson, Senior Lecturer in Botany at the university, describes the colonies growing out of the river-bank and waste ground of the Cunningar Loop as 'one of the most remarkable natural history sights of the Glasgow area'.[93]

Glasgow citizens seem to have reached a better *modus vivendi* with the plant, too, than their southern counterparts: 'People in the Glasgow area have brought it in indoors for flower arrangement, the older terraced houses having the necessary high ceilings. People are aware of the plant and incidents of dermatitis are rare.'[94]

The irony is that more cases of photodermatitis are caused by two much commoner and certainly less vilified umbellifers – common hogweed and wild parsnip.[95] Since the introduction of the strimmer, anyone clearing rough grass which includes either of these species risks spraying their skins with a fine mulch of furocoumarins. An ecology lecturer remembers what was widely known as 'dreaded plod rot' erupting routinely amongst her students when they were doing fieldwork amongst common hogweed on Skokholm Island in the late 1960s.[96]

Buddleia or **Butterfly-bush**, *Buddleja davidii*. Since its introduction to this country from China in the 1890s buddleia has spread across almost the whole of Britain, except the far north, and could be said to have been the saving of many butterfly populations in urban areas. Its long, honey-scented purple flower-spikes, in bloom from July to October, are the favourite source of nectar for almost all butterflies and moths that haunt gardens and waste places. In my own garden in August I have regularly seen more than 50 individuals of up to ten species together on a single bush.

Buddleja davidii was first found in the mountains near the Tibetan–Chinese border in 1869 by the French missionary Père David, a discovery which is commemorated in the plant's Latin name. The first specimens were sent to Europe some 20 years later by another French missionary and plant-collector, Jean André Soulie. The early imports were apparently weak and semi-prostrate specimens, and poor in colour, and were rapidly superseded by a more vigorous and attractive variant raised in Paris in 1893 by the famous nursery firm of Vilmorin.[97]

Once established, buddleia rapidly began to colonise waste ground. Its seeds are light and winged, and can be blown some distance on the wind. And, like many species from exotic stony habitats, it seems to find the ballast along the edge of railway lines a particularly congenial habitat. The railway system provided a network of corridors along which the seeds could be dispersed over long distances, sometimes, no doubt, being drawn along by the slipstream of trains (cf. Oxford ragwort, p. 17). From its strongholds on railway embankments it spread to waste ground, bomb sites, allotments, walls, sometimes even being blown upwards to take root in chimneys. An admirer from Cheshire describes a typical invasion:

'In the early 1980s there were several large demolition jobs going on in Chester. In one area a large piece of derelict land was left isolated at the junction of five roads. Within a few years the whole island was covered with purple buddleia to the extent of it becoming a recognised "show". Not satisfied, this enterprising plant soon crossed the roads and is now sprouting from bridge brickwork, tiny corners of wasteland, pavements and factory buildings on the north side of the city. I see a distinct plea in all this to be recognised as British, having shown such fertility and enthusiasm for our least favoured growing sites.'[98]

In many southern cities it can form dense shrubberies that, mixed with birch and scrub willow, amount to a unique form of urban woodland. 'Its abundance in towns like Bristol is amazing; it forms thickets everywhere, colonising ledges on buildings as well as covering waste ground. A visit to the city makes it easy to visualise the description of an early visitor to China who reported that buddleia thickets on shingle beside the Satani River provided "famous harbourage for tigers".'[99]

Various colour variants, including purple and white, sometimes crop up amongst naturalised colonies, but are not usually rich in nectar.

Ivy-leaved toadflax, *Cymbalaria muralis* (VN: Mother of thousands, Travelling sailor). A delicate but aggressive creeper that trails over walls, banks and pavements, ivy-leaved toadflax was introduced from southern Europe early in the seventeenth century. William Baxter, writing in the 1830s, described 'this very pretty plant' as 'a

Railside buddleia. The granite chips of the permanent way are a fair imitation of its native habitat in China.

native of Italy ... said to have been originally introduced into England by means of its seeds having been brought in some marble sculptures from that country to Oxford, where it has long established itself on the walls of the Colleges, gardens, &c. in such abundance, as to have obtained the name of "Oxford-weed".'[100] It is virtually unknown in natural habitats in this country.

Ivy-leaved toadflax has a mechanism which makes it easy for the plant to colonise walls vertically upwards. When it is in bloom, the flower-stalks bend towards the light; once the flowers are over, the seed-heads bend the other way, so that the seeds are more likely to be shed into cracks in the supporting stones. Its small, neat, purple and yellow snapdragons made it very popular as an ornamental plant between the seventeenth and nineteenth centuries, when there were many new walled gardens which it could exploit. It is no longer deliberately planted, but it is now found throughout Britain.

'My daughter grew up believing that a plant growing on walls was called "I believe in toadflax". It is now a family name.'[101]

Canadian goldenrod, *Solidago canadensis.* Our native goldenrod was upstaged when its tall and showy relative from the New World was introduced to this country in 1648. Canadian goldenrod was a popular border plant, until its tremendous capacity for self-seeding and spreading was realised in the Victorian garden, when –

along with the Michaelmas-daisy (see below) – it was consigned to the rubbish-heap or the wild garden. This century it and **early goldenrod**, *S. gigantea*, have become two of the dominant flowers of urban wasteland in late summer and early autumn.

Michaelmas-daisies, *Aster* species. Michaelmas-daisies of all kinds are widely naturalised in waste places. They have a particular liking for railway embankments, and the drifts along some lines, in pastel shades that range from palest blue to mauve, mark the year's last great show of wild-flower colour, often continuing well into November.

They were first introduced to this country from North America at the start of the eighteenth century. But it was the taste for wilder

Ivy-leaved toadflax, introduced to Britain in the seventeenth century as a wall plant.

gardens in the mid-Victorian period that prompted their much wider spread. William Robinson, as usual, was perceptive and unwittingly prophetic about the role they might play in the landscape. In 1870 he wrote of 'Starwort, or Aster': 'they form a very good example of a class of plants for which the true place is the copse, and by wood-walks, where they will grow as freely as any native weeds, and in many cases prove charming in autumn … Associated with the Golden Rods (*Solidago*) – also common plants of the American woods – the best of the Asters or Michaelmas Daisies will form a very interesting aspect of vegetation. It is that which one sees in American woods in late summer and autumn when the Golden Rods and Asters are seen in bloom together. It is one of the numerous aspects of the vegetation of other countries which the "wild garden" will make possible in gardens.' [102]

And it is precisely with naturalised goldenrods that Michaelmas daisies provide such an adornment to urban wasteland – though here they are echoing their other North American native habitat, the plains and prairies, rather than the woods.

Martagon lily, *Lilium martagon*, is a species from mainland Europe with usually pale purple, black-flecked 'Turk's-cap' flowers, naturalised in a scatter of woods, mainly in England. It may possibly be native in a few woods in the Wye Valley and Surrey. **Pyrenean lily**, *L. pyrenaicum*, is a native of the Pyrenees with greenish-yellow 'Turk's-cap' flowers, well naturalised in woods and on hedge-banks chiefly in the West Country. Two Devon villages, only five miles apart, have both claimed it as their own. In one it is known as 'the South Molton lily', and in the other as 'the Molland lily'. [103]

WILD PLANTS IN THE GARDEN
Many attractive native species have gone the other way from the immigrant plants described above and have been taken into gardens almost unchanged from their wild state: primroses, meadow crane's-bill and setterwort, for instance, as well as the plants that follow.

Columbine, *Aquilegia vulgaris* (VN: Granny's bonnet, Granny's nightcap). This cottage-garden favourite, a true British native, is named after two rather incompatible birds. The Latin name, *Aquilegia*, is derived from *aquila*, an eagle, because of a fancied similarity between the petals and eagles' wings (perhaps because of the upturned tips?). Columbine is from *columba*, a dove, and from the more striking resemblance of the bases of the petals to five pigeons perched in a ring. Columbines have been popular subjects for church carvings. They are, for instance, figured

Wild columbines are usually blue or purple, though occasionally white.

on misericord supports in Manchester Cathedral (*c.* 1506) and Ripon Cathedral (*c.* 1490); on a bench-end at St Petroc's in Lydford, Devon; and in a window border with fritillaries at St Bartholomew's, Yarnton, Oxfordshire.[104]

Columbines are scarce but widespread flowers of woods, fens and damp grassland on calcareous soils. Truly wild specimens are usually blue or purple (though I have found colonies with pure white flowers in the Derbyshire Dales). Other colours, and double- and large-flowered forms, increasingly common on road-verges and the edges of woods, are usually garden escapes.

Tutsan, *Hypericum androsaemum*, is a bushy plant, with a procession of bright yellow flowers from June till September, which give way to shiny berries, green at first, then tinged with red, and finally purplish-black. The leaves are heart-shaped, up to four inches long, and when dry have an evocative, fugitive scent, reminiscent of cigar boxes and candied fruit. For this reason, as well as their convenient shape, they were used as bookmarks – especially in Bibles ('Bible leaf' is an obsolete West Country name), perhaps because of the plant's reputation as a benign and healing herb. ('Tutsan' is itself a corruption of the French *toute-saine*, meaning, roughly, 'all-heal'.) Tutsan leaves were still being used as Bible markers in parts of Somerset up to the Second World War.[105]

Tutsan is very much a plant of the west, of damp woods and shady banks. In Devon and Cornwall it is one of the most characteristic plants of hedge-banks, and even grows on some sea-cliffs. But it also occurs scarcely in moist and sheltered places throughout Britain, and is always an intriguing plant to find, lurking deep in a crevice in the limestone pavements below Ingleborough in Yorkshire, or in a sunken lane in the Hampshire Weald. Rather surprisingly, given the popularity of the berries with birds, tutsan cultivated in gardens rarely seems to become established beyond them.

The delicately bronzed leaves of tutsan, here growing in a limestone pavement, Gait Barrows, Lancashire.

The dog-rose, the most abundant of our native rose species.

Wild roses, *Rosa* species. The rose is England's national flower, but none of the likely candidates for this honourable position is a native wild species. The Red Rose of Lancaster is the Mediterranean *Rosa gallica*, the White Rose of York almost certainly a hybrid between the native field-rose, *R. arvensis*, and the damask rose *R. × damascena*. Even the heraldic roses carved on churches and memorials throughout the land are modelled more on the Holy Rose of Abyssinia (*R. richardii*), the oldest of all cultivated roses and figured in paintings on the murals at Knossos in Crete, than on any indigenous briar.[106]

But our native roses are amongst our best-loved and most familiar flowers, even though the barbarous schedules of modern hedge-cutting rarely allow them to flower. There are 14 species currently accepted as native to Britain. Four of these – dog-rose, *R. canina*, field-rose, *R. arvensis*, harsh downy-rose, *R. tomentosa*, and sweetbriar, *R. rubiginosa* – are common hedgerow climbers. Numerous subspecies and hybrids occur naturally, and three of these species have played a modest part in the evolution of various groups of cultivated rose. (Wild roses have also frequently been been used as grafting stock for cultivars. A Buckinghamshire contributor recalls how cottagers would take wild roses from the hedges to graft garden roses, 'if they got given a bit from one of the wealthier houses'.[107])

Dog-rose, *R. canina* (VN: Ewemack), is the most abundant and widespread species, and also the most variable. It can be a low-growing

scrambler or climb 30 feet up a woodland tree to
flower in the crown, like a rain-forest vine. The
sweet-scented blooms vary in colour from deep
pink to white. *R. canina* has produced a small
number of cultivated varieties, the best known of
which is 'Abbotswood', a chance hybrid with an
unknown garden variety, which has scented,
double, pink flowers. (It originally appeared in
the garden of Harry Ferguson, of tractor fame.)
It is also in the breeding line of the 'Alba' group.

An old riddle, 'The Five Brethren of the
Rose', gives an effective way of identifying roses
of the *canina* group. It is a folk-riddle that has
been passed on orally since medieval times. This
is a version transmitted through a line of distinguished gardeners, from Canon Ellacombe to
Edward Bowles to William T. Stearn:

> *On a summer's day, in sultry weather,*
> *Five brethren were born together.*
> *Two had beards and two had none*
> *And the other had but half a one.*[108]

(The 'brethren' are the five sepals of the dog-
rose, two of which are whiskered on both sides,
two quite smooth and the fifth whiskered on one
side only.)

Field-rose, *R. arvensis*, is a scrambler, whose
arching stems rarely reach more than three or
four feet above ground level. It always has pure
white flowers, with conspicuous golden anthers,

Sherard's downy-rose, common in Scotland but very rare in southern England.

a pin-like column of styles and a musky, honey scent. It is the ancestor of the Ayrshire roses, now very rare in cultivation. **Sherard's downy-rose**, *R. sherardii*, is commonest in northern Britain. It is a beautiful and subtle rose with downy leaves and deep pink, velvety petals, which surprisingly has not been taken into cultivation at all.

Sweet-briar, *R. rubiginosa*, the 'eglantine' of Shakespeare and early writers, is noticeable for its sticky, apple-scented leaves, which become especially fragrant after rain. It is scattered throughout Britain, but most frequent in chalk scrub in southern England. A semi-double sport (reputedly discovered in a Cheshire lane) was named 'Janet's Pride' and was the precursor of a group of spectacular and vigorous sweet-briars bred by Lord Penzance in the 1890s, including 'Amy Robsart', 'Meg Merrilies' and 'Lady Penzance'. Most of the earlier cultivars are probably extinct. They included var. *concava*, in which both the deep pink flowers and the leaves were concave, like little spoons; various doubles, including the very fragrant 'William's Sweet-briar' (var. *multiplex*); and var. *marmorea*, with marbled flowers.[109]

'A local farmer's wife [Whitby] recalls, on the way to school, picking the tender young shoots of wild roses, to suck in the place of sweets which were not available to country children. I think this could have arisen in more calcium-rich areas, where the sweet-briar rose grows. This has glands which secrete an apple-smelling liquid leaving a pleasant taste.'[110]

Burnet rose, *R. pimpinellifolia*, is a low-growing species, largely confined to dry sandy places near the sea and to calcareous areas inland. It has white flowers, frequently tinged with cream (or more rarely with pink), prominent golden stamens, and the sweetest smell of any native rose – a mixture of honey and jasmine. The hips are almost round, blackish-purple in colour, and the leaves are small and oval, very like those of salad burnet (hence the name).

A colour variety with slightly yellower flowers is known to rosarians as the Dunwich Rose, from its discovery on the sandy cliffs of Dun-

Burnet rose, whose flowers have the finest scent of any of our wild species – a mix of honey, clotted cream and jasmine.

wich in Suffolk in 1956. It has gone from the cliffs, but still survives in heathland a mile or two inland – and, it hardly needs to be added, in several local gardens.[111]

R. pimpinellifolia has been used in rose-breeding as far back as the early 1800s, when the double varieties known as 'Scotch roses' were fashionable. The best known is 'Stanwell's Perpetual', with very double, soft pink flowers.

The hybrid between the burnet rose and the dog-rose, *R.* × *hibernica*, occurs occasionally in

Japanese rose, widely naturalised – as here, in the steelworks area of Sheffield.

enough to have become local landmarks include those along the railway embankments at Bletchley, Buckinghamshire; in the sandy fen behind the coast road at Aldeburgh, Suffolk; covering the cliffs between Coldingham Bay and St Abb's Head in Berwickshire; and on beaches at Flimby, Cumbria, and Carylon Bay, Cornwall, not far from the St Austell china-clay works.[112] An exceptionally large colony is along the York ring road, though this is probably an extension of an ornamental planting: 'They are growing on rough ground adjacent to and overlooking the roadway, in some cases with other bushes, to a depth of 10 yards, and extend along the road for almost 800 yards.'[113]

Japar se rose was one of the spiny species chosen by the Essex police in 1993 for planting as anti-thief barricades. These also included *Berberis* spp., hawthorn and gorse, and were collectively nicknamed, in a fine example of Estuary Latin, '*Burglaris disembowelis*'.

'These plants make an attractive alternative to conventional fencing or the use of barbed wire on walls.'[114]

Red-leaved rose, *R. glauca*, better known to gardeners as *Rosa rubrifolia*, is a species rose from central Europe, quite widely naturalised from bird-sown seed. It is striking for its greyish, red-tinged leaves and diminutive pink flowers, more like a bramble's than a rose's.

There are many other foreign rose species and cultivars which have naturalised from gardens – or lived on there after the house itself has vanished. A few have been thought lost, but have then been rediscovered in abandoned corners and brought back into cultivation. The most celebrated is the deep-coloured Victorian rose that was found by the late Humphrey Brooke, scrambling up the wall of Woolverstone Church in Suffolk. The bush was over a hundred years old but still flowering. Brooke, an eccentric but distinguished and knowledgeable rosarian, thought it had the strongest scent of any rose he knew and once recounted to me how a blind friend had 'put his nose in a bloom and said that if this scent was available in a bottle it would put every tart in Europe out of business'. The Woolverstone

the wild. (I have seen it in the Yorkshire Dales.) It has bright pink single flowers, but most of its other characteristics are midway between those of its parents.

Japanese rose, *R. rugosa*, is a low-growing, viciously spiny Asian species with single pink flowers, often planted in masses on urban roadsides and roundabouts. It can expand into very large clumps by suckers and is increasingly naturalised on banks, dunes, waste ground and the sites of old gardens. Thickets conspicuous

Church rose is now back on the market as 'Surpassing Beauty of Woolverstone'.

Rosebay willowherb, *Chamerion* (or *Epilobium*) *angustifolium* (VN: Bombweed, Fireweed, Ranting widow). Something has happened to rosebay over the past century. What had been a comparatively scarce woodland plant has turned into one of the most successful and colourful colonisers of waste places – car parks, railway embankments, roadsides, even cracks in chimneys. The records track the change, but do not by themselves explain it.

Up to the mid-eighteenth century most writers seemed to regard rosebay as a garden plant which occasionally escaped into the wild. The first convincingly wild records are all from rocky or riverside sites. In Northumberland in 1769, for example, rosebay could be found 'Among the rocks and bushes under the Roman wall on the west side of Shewing-sheels, and by the Crag-Lake … It is introduced into some of our gardens under the name of French willow; but being a great runner, it makes a better figure in its more confined situation among the rocks, than under culture … It is reputed a scarce plant.' [115] In Hertfordshire, in the 1840s, it was described as 'rare' in 'woods on a moist sandy soil, and in osier beds'.[116] At about the same time, one of the women from the Clifford family of Frampton on Severn in Gloucestershire, who collectively painted a remarkable and normally reliable Flora of their neighbourhood, produced a meticulous illustration of rosebay, but misidentified it as 'Great hairy willowherb or Codlings and Cream'. From the amendments to the label it is clear that she was not entirely sure of what she had found.[117] In Hampshire, too, the Revd C. A. Johns, author of the seemingly immortal *Flowers of the Field* (1853), described 'the Rose-bay, or Flowering-willow' as 'not often met with in a wild state, but common in gardens'.[118] In Wiltshire in 1888, the Revd T. A. Preston had it confined to 'gravelly banks' (with a first county record as late as 1864) and considered it 'very doubtfully native'.[119]

But by 1867, the Worcester botanist Edwin Lees had begun to notice a change in its habits: 'Quite recently the Rosebay Willow-herb has

The wild rose screen at Great Warley, Essex. The white roses at the top of the screen represent purity; the lower, earthbound red roses, blood and passion.

become numerous in several parts of the Vale of Severn, and promises to spread, incited to take possession of new-made roads and embankments. I have observed it by the side of a diverted road near Shatterford, and in the cutting of the Birmingham and Gloucester Railway, near Croome Perry Wood.' [120]

During the First World War, rosebay's populations exploded, especially in the extensive areas of woodland that had been felled (and often burned) to supply timber for the war effort. In World War II, there was a second wave of expansion. Rosebay relishes areas where there have been fires, and the summer after the German

One of the earliest portraits of rosebay, painted in
Frampton c. 1840 and misidentified as 'Great Hairy
Willowherb or Codlings and Cream'.

bombing raids of 1940 the ruins of London's
homes and shops were covered with sheets of
rosebay stretching, according to some popular
reports, as far as the eye could see. There is, alas,
no record of how Londoners themselves felt
about this purple haze rising from the rubble.
Did they see it as a symbol of life triumphing
over destruction, or as a weedy invasion that
simply added insult to injury? But it did generate
one popular name – 'bombweed' – that became
current throughout the south-east.[121]

In Gloucestershire – where rosebay had been
a confusing rarity just a century before – there
were certainly mixed feelings about the plant.
In 1948 the new county Flora edited by H. J.
Riddelsdell could say: 'This species has spread
with great vigour since about 1914 owing to the
clearing of woods … The seed is easily carried, of
course, and the railway has been a great agent in

its spread. Beautiful as the plant is in its flowering season, when it is in seed it creates desolation
and ugliness over the whole of its area.'[122]

In 1953, Professor T. G. Tutin attempted to
relate the new expansiveness of rosebay to the
existence of two apparently different varieties:
var. *macrocarpum*, the true native confined
chiefly to rocky places and damp woods; and var.
brachycarpum, an alien strain from Scandinavia
or perhaps Canada, which thrived on disturbed
ground and had been the kind most commonly
cultivated as 'French willow'. It was this second
variety, he suggested, which had expanded to
take advantage of the new open areas created by
bombing and forest clearance.[123] But subsequent
research has failed to find any physical or genetic
differences between the undoubtedly wild populations and the supposedly naturalised colonies
in the lowlands. It now looks as if the Gloucestershire Flora's suggestion that the spread was
due to the railway system opening up new corridors of expansion may have been correct. Rosebay's seeds – and each plant produces about
80,000 – are certainly equipped to take advantage
of such opportunities. They are fitted with
plumes of featherweight hairs which, in warm,
dry conditions, open like parachutes and enable
the seeds to drift long distances on the breeze –
or in the slipstream of trains. These days most
people would take a more tolerant view of the
resultant blizzards than the Revd Riddelsdell,
and the difficulties they present are strictly local:
'I have seen a Gloucestershire woodland in early
September as though in a summer snowstorm
with the multitude of plumed seeds that appeared to fill the air.' (1961)[124] 'The local hunts-
man does not like letting the hounds go through
stands of this when cubhunting as the downy
seeds get up his hounds' noses so that they are
unable to smell.' (1993)[125]

In parts of the north of England the rosebay's
seeds (along with other airborne downy seeds)
are known as 'sugar stealers'.[126] There has been
no explanation for this name as yet, and I wonder
if it might stem from their resemblance to the
downy mould that often forms on the top of
home-made jam.

Lily-of-the-valley, *Convallaria majalis*, has one of the most beautiful fragrances of any of our native plants, yet demands the poorest soils to flourish. In a manner that echoes juniper, it occupies two distinct habitats in Britain. In the lowland south and east of England it favours ancient woods on sandy, acidic soils, such as the heathy reaches of Danbury in Essex and the greensand woods round Brickhill and Woburn in Buckinghamshire. George Claridge Druce marvelled at the 'wonderful sight' it offered there in the 1920s 'despite the raids that have been made on it in recent years'.[127] It even grew on Hampstead Heath until the middle of the nineteenth century.[128] The most celebrated (though not always the most free-flowering)[129] of these southern colonies are the 'Lily Beds' of St Leonard's Forest in Sussex, which are extensive enough to be marked on the Ordnance Survey map.

But in the west and north it is almost totally confined to limestone woods, from the Cotswolds up to the Yorkshire Dales. Lightly wooded limestone pavements such as Great Scar Close are the place to see them, with their glossy leaves clattering against the pale stone and the pure scent of their white bell-flowers drifting over the surrounding pastures. June is their peak flowering month in Britain, but in France and Germany they are one of the symbols of May Day and are known as *muguet de mai* and *Maiblume*.

All parts of the plant, including the red berries that follow the flowers, are highly poisonous, acting on the heart in a similar way to *Digitalis*.

Lily-of-the-valley at the famous 'Lily Beds' in St Leonard's Forest, Sussex.

Urban Commons

IN THE 1980s the phrase 'urban commons' became a widespread but informal description for the undeveloped 'white' land in and around towns and cities (which I had nicknamed 'the unofficial countryside' in a book in 1973).[1] The term covers a huge range of habitats – railway embankments, factory buffer-land, demolition sites, rubbish-tips, cemeteries, old docks, canals, even 'vertical land', such as walls and bridge-work.

Dr Oliver Gilbert is the acknowledged expert on the vegetation of the urban common, and in 1993 published a fascinating acount of how this varies from city to city, depending on climate, geography and economic and social history.[2] Below, reproduced with his permission, are précis of some of the highly local and distinctive plant communities of our big cities.

Birmingham has an abundance of Canadian goldenrod, probably a consequence of its being very much an allotment plant. (The city has a long history of 'guinea gardens' and allotments.) The local Urban Wildlife Group have adopted greater bindweed as a motif for their publications, as it is conspicuous in the city, scrambling up chain-link fences and over walls.

Bristol is dominated by buddleia (see p.170), and a slogan on one wall reads 'Buddleia rules OK'. At a site by the Royal Hotel it is beginning to be overtopped by sycamore, probably its natural successor in towns. There is a good deal of traveller's-joy in the city centre, windblown seeds from the local limestone cliffs readily establishing themselves on stony rubble, and red valerian on the older stone walls.

The River Don corridor through the heart of the old steelworks area in Sheffield, fringed by fig trees, willow scrub and lush exotic flowers such as Indian balsam and Michaelmas-daisies.

Fort William is one of the few urban areas of any size in north-west Scotland. The infill and rubble are largely acidic and the climate wet and cool. This has a dramatic effect on the vegetation of the urban commons, which includes heather, gorse, foxglove, Nootka lupin, rhododendron, larch and Sitka spruce.

Glasgow also has a wet climate, with moorland close by. 'The vast site formerly occupied by the Dalmarnock Generating Station is being colonised by an assemblage of woody plants that include birch, Scots pine, grey alder, common alder, broom, goat willow and cotoneasters. Nothing similiar is known in other UK cities.' There is also an abundance of elm seedlings, Dutch elm disease having spared many local trees, and a new orchid, Young's helleborine.

Leeds is one of the few cities where poplars regenerate from seed. In waste ground near the city centre there is a hybrid swarm of crosses between native black-poplars and balsam-poplars.

Liverpool has relatively few mature urban commons, owing to extensive landscaping work by environmental agencies. But there are enormous colonies of evening-primrose on sand-dunes just outside the city.

Manchester is distinctive for its abundance of Japanese knotweed, major thickets of which occur at almost every site, often with the even taller giant knotweed.

Norwich has the most continental climate of all the cities surveyed by Oliver Gilbert. As a result of summer warmth, several colourful garden annuals such as larkspur, blue lobelia and white alyssum are becoming established on pavements and on the bare edges of waste ground.

Sheffield has large numbers of colourful garden escapes, including hillsides covered with spectacular displays of pink-, purple- and white-flowered goat's-rue. 'A Sheffield miner told me that he remembered his father recounting how in the early part of this century horticultural traders used to work the poorer parts of the city suburbs selling garden plants which only just merited that description. They were aggressive species like tansy, Michaelmas-daisy, feverfew and goat's-rue, all of which have naturalised widely in the

Rosebay willowherb on industrial patio. Derelict gasworks at Beckton, east London.

city. He recalled his father purchasing Japanese knotweed and how friends were invited round to marvel at the spotted stem and attactive foliage and how later the plant was divided up for exchange [see p. 151].'

There are also the celebrated fig trees along the River Don (see p. 148), whose banks carry large populations of soapwort, wormwood and Indian balsam.

Southampton is a south-coast city that has characteristic communities of warmth-loving species. In several areas of railway land there is a remarkable, species-rich scrub developing amongst buddleia thickets. Up to 16 species can be involved, including firethorn, seven different cotoneasters, Norway maple and the bramble 'Himalayan Giant'.

Swansea is also dominated by Japanese knotweed, which is known locally as 'rhubarb' and 'cemetery weed'. It is often joined on waste ground by buddleia (butterfly-bush), and the combination of these two species with hemp-agrimony and pale toadflax is very characteristic. Swansea also, unusually, has large populations of the fern polypody on many walls.

Teesside has a long history as a port, and a number of its specialities are believed to have been introduced in ships' ballast. Perennial wall-rocket is unusually abundant; it was established on ballast hills by the middle of the nineteenth century and is now ubiquitous. Chalk-loving species such as carline thistle, centaury and yellow-wort, formerly associated with calcium-rich spoil-tips near steelworks, are spreading.

The orchids make up the most glamorous and mysterious of our wild plant families. They have extraordinary life-cycles, sometimes blooming only once in a decade. A little imagination can make their flowers resemble insects, reptiles, ball-gowned ladies, even monkeys, and a little more can bridge the gap between modest English woodlands and distant rain-forests. Yet there is surprisingly little mythology or cultural association attached to them, beyond the rather negative (and not particularly accurate) belief that they are all rare, endangered and highly sensitive. Although this is true of some species, others are proving themselves highly adaptable and capable of moving into the most improbable habitats. This has a lot to do with their being a youthful family in evolutionary terms, still throwing up new forms and hybrids; and also with the fact that many orchids produce enormous quantities of exceptionally lightweight seed, which can be blown long distances. These days this often fetches up on artificially open habitats, low in nutrients and free of competition (quarries, for example), which replicate orchid-rich natural habitats such as sand-dunes and cliff-tops. It is this paradoxical, opportunistic quality of many orchids – the exquisite bloom transforming the spoil tip – that has become the basis for the true modern myth of the family, a botanical version of Beauty and the Beast. Increasingly, orchids are found on the lime-rich waste-tips of old chemical factories, on abandoned colliery land, reclaimed airbase runways and bunkers, urban recreation grounds, motorway verges, roundabouts, and power-station fly-ash tips.[3] Orchids invading garden lawns are a source of particular satisfaction:

'We had 198 blooms of spotted orchids on our lawn this year [1993] and we are very proud of them. We originally had two plants – one came in on its own and the other we rescued from someone who had dug one up and put it in a pot, and after talking to us felt thoroughly ashamed. They have increased to this number over about 15 years. We mow them in the early autumn, and in the spring, we go down on our hands and knees and mark the orchids as they come up, even the tiny seedlings ... We also rescued some lady's tresses from a friend who had a ruthless gardener and feared for their safety. We swapped a deep cut turf. We now have 10 plants.' (Hampshire)[4]

'I have observed an abundance of pyramidal orchids growing quite freely in my front garden. Unfortunately, this is not the result of any strongly held conservationist views, but is a direct consequence of a somewhat precarious financial state. Early in 1992, I was made redundant. This was followed by a whole series of home appliance failures, i.e. the washing machine, the cooker, the fridge and yes, the lawn mower. Unable to purchase a replacement mower I decided to neglect the garden and let nature take its course. In the June of this year [1993] I observed a number of the purple conical-shaped flowers appearing on the now overgrown lawn.' (Clwyd)[5]

Pyramidal orchid, *Anacamptis pyramidalis* (often inexplicably pronounced py*ram*idal orchid by many botanists), is quite widespread on chalk and limestone areas throughout Britain. It has a preference for old, semi-natural grassland, including churchyards, but is also beginning to

Pyramidal orchids on chalk downland in Dorset.

appear in much more artificial habitats. Colonies have been noted, for instance, on the verges of both the A66 and the M66 in Lancashire; on the Oxford ring-road and the banks of the Marina at Maryport, Cumbria; and 'at the famous Mucky Mountains, St Helens, alongside the Sankey canal ... this is waste from the Alkali industry forming grasslands resembling limestone grassland'.[6]

'A large population at Stansted airport, growing on rubble left after the Second World War, was successfully "translocated" in 1986 into a new specially designated "wildlife area" close to terminal access roads. In 1986, when the grassland was moved, it had a population of 60 pyramidals. Now there are more than 660, with a scatter of bees and common spotted.'[7]

'Several years ago a road improvement scheme was carried out on the A420 between Giddeahall and Ford, Wilts. Because of the unstable nature of the limestone the cutting was extended well beyond the road surface, leaving a flat area which remained sterile for many years. However, soil has gradually formed, and a few years ago a small group of pyramidal orchids appeared. This year [1993] they have spread along the entire length of the cutting, with many hundreds of flowers present. The colour ranged from deepest magenta to two specimens which were a lovely pure albino.'[8]

The most famous roadside sites, which have both become traffic-slowing landmarks in June, are the Claydon and Coddenham roundabouts on the A14 in Suffolk: 'The roundabouts were constructed in the late 70s. By the early 1980s a few pyramidal orchids were growing on both roundabouts. By the summer of 1992 the numbers had increased markedly to between 5,000 and 6,000. At this stage both sites were designated as roadside nature reserves under the scheme operated by the Suffolk Wildlife Trust and the County Surveyor's Department. Management entails a late summer cut with the cuttings being raked and removed. Some thinning of the trees has also occurred to allow the orchids to further colonise each site. Possibly because of this the total number of flowers increased to 11,000 in 1993.'[9]

Pyramidal orchids can occur in many shades of pink, and occasionally white. Sometimes the individual flowers in the spike occur upside down.

The marsh- and spotted-orchids (*Dactylorhiza* spp.) are generally the most widespread and most catholic in their choice of habitats. They are also extremely variable, and there are many sub-species and hybrids as well as simple colour variants. **Common spotted-orchid**, *Dactylorhiza fuchsii*, is the most frequent British orchid and can be found in open woods, scrub, fens and grassland (usually on chalky soil) as well as spoil-tips, railway embankments and old quarries. It can vary in colour from almost pure white to deep pink, and in height from a few inches to two feet. Large populations, including hybrids with **southern marsh-orchid**, *D. praetermissa*, are frequent on damp ground at old industrial sites,

Common spotted-orchids, commonest of the tribe in Britain.

Marsh-orchids growing at Saltfleetby, Lincolnshire.

including the fly-ash tip at Aberthaw Power Station near Barry in Glamorgan, and on the spoil around British Steel's deep ore mines at Scunthorpe.[10]

Heath spotted-orchid, *D. maculata*, is similar, but prefers damp places in bogs, marshes and acid grassland. It is the commoner of the two in northern and western Britain, and is plentiful enough on peaty roadsides in parts of Scotland to be picked for vases.

Bee orchid, *Ophrys apifera*. The first sight of a bee orchid is an experience few flower-lovers ever forget. There is nothing quite like the sculptured *oddity* of the blooms, perched like sunbathing, pink-winged bumble-bees on the stalk. They are beautiful, bizarre (the brown 'body' is even furry to the touch) and exotic. Yet bee orchids sometimes behave like rampant weeds. They appear in huge numbers on disturbed chalk soils, linger for a few years and then vanish. Large populations have exploded like this on, for example, a new roundabout near Hitchin, Hertfordshire; shingle banks bordering the Telephone Exchange car park in Milton Keynes, Buckinghamshire; and at the old limestone quarries near Worksop, Nottinghamshire.[11] They can also appear on lawns, sometimes miles from the nearest wild colony.[12]

Bee orchids can be frequent on short, calcareous grassland, sand-dunes, spoil-heaps, railway embankments and woodland rides. They also haunt damp places, such as shallow fens (where the spikes can often grow immensely tall, bearing as many as ten separate flowers) and damp, clayey meadows: 'Three years ago orchid leaves were noticed on the running track and hockey pitch of our playing fields, which are on heavy clay soil and permanently waterlogged in winter. These plants were moved in large turves to our meadow area, where they should escape mowing and trampling. I expected some sort of marsh orchid, but to our surprise they turned out to be bee orchids.' (Oxfordshire)[13]

The bee orchid flower is believed to have evolved originally as a decoy, to trick real bees into attempts to mate with successive flowers and so help with pollen transfer. But this has

Bee orchid, often appearing in large numbers on disturbed roadsides, quarries and mine spoil-heaps.

never been reliably observed, and in Britain the flowers are self-pollinating. Some human enthusiasts, however, remain optimistic about the flower's capacity as a lure. 'One of my very favourite flowers from an early age has always been the bee orchid. We used to visit an uncle and aunt in Dorking and often walked on Box Hill, so I got to know the orchids well as a child. When I was at university I went to a fancy-dress party *as* a bee orchid, with the outer perianth represented by a head-dress which I fashioned out of wire, coloured tissue paper and odd bits of cloth, the lip represented by a sort of bib made in the same way. I had a green pullover and borrowed some green trousers.'[14]

Churchyards

IN ENGLAND (though much less so in areas of Scotland and Wales) wild plants figure conspicuously in both churches and churchyards. There are good historical reasons for this. The parish church was not only the focal point of the community but one of the main custodians of its continuity. Christian churches often developed on the sites of pre-Christian and Celtic holy places, inheriting some of their nature-worship icons – old yew trees, for example – and Christianising practices such as the hanging-up of winter greenery. They were also centres of culture and craftsmanship, where wood-carvers could work, where medicinal herbs were cultivated, and where ceremonies and rituals involving plants – weddings, funerals, harvest festivals, beatings of the bounds – were centred.

Over a period of more than a thousand years, all this activity has left a rich legacy of plants, both real and representational, inside the territory of the church. From the late thirteenth century, carvings of recognisable flowers began to appear on the capitals of pillars, especially in the larger churches and cathedrals, where skilled masons (sometimes itinerant workers from the continent) could be employed.[1] Misericords, bench-ends and pulpits were favourite sites for local carvers to add distinguishable wayside flowers amongst the more formal rose and vine motifs. Since then wild plants have increasingly figured in stained-glass windows, pew-ends, altar-cloths and kneelers. In tiny churches in the Norfolk Broads, wild plants – sawn-off tussock sedges – *were* the kneelers.

The churchyard has also become a sanctuary for plants. At a time when unimproved grassland has all but disappeared across much of agricul-

Meadow saxifrage is now confined to old grassland, including churchyards. Rockbourne, Hampshire.

191

tural Britain, these small patches of turf – 'God's Acres' – are in many parishes the last refuges for species such as meadow saxifrage, green-winged orchid and hoary plantain.[2]

There are also churches in woods, hedged churches (for instance All Saints, South Elmham, in Suffolk, which has an abundance of pyramidal orchids and sulphur clover), and ditched churches (including a tenth-century example at Hanbury, Warwickshire, with a churchyard surrounded by an eighteenth-century ha-ha).[3] At Tilbury-juxta-Clare in Essex, the circular churchyard of St Margaret's rises above the vast arable fields like an oasis and is surrounded by a hedged medieval bank-and-ditch. In it can be found

scarce woodland plants such as stinking iris and stinking hellebore. There is a remote possibility that they are native relics on this ancient site; but more likely they are relics of herbal cultivation or of winter grave decorations.

Many other species have become naturalised from memorial posies and wreaths: lily-of-the-valley, snowdrop (also planted for Candlemas, see p. 138), primroses (on young children's graves especially), including the pink 'churchyard primrose', garden forget-me-nots, and even rosemary 'for remembrance'. Occasionally ornamental plants such as teasel (and even woad), used for flower arrangements inside the church, seed themselves near the porch.

St Enodoc's, Cornwall. The church is surrounded by a tamarisk hedge.

Yew, *Taxus baccata* (VN: Hampshire weed; Snotty-gogs (for the berries)). A mature yew is a compelling tree whatever its situation. It has the densest, darkest foliage of any evergreen and a buttressed trunk that comes close to the colour of mahogany. Its wood reputedly outlives iron. A 250,000-year-old yew-spear found at Clacton in Essex is the world's oldest known wooden artefact.[4] Yet what sets yews most decisively apart from other trees in Britain is the remarkable and probably unique association they have with ancient churches. At least 500 churchyards in England and Wales alone contain yew trees which are certainly as old as the church itself, and quite likely a good deal older. Yews of great ages are rare outside churchyards, and no other type of ancient tree occurs so frequently inside the church grounds. I do not know of any similarly exclusive relationship between places of worship and a single tree species existing anywhere else in the Western world.

It is obviously a meaningful association, however cryptic, and when you contemplate yews of extreme age it is hard not to believe that the meaning is a profound one. In the village of Fortingall, Perthshire, at the geographical heart of Scotland, there are living fragments of the shell of a stupendous yew. It stands in the corner of a churchyard where there has been a building for worship since at least pre-Reformation times. Nearby there are groups of ancient, possibly Druidical stones. In 1769 Daines Barrington measured its girth at 52 feet, but it was already a hollow ring of wooden pillars, like a wood-henge, and funeral processions reputedly passed *through* the trunk. There is a legend that Pontius Pilate (whose father was supposedly a legionary stationed in Scotland) played under its branches.[5] Guesses about its age range from 2,000 to 9,000 years.

Even modest, middle-aged yews can have a powerful presence. The tree which stands on a mound at the southern corner of St Peter's church in Berkhamsted is probably no more than 350 years old. It was a local tradition for towns-people to gather under it on New Year's Eve, which I can remember persisting until the early 1960s. On windy nights in the heart of winter, the twigs still stream above the High Street like ceremonial bunting.

It is no wonder that ancient yews have been the subject of all manner of theories and myths about their origins, age and meanings. At school we were taught that the mound on which the Berkhamsted tree stands contained our town's plague victims; and yews were certainly once planted over graves to protect and purify the dead. This was a business which could create perils of its own: 'if the Yew be set in a place subject

The extraordinary texture of the wood inside a hollow yew.

to poysonous vapours, the very branches will draw and imbibe them, hence it is conceived that the judicious in former times planted it in churchyards on the west side, because those places, being fuller of putrefaction and gross oleaginous vapours exhaled out of the graves by the setting sun, and sometimes drawn by those meteors called *ignes fatui*, divers have been frightened, supposing some dead bodies to walk, etc.'[6]

There have been more mundane explanations for yews' presence in churchyards. They were planted in these protected plots to provide wood for long-bows and to keep their poisonous foliage out of the reach of browsing cattle; to provide decoration for the church, or as a *memento mori*.

The distribution of old yews in old church-yards (they are concentrated in south-east and central England, Wales and the Lake District) is reflected in the tree's distribution in the wild. Yew is principally a species of well-drained chalk and limestone soils. In ancient woods it grows in the company of beech, maple and ash, and on sheer slopes such as Stoner Hill in Hampshire it can look dramatic in winter, silhouetted against the white plumes of old-man's-beard. But yew's sticky red berries are popular with birds, and bird-sown seedlings will colonise open chalk downland as well, forming dark thickets under which nothing else can grow. The trees live so long that woods formed in this way can become at least a temporary 'climax' vegetation and per-sist for centuries. 'Nunton Ewetrees' in Wilt-shire, first described by John Aubrey in 1685,[7] still survives near Downton in Wiltshire (though none of the individual trees look very old or large, and some appear to have been coppiced). The famous horseshoe of chalk at Kingley Vale in Sussex has been invaded by yew largely over the past hundred years. But in the heart of the thickets of younger trees is a group of more ven-erable yews, probably 500 years old. They are spectacularly split and sinuously interwoven, and in places they have welded together to form multiple trunks. Many of the larger boughs have sagged down to ground level, and the experience

of scrambling through this twilit wooden labyrinth, over damp and musty leaf litter, is not unlike being in a series of subterranean caverns.

An early theory about the link between yews and churchyards occurs in Sir Thomas Browne's *Hydriotaphia* (1658). He wrote, 'Whether the planting of yewe in Churchyards, hold not its originall from the ancient Funerall rites, or as an Embleme of Resurrection from its perpetual ver-dure, may almost admit conjecture.'[8] A century later, when Gilbert White wrote a detailed de-scription of what was to become England's most famous (and most measured) yew, he took a slightly different view of its symbolism:
'In the church-yard of this village [Selborne, Hampshire] is a yew-tree, whose aspect bespeaks it to be of a great age: it seems to have seen several centuries, and is probably coeval with the church, and therefore may be deemed an antiquity: the body is squat, short, and thick, and measures twenty-three feet in girth, supporting an head of suitable extent to it's bulk. This is a male tree, which in the spring sheds clouds of dust, and fills the atmosphere around with it's farina.

As far as we have been able to observe, the males of this species become much larger than the females; and it has so fallen out that most of the yew-trees in the church-yards of this neighbourhood are males: but this must have been matter of mere accident, since men, when they first planted yews, little dreamed that there were sexes in trees …

Antiquaries seem much at a loss to determine at what period this tree first obtained a place in church-yards. A statute passed AD 1307 and 35 Edward I. the title of which is "Ne rector arbores in cemeterio prosternat." ['To prevent the rector from felling trees in the graveyard.'] Now if it is recollected that we seldom see any other very large or ancient tree in a church-yard but yews, this statute must have principally related to this species of tree; and consequently their being planted in church-yards is of much more ancient date than the year 1307.

As to the use of these trees, possibly the more respectable parishioners were buried under their shade before the improper custom was introduced of burying within the body of the church, where the living are to assemble …

The farther use of yew-trees might be as a screen to churches, by their thick foliage, from the violence of winds; perhaps also for the purpose of archery, the best long bows being made of that material: and we do not hear that they are planted in the church-yards of other parts of Europe, where long bows were not so much in use. They might also be placed as a shelter to the congregation assembling before the church-doors were opened, and as an emblem of mortality by their funereal appearance. In the south of England every church-yard almost has it's tree, and some two; but in the north, we understand, few are to be found.

The idea of R.C. that the yew-tree afforded it's branches instead of palms for the processions on Palm-Sunday, is a good one, and deserves attention. See Gent. Mag. Vol. L. p. 128.'[9]

Some of White's hypotheses do not really hold water. Individual yew trees would not provide much protection from the wind; and, in any case, this function would hardly have been compatible with their harvesting for long-bows, which were cut from the trunks, not the branches. In fact English yew was regarded as being too brittle for use in long-bows, and the

Most ancient British yews are associated with churchyards.

wood was usually imported from Spain and Italy.[10] (This also meant that there was little point in conserving yews – and thus separating them from stock – within the confines of the church-yard walls, especially as animals were frequently allowed to graze in churchyards.)

But the use of yew branches as 'palm' was certainly widely practised, especially when Easter occurred too late for gathering sprays of pussy-willow, the usual English substitute for real palm and olive branches. In the churchwarden's accounts of some parishes, presumably those without yew trees of their own, there are entries for payments made for the purchase of yew 'Palme'.[11] At Kington, in Herefordshire, yew was also used in Whitsuntide celebrations and brought into churches to decorate the tops of the pews.[12]

Since White's time it has generally been presumed that yews were planted in churchyards not as emblems of mortality, but, because of their evergreen foliage, of *im*mortality and resurrection. Yet there have been difficulties in relating this theory to a specifically Christian tradition. As more and more ancient yews have been examined by naturalists and antiquarians, the more it has seemed that many are not just 'coeval' with the church, but vastly older. Circumstantial evidence in the form of earthworks, local legends and the sheer physical bulk of many of the trees has suggested ages of up to at least 2,000 years.

In the 1940s Vaughan Cornish surveyed many of the yews in British dioceses and parishes, and concluded (though without a great deal of solid evidence) that the oldest were not Christian plantings at all. They were the sacred trees of ancient religions, some Druidic, some Celtic, and a few, maybe, relics of pre-Celtic Iberian settlers (hence their frequency in Wales). And, like many pagan icons and practices, they were retained and

One of the giant yews – probably five centuries old – in Kingley Vale, Sussex. This remarkable valley on the southern chalk has yews of all kinds: a central core of ancient trees and spreading new woods of bird-sown specimens up to a hundred years old.

pragmatically sanctified by the Christian church. Moreover, from the medieval period it became the custom to plant two yews in churchyards, one close to the pathway which leads between the principal entrance of the church and the funeral gateway, and the other beside a path which leads to a second and lesser doorway. Coffins would probably pass both trees during funerals.[13]

The problem with the historical basis of Cornish's theory is getting any accurate confirmation of the ages of the trees. After 400 or 500 years almost all yews begin to lose their heartwood and become hollow, making dating by ring-counts impossible. They also enter long periods of suspended growth, when they put on virtually no extra girth at all. The great yew at Crowhurst in Surrey apparently grew only nine inches in girth in two and a half centuries, from 30 feet in 1630, to 30 feet 9 inches, recorded in both 1850 and 1874.[14] The Selborne yew seemingly *shrank* between 1950, when Sidney Scott reckoned it 'nearly 28 feet',[15] and 1981, when it was more precisely measured at 25 feet 10 inches.

The last record was made by Allen Meredith, who has made a long study of the sizes, positions and archaeological associations of ancient British yews. From this, and the limited documentary evidence that is available about the dates when some church yews were planted, he has drawn up a tentative table linking girth and age. Young trees, whose ages are verifiable by ring-counts, raise no problems, and a yew 12 feet in girth, for instance, is given the uncontentious age of 300 years. The laboriously slow growth of extreme old age, though also partially quantifiable by ring-counts in the trunk's shell, is altogether more speculative. Meredith puts trees with a girth of 30 feet at 2,400 years, and of 33 feet at 3,000 years. This would put three trees in three churchyards in Powys (Defynnog, Discoed and Llanfaredd), all of which exceed 35 feet, at more than 4,500 years of age. (A younger tree – a mere 22 feet in girth, at Strata Florida, over the Powys border – is the burial site of the medieval poet Dafydd ap Gwilym.)[16]

The extrapolation of the growth-curve, back

not just into the pre-Christian period but into prehistory, is done with not much more solid evidence than Vaughan Cornish had access to. There is no living heartwood from British yews older than 400 years, no datable ancient timbers (as there are for most other species). No one is sure, yet, at what age they begin to go hollow, or when or why they go into slow-growth mode.

And there is one more complication. The planting of wild tree species was very rare before the Middle Ages – which suggests that the original sacred sites were situated close to existing yew trees, rather than vice versa. Yet can the architects of at least 500 Christian churches really have wedged their buildings into already established ground-plans?

But there is no doubt that old yews have an irresistible aura of extreme antiquity, and it is hard not to believe that they antedate their attendant churches. At Hambledon, Surrey, there is a tree with a girth of 35 feet and an enormous spread, so that the lower branches are propped up on tombstones. The hollow trunk is covered with burrs, which have the look of green pincushions from their bristling epicormic shoots. At Stedham, West Sussex (12 miles south of Hambledon in this concentrated zone of churchyard yews), the yew is slightly thinner (30 feet in girth), shorter and squatter, and the trunk is held together by wire hawsers. Yet its interior has a quality missing in the Hambledon tree, and found in other hollow yews with dryish interiors. The shelved surfaces of the dead wood have a lustrous, satiny finish, close to the texture of wasp-nests. In places they are bleached like driftwood; but here and there patches of colour break through – the orange of living yew-wood, a violet sheen of the kind sometimes seen in mother-of-pearl, small invasions of green algae.

These brooding, gothic trees frequently became landmarks when they grew in the wider countryside. A venerable yew stands over the site of the ancient holy well of Glangwenlais, in the Carmel Woods near Ammanford, Dyfed. Wordsworth's yew in Lorton Vale, Cumbria ('Of vast circumference and gloom profound/ This solitary Tree! a living thing/ Produced too slowly ever to decay;/ Of form and aspect too magnificent/ To be destroyed ...'),[17] still stands by White Beck, High Lorton.[18] The Celtic 'iw' is one of the oldest tree names and, transmuted into 'ew' or 'ewe', is an occasional component of place names, as in Ewhurst (Hampshire, Sussex and Surrey), meaning 'yew-tree wooded hill', and Ewshott (Hampshire). In Cheshire Jill Burton surveyed yew place names, and found 74, mostly attached to isolated farms or cottages: 'The majority of Yew places are in a central band up the Weaver/Dane valley, from the southern border with Staffordshire. There is only one in the Wirral, one in South West Cheshire and one on the extreme East border with Derbyshire. 67 per cent are actually on or very near roads, with 22 per cent being near "old roads". Some 52 per cent are within 500 metres of a boundary. Surprisingly, only 6 per cent are near a church ... 28 per cent are at junctions of roads and footpaths, with the inference that the roads and paths led to them, or even that they could have been used as markers for crossings. Less than 12 per cent are in hamlets *and* near roads.'[19]

There are many 'Yew Tree' inns, too (though the trees are invariably much younger than those in churchyards), as, for instance, in Lower Wield, Hampshire, Odstock, Wiltshire, and near Newent, Gloucestershire. A gateway yew at the North Star pub at Steventon in Oxfordshire has been divided into two for access and has a lamp attached.[20]

'On the old drove road across Ashdown Forest two yews were a sign for travellers of the availability of overnight accommodation. Three yew trees indicated additional provision for animals. Three such yews can be found at Duddleswell Crossroad on Ashdown Forest. One of these old yews was uprooted during the 1987 gale; but before the Forest Rangers had an opportunity to right it, most of the wood was cut up and it disappeared.'[21]

'When the very ancient yew in The Lee Graveyard blew down in the 1990 storm, the bellringer told me that it was very unfortunate for the vergers, etc, as it was always used as a WC. Its huge, hanging branches concealed all.'[22]

Hollow yew in Much Marcle churchyard, Herefordshire. There is a cluster of ancient churchyard yews in the area and this one is believed to be over 2,000 years old.

'A famous Derbyshire yew is in Shining Cliff Wood near Ambergate – a yew supposedly the inspiration for the nursery rhyme "Rock-a-bye-baby". It is known as the Betty Kenny Tree ... Apparently one of the boughs was hewn out to create a cradle. A family used to live in it, hence Rock-a-bye-baby ... Also in Derbyshire, one at Churchtown, near Matlock, is probably nearer 2,000 years old. The font is made from its wood.'[23]

'A wood carving of a dove in flight, as the

handle for the font cover for Hastingleigh Church [Kent], was made from one of the yews blown down in the storms.'[24]

'On their smallholding in Torver near Coniston, my uncles used to make walking sticks and shepherding sticks from the branches of yew trees. They would choose a small branch which had grown from the underside of the yew, and which therefore had to turn up towards the light, forming a ready-made handle for the stick, which was then smoothed and finished.'[25]

The story of the yew in St Mary's churchyard, Selborne, encompasses all these aspects, sacred, secular and commonplace. Its abrupt collapse during the great gale of 25 January 1990 has been graphically described by the vicar, James Anderson: 'The massive trunk lay shattered across the church path and a disc of soil and roots stood vertically above a wide crater. The bench around the trunk was still in place, looking like a forgotten ornament on a Christmas tree. A stormy sea of twisted boughs and dark foliage covering the churchyard was pierced here and there by a white tombstone like a sinking ship.'[26]

There were also white bones showing through, brought up to the surface from ancient burials or lying tangled in the root-ball. They were quickly taken into custody in the nearby Field Studies Centre, to protect them from dogs and other predators, and permission for an emergency archaeological dig was obtained from the Diocese, on the understanding that all human remains would eventually be reburied in the churchyard. In the course of the next week, two archaeologists from the Hampshire Museums Service uncovered the remains of about 30 individuals, several of which were complete burials in their original positions. They were all apparently Christian burials, in shallow graves *beneath* the root-mass. The earliest, and the deepest, was dated by pottery from the grave-fill to about AD 1200. A number of nails suggested that the man had been buried in a coffin. He had been placed right against the south side of the yew when it was probably about 10 feet in girth. The original site of the young yew was estimated by the archaeologists to be a patch of undisturbed soil with no remains of any kind, just north-west of the centre of the old tree.[27]

Meanwhile, the fallen yew had become the scene of extraordinary activity. People from all over Britain who had once lived in Selborne, or just visited it, came to pay their respects and to buy or beg a piece of the wood. One man remembered having his daily lunch-break in its shade. Another came to retrieve a fragment for his parents, who had become engaged under it. The source of the wood (some of which was sold for the church funds) was the vigorous lopping the tree received before an attempt to winch it back into the vertical and, in effect, replant it. By mid-February almost the entire crown had been removed, and on the 13th the tree was ready to be raised. A time capsule (containing, amongst many other things, a paperback edition of Gilbert White's book, with its early history of the tree) and a probably superfluous load of tree-planting compost were inserted in the root-hole amongst the resettled medieval skeletons, and a three-ton crane began laboriously to winch the tree upright. By dusk it was done. Later, the vicar and children from the local school linked hands round the tree and said prayers for its survival. And providentially (or so it seemed at the time) a water-main promptly burst close by and bathed the yew's roots in water for the next 36 hours.

The prognosis looked good to start with. That summer, the tree put out a bristle of new shoots on the west side, both on its pollarded branches and from the base of the trunk. For once it looked remarkably like the illustration of the tree that Hieronymus Grimm had made for the first edition of White's book, suggesting that the tree may well have been pollarded in the past.[28]

But in the hot summer of 1991 the shoots withered, and by 1992 it was clear that the tree was dead – the result, some pundits believed, of a surfeit of water. Later that year, in a touching ceremony on 28 November, a cutting taken whilst the tree was still alive was planted in the churchyard by the youngest and oldest citizens of the parish together.

Yet the old hulk lives on in its own way. Its hollow shell (which still has patches of that lustrous, layered, satiny deadwood) has been colonised by young hazel and foxgloves, and a honeysuckle of more exotic origins is beginning to cloak the fluted exterior. Some of the wood taken from the larger branches has been made into artefacts for the church, and a yew font-cover and altar screen now join the rough yew cross which has long hung over the nave. A lute has also been constructed from the wood (a very traditional use), with the curved back of the instrument using alternating strips of the dark heartwood and paler sapwood.

Most yew plantings these days are not of the wild variety, but of the tidier but blander fasti-giate variety, or Irish yew, whose branches all sweep evenly upwards, as if they had been bound into a bundle. They are mostly descendants of two trees found on a limestone crag in Fermanagh in the 1760s, and presumably ousted 'normal' wild trees because of their resemblance to Mediterranean funereal cypresses, and for the ease with which they could be clipped – and even 'topiarised' – into order. (The clippings have recently become commercially valuable. An alkaloid named taxol, which seems effective against ovarian cancer, has been discovered in yews, and research laboratories and drug companies are offering to buy the foliage in bulk.)

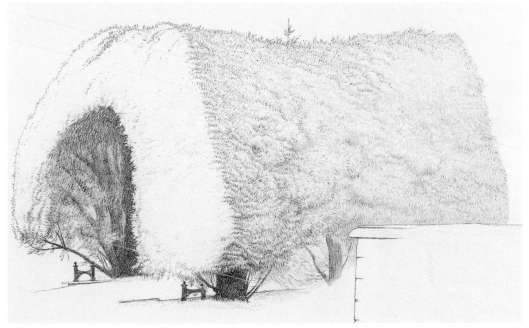

Clare Roberts's sketch of the living lich-gate of yew at St Margaret's, Warnham, West Sussex. It is well over a hundred years old and was previously much larger, but had to be clipped back to avoid obstruction to the pavement.

Midwinter Greenery

THE USE of evergreen plants to decorate houses at the midwinter solstice is a custom which long antedates Christianity in Europe and Asia. Evergreens, flourishing when all other plant life seems dead or dormant, were regarded as symbols of the continuity of life through the dark season.

In ancient Rome, for example, garlands were made from Mediterranean bay, box, rosemary, pines and evergreen oak. In Britain the native holly, ivy and mistletoe were (and still are) the favoured plants, and their various roles are discussed under their separate entries. But they were often used together, in wreaths hung on the door or over the porch, for instance. A favourite decoration in late medieval England was the kissing bough, which was a garland of greenery shaped roughly like a crown and adorned with fruit, coloured paper rosettes, candles and, most importantly, a bunch of mistletoe hanging from the centre.

There have been strict rules about when the midwinter greenery should be put up, when it should be taken down, and how it should be disposed of. Twelfth Night (6 January) has long been a watershed. But in some areas the greenery was kept until Candlemas Eve (see snowdrop, p. 138). In some it was ceremonially burned, in others fed as a charm to cattle. Most of these local customs have faded and been absorbed into the national pattern. But there are still places where the rituals associated with midwinter greenery kept a distinctive local flavour until recently: 'The parish church of Hest Bank, Lancaster (its full name is St Andrews, Slyne-with-Hest), kept until recently a curious and almost certainly pre-Christian custom, of the men of the church processing in company carrying

A group of hollies lopped for cattle food (a 'hollin') in the Olchon Valley, Herefordshire.

203

small conifer trees, about three feet tall, on their shoulders. About a dozen in all, on a Sunday near Christmas.'[1]

'When I first went to live in Peel, on the Isle of Man, I was surprised to see that the holly and other Christmas greenery was still in place after Twelfth Night. I commented on this, and was told that here they are left up until Shrove Tuesday. There was a practical reason for this in addition to any regard for custom. The fierce heat which they gave when burnt in the range was just what was required for the cooking of pancakes.'[2]

Norway spruce, *Picea abies*. Across most of northern Europe and America, Norway spruce trees have become known simply as Christmas trees. Ever since Prince Albert and Queen Victoria introduced an old German custom to this country in 1841 and hung lights and decorations on a tree at Windsor Castle, a decked-up spruce has been the centrepiece of northern Christmases. In 1850 Charles Dickens called it 'the new German toy', but there was really nothing new about it. Tree-dressing has been practised around the globe and decorated greenery brought into European dwellings for the winter solstice as far back as the Iron Age. And what is often cited as the prototype English Christmas tree – the branch of evergreen nailed to a board and decorated with gilt oranges and almonds, which a German member of the royal household arranged for a children's party in 1821[3] – is not so different from the ancient kissing bough. But Albert and Victoria's patronage made the notion of decking up conifers at Christmas decisively fashionable; and the Norway spruce (introduced to this country around 1500) quickly proved to be a species which could be grown and marketed on a sufficiently commercial scale to meet the new demand.

Many towns and villages now have communal Christmas trees, erected in market places or on greens. The most famous is the one which is set up in Trafalgar Square, London, close to Nelson's monument. Since 1947, this has been donated to the people of London by the people of Oslo, as a gesture of appreciation for the help Britain gave to Norway during the Second World War.

Yet considered purely as a tree, a piece of living greenery, the Norway spruce hasn't much to commend it beyond a symmetrical profile, which makes a kind of conical clothes-horse ideal for hanging decorations on. The twigs are rough, the bark scaly, and the needles hard, spiny and notoriously liable to be shed in centrally-heated rooms. This habit has inspired one nickname for the tree which deserves a wider audience. It appears in some Christmas greetings doggerel from a London industrial cleaning firm, printed on a free Hoover bag and entitled 'On the Trail of the Lonesome Pine Needle':

The Trafalgar Square Christmas Tree, first donated by the citizens of Oslo to the citizens of London in 1947.

You'll find them in the budgie's cage
  And in the baby's cot.
You can afford to leave no stone
  Unturned, no tender foot unsocked.

It's mid-July, you cry out 'Waiter,
  What's this in my soup?'
He replies 'Norwegian Tarragon,
  According to the cook'.[4]

Norway spruce plantations are now a common feature of the British landscape. Some are cultivated solely for the Christmas tree market, but the majority double up as softwood timber plots, with some trees cut for Christmas and the more mature specimens being grown on for pulp or light lumber. It has the advantage over its even more widely planted cousin, the Sitka spruce, of being thoroughly frost-hardy.

Mistletoe, *Viscum album*. Mistletoe traditions are amongst northern Europe's last surviving remnants of plant magic. Everyone knows the custom of kissing under the mistletoe, even if they don't indulge in it. Whether a sprig is hung traditionally above the door and a berry removed with each kiss, or carried in a pocket or buttonhole and flashed opportunistically like a calling card, the obligation is the same: a kiss can be claimed. Even when the real plant seems to have been forgotten – as it often is in television dramas, for instance, replaced by some notional pastiche made from bay leaves and white plastic balls – the old ritual itself is plainly bedded in the national folk-memory. And if we sometimes assume that it is all just a frivolous, albeit ancient, party game, it is worth pondering that, at least until the 1960s, the inclusion of mistletoe in church decoration was frowned on in many parishes. A more complicated and maybe darker past is also lurking in the folk-memory.

Looking at mistletoe against a low winter sun – the great tresses glistening the colour of tarnished brass, the tiers of twigs like wishbones, the whole plant's unearthly vitality in the leafless trees – it is not hard to imagine how it became one of the most revered plants of early herbalists. We know it to be a partial parasite, making some of its own food, but taking minerals from its host

A mistletoe lot for sale at the Tenbury Wells mistletoe market.

tree. But to early people, especially the fearful medievals, it was entirely magical – a plant without roots or obvious sources of food, that grew way above the earth and stayed green-leafed when other plants were bare. It seemed the supreme example of spontaneous generation and continuing life. It is no wonder that it was credited with extraordinary powers. In the Middle Ages, it was believed capable of breaking the death-like trances of epileptics, of dispelling tumours, divining treasure, keeping witches at bay, and protecting the crop of the trees on which it grew. And with its milk-white berries suggestively held between splayed leaves, it seemed 'signed' as a human fertility potion and aphrodisiac too. Women who wished to conceive would tie a sprig round their waists or wrists.

It may seem a long jump from these ancient beliefs to Christmas kissing. Yet in mistletoe's heartland, the border country between England and Wales (and Saxon and Celt), the plant has never entirely lost its magical role. Although mistletoe is widely scattered across southern England and Wales, it needs both a mild, humid climate and a good concentration of trees with soft bark in which its sticky seeds can be deposited by berry-eating birds. These requirements are met most successfully in a wide circle of land around the Severn estuary, where the valleys are moist, mild and sheltered from the worst of the west winds, and where there is a long tradition of fruit-growing. In the mid-nineteenth century, Dr H. G. Bull of the Woolhope Naturalists' Field Club, found that mistletoe grew on no less than 34 per cent of the apple trees in Herefordshire orchards.[5]

In this region arcane fertility rites involving the plant persisted until the early years of this century. In most Herefordshire cottages the practice was to cut the mistletoe bough on New Year's Eve and hang it up as the clock struck twelve. The old bough, which had hung there throughout the previous year, was taken down and burnt at the same time. But on many farms

the more elaborate and mysterious custom of Burning the Bush persisted until the outbreak of the First World War. The Bush was a globe made of twisted hawthorn twigs and mistletoe. Early on New Year's Day it was taken to the first sown wheatfield and burnt on a large straw fire. At Brinsop, north-west of Hereford, the globe was filled with straw and set alight, and a man ran with it over the first twelve ridges of the field. In other villages the ceremonies had their own quirks. At Birley Court near Leominster two globes were used. These were thrown on the fire together, the smaller inside the larger. Whatever routine was followed, it was regarded as an omen of bad luck if the flames went out before the end of the run, and it was thought that the soil would not then have been purified and made fer-

The holly and mistletoe market at Tenbury Wells.

tile. In almost all villages the ceremony ended with cider-drinking and general carousing.[6] While these rites went on outside, a new Bush was made indoors to replace the old one. E. M. Leather heard one farm-worker from Shobdon tell her that cider was poured onto the globe of thorn and mistletoe 'to varnish and darken the bush like'.[7] In neighbouring Worcestershire, mistletoe formed part of the Christmas greenery hung in halls and over doorways, and was dressed with apples and ribbons. It was almost certainly kissed under as part of the general medieval enthusiasm for embracing.

But it was the eighteenth-century fad for Druidism that turned these local customs into a national fashion, and revived echoes of the plant's old aphrodisiac magic. The eccentric antiquarian the Revd William Stukeley, prompted by little more than a few remarks in Pliny's *Natural History* about how the Druids revered mistletoe grown on oak, elevated the plant into the most important accoutrement of the whole religion, and argued that its priests were religious philosophers and the harbingers of Christianity in Britain. By 1728 he was creating a Druidic temple in the orchard of his Lincolnshire garden, around the centre-piece of an 'antient appletree oregrown with sacred mistletoe'.[8]

One of the practices he popularised was 'inoculating' (bud-grafting) trees with mistletoe. There was a good deal of argument at the time about how mistletoe was propagated in the wild. Some writers, like Pliny, believed that the seeds would not germinate until they had been 'ripened' by being passed through a bird. Sir Thomas Browne disputed that the plant grew from seed at all. He thought it 'an arboreous excrescence bred of a superfluous sap which the tree itself cannot assimilate'. But soon gardeners and botanists were successfully propagating mistletoe by 'incising' the seeds under the bark of trees such as poplars and apples.

They had little luck, though, with growing it on oak – which, thanks to the fascination with all things Druidic that Stukeley's writings were helping to fuel, was the kind the public wanted. So the market was ripe for botanical fakes, and

Philip Miller, curator of the Chelsea Physic Garden, remarked that supplies reaching London were frequently passed off as 'oak-mistletoe' regardless of their origins. Such mistletoe, he wrote, was so rarely met with that 'whenever a Branch of an Oak-tree hath any of these plants growing upon it, it is cut off and preserved by the Curious in their Collections of Natural Curiosities, and of these there are few to be seen in England'. He also discovered that simply smearing the sticky seeds onto a suitable tree was sufficient to establish it; this, after all, was how the eponymous mistle-thrush spread the plant about: 'for the viscous Part of the Berry, which immediately surrounds the seed, doth sometimes fasten to the outward Part of the Bird's Beak; which to get disengag'd of, he strikes his beak against the Branches of a neighbouring Tree, and thereby leaves the Seed sticking by this viscous Matter to the Bark; which, if it light upon a smooth Part of the Tree, will fasten itself thereto, and the following Winter will put out and grow.'[9]

Border country farmers must have welcomed the growing interest in this orchard familiar, and no doubt much inoculating, incising and smearing went on to supply the growing demand. By the early nineteenth century, it was even possible to buy small trees already sporting mistletoe bushes. The mythology surrounding the plant had also become available off-the-peg. The Druidical and Celtic fertility rites, involving (probably apocryphally) golden sickles and white-robed virgins, were sanitised to a Christmas kiss, and in 1842 even that austere poet Tennyson could write: 'The game of forfeits done – the girls all kiss'd/ Beneath the sacred bush and past away...'[10]

The Victorians also resurrected the Scandinavian myth of Balder the Beautiful, in which Balder is killed by a spear of mistletoe guided by the jealous god Loki – for which his grieving mother Frigg banished it for ever to the tops of trees. (Read Enid Blyton's version of this story – and her accurate, unsentimental and uncompromising botanical and historical preface.)[11]

But the mythology was worn increasingly lightly. By the second half of the century the

Woolhope Naturalists' Field Club, a third of whose 150 members were clerics, were able, without any apparent embarrassment or Christian guilt, to act out an affectionate parody of the rites of their priestly ancestors. On their spring field outing on 24 May 1870 they assembled under a mistletoe oak near Aymestrey:

'The bunch of mistletoe in the oak was so large that it could be exceedingly well seen from the adjoining lane, notwithstanding the foliage of the tree. "There's no mistake about it," said one gentleman, as if he thought there possibly might have been, its portrait and the description in last year's volume of the Club notwithstanding! A ladder had been placed against the tree, with the same thoughtful consideration to every detail that could add to the pleasure of the visitors that prevailed throughout the reception, and it was soon mounted. There was no white yearling bull with garlanded horns to sacrifice beneath the tree for the festivities, nor was there an Archdruid to cut the mistletoe with a golden sickle – indeed the Druidical programme was rather reserved on the present occasion – but anyway the mistletoe bunch was reached and gathered amidst three rounds of applause that were given by the assembled multitude below, and small sprays of the "heaven born plant unpolluted by any touch of earth" were distributed to the ladies present and to all others who wished for it.'[12]

Today a similar scepticism exists hand in hand with a willingness to play along with the old beliefs. A member of an old Scottish family wrote to us in the same spirit, and with more than a touch of *Cold Comfort Farm*:

'The plant is the ancient badge of Clan Hay. Frazer's *Golden Bough* relates how the fate of the Perthshire Hays was influenced by mistletoe. A sprig cut by a Hay with a new dirk on All-hallowmass Eve was a sure charm against witchery and against wound or death in battle. The two most unlucky deeds that could be done

Lime and apple are mistletoe's favourite hosts. The lime avenue at Burton Pinsent, Somerset …

in the name of Hay, was to kill a white falcon and cut down a limb from the oak of Errol. These beliefs were set down by Thomas the Rhymer:

> But when the aik decays
> And the mistletoe dwines on its withered
>   breast,
> The grass shall grow on Errol's hearthstone
> And the corbie roup in the falcon's nest.

Well the oak crashed down and the grass grew and I'm down here in Derbyshire – with dandruff.'[13]

These days, not even churches prohibit the use of mistletoe in Christmas decorations, and maybe the disapproval was always ambivalent. Stukeley himself wrote that the plant had been carried to the High Altar of York Minster on Christmas Eve. And it is carved, with holly, in a nineteenth-century addition to the galaxy of medieval plant decoration in Southwell Minster.[14] A more modern representation is an embroidered poem, 'The Mistletoe Bough', done entirely with black and white threads, on a wall at Bramshill Police College in Hampshire.[15]

Mistletoe for sale at Christmas is now mostly imported from northern France, especially from poplars in Picardy and the cider-apple orchards of Normandy and Brittany. The home-grown trade is largely channelled through Tenbury Wells in Worcestershire. For a month before Christmas, part of the market is given over wholly to mistletoe and holly sales, and small-holders bring in their bundles to be auctioned to wholesale greengrocers from the Midlands.

Home-grown mistletoe has also cropped up at Weston-super-Mare Sunday Market, and at Stroud: 'All along the Gloucestershire part of the A38 there are the remains of ancient perry orchards, and many of them have great clumps of mistletoe growing high up in their branches. In Stroud market in Christmas 1991, local mistletoe was being sold along with that from France.'[16]

Sometimes rather unconventional gathering techniques are used: 'At the Berkshire College of Agriculture, there are numerous lime trees, which are over 200 years old. Many of these sup-port large mistletoe plants, most of which are in the higher branches ... [this] is harvested by shooting down with a shotgun.'[17]

But in a few places mistletoe is still nurtured as a catch crop. At the Evans family's farm, for instance, at Lower Rochford near Tenbury Wells, mistletoe grows in the ancient fruit trees in their mixed orchards, above grazing sheep and free-range hens. They are happy to have it there, and harvest it for the Tenbury Wells market. But they do not cut it every year. Mistletoe is dioecious, with separate berryless male and berried female plants, and stocks of the latter need building up periodically.

Sadly, old orchards are increasingly being grubbed out, and native mistletoe is a declining plant in Britain's farming landscape. But there is some compensation in its increasing colonisation of soft-barked trees in parks and gardens. The border country can again boast a great variety of hosts. Mistletoe has been recorded on japonica and walnut in Ledbury and Ross-on-Wye, on cotoneaster and laburnum in Hereford, on a weeping ash in Bridgnorth, and on almond in Westbury-on-Trym, north-west of Bristol.[18]

The rose family, as can be seen here, forms an important group of hosts. (Mistletoe is very rare on the wild rose itself, though John Morton reported one from a copse near Kirby, Northamptonshire, in 1712.)[19] Cotoneaster mistletoes have been found in Gwent, at Shillingstone, Dorset, and at Upton St Leonards, near Gloucester. Mistletoe grows on rowan in Taunton, and on an amelanchier in Essex.[20] And hawthorn is one of the most frequent hosts: 22 per cent of Shropshire mistletoe, for instance, was found on hawthorn in the 1980s;[21] and over the Welsh border, at Fforest Coalpit, 'there is a hawthorn bush near our farm with a good clump of mistletoe growing on an exposed mountain side at 1,200 feet'.[22] (Hawthorn mistletoe must have been thought to pick up some of the host tree's magical potency. A woman from Somerset remembered: 'I am in my seventies; a few old-fashioned cures were used for various complaints when I was a child ... Mistletoe from a hawthorn bush for measles; this was made into a tea.')[23]

Other hosts include false-acacia, in many places, including Sible Hedingham, Essex, Warborough, Oxfordshire, and Cowes, and, unusually, a cemetery cypress in Stratford-upon-Avon, which is one of the very few records for a coniferous species.[24] Mistletoe oaks remain rare (except in Epping Forest),[25] and the commonest large tree hosts are much as they have always been: apple, hawthorn, lime, poplar, field maple, elm, sycamore and ash.

In 1991 Angus Idle surveyed all the mistletoe growing in the vicinity of High Wycombe, Buckinghamshire. This is outside the species' heartland, but the general pattern of hosts was repeated:

'I asked for information from people who knew of the location of mistletoe. This produced a number of replies, which included known plantings, but also sightings which turned out to be things like witches' brooms, rooks' nests and squirrels' dreys. Nevertheless it was found that mistletoe was locally very common, with a great deal growing in lime trees, particularly those planted up to 100 years ago in large estates such as West Wycombe Park, Wycombe Abbey, Cliveden and Bulstrode. Mistletoe also occurs on apple, especially when close to the invaded limes, so it seems probable that these have been the sources from which it has spread to other tree species in the district. I have found that

... and an apple orchard in Aymestrey, Hereford.

mistletoe does in fact grow on a number of other species in this area, even if not commonly. I have found two lots of mistletoe growing on false acacia. In addition to growing on apple in gardens near The Rye, a large grass recreation area near the centre of Wycombe, it also grows on ornamental *Prunus* and hawthorn and poplar. I have also found it on horse chestnut and turkey oak, and I have an as yet unconfirmed report of it on *Hamamelis* "Red Glow" at Bulstrode Park.'[26]

It is finding mistletoes that are exceptions to the rule, which grow on ill-matched trees, or in incongruous (or pleasantly appropriate) places, that makes mistletoe-hunting such an agreeable pastime. The most enchanted mistletoe I have seen was in the dim heart of a hazel bush in Wales. The most aptly sited are the many bunches that grow in a lime overhanging the entrance turnstile to the Oxford Botanic Garden. More grow enticingly from trees overhanging the nearby punt-routes along the River Cherwell. But the most romantic must be in what remains of the Revd William Wilks's (of Shirley poppy fame, see p. 42) garden near Croydon. Here there are two old apple trees with their lower branches fused into a natural arch, which is densely draped with mistletoe.[27] The most dramatically beautiful festoon the long avenue of limes at Kentwell Hall in Suffolk. The trees were planted in 1678, and are covered with large fig-shaped swellings produced by centuries of mistletoe growth. On moonlit nights in winter the clumps glisten in the upper branches like balls of mist. It is easy here to understand the awe which early physicians felt about the plant.

And maybe it wasn't an entirely superstitious awe. Recent medical research has suggested that some of the chemicals in mistletoe may indeed have anti-tumour and sedative properties. The Druidical panacea certainly worked for one family:
'Winkburn Park, Notts, has always been known for mistletoe. It grows on thorn, lime, poplar ... One of the interesting things about Winkburn mistletoe is that it cured a boy in the village of epileptic fits. He could not attend school

regularly, and wasn't safe to go out unattended. A gypsy woman visiting the village told his father to boil some mistletoe and give the boy a wine glass of the water to drink. His father did this, but before giving it to the boy, drank some himself as a precaution, but felt no ill effects. He then gave the boy a wine glass full, and afterwards he never had another fit. He is now sixty-six [1993].'[28]

Holly, *Ilex aquifolium* (VN: Hulver, Holm, Hollin). Compared to mistletoe and its cryptic links with pagan magic, holly seems an uncomplicated festive plant. There is nothing intrinsically mystical or mysterious about gathering bright red berries and shiny leaves to decorate a house in the darkest days of winter. We would probably find ourselves doing exactly the same if holly was a new plant-breeders' sensation, instead of our commonest native evergreen.

Yet scratch below the surface familiarity, and holly too has a complex and paradoxical history. Although lopping boughs for Christmas is 'allowed', for instance, there is still a widespread belief that cutting down whole holly trees will bring bad luck. We use the berries, too, in a kind of informal divination, seeing bumper crops as an ominous sign of hard weather to come rather than as a result of a good spring.

Holly occurs throughout north-west Europe – even, sparsely, in the mountain regions of the Mediterranean. But true holly-woods, of the kind that can be found in, say, Epping Forest, the Welsh Marches and in the groups of huge, unpollarded trees near Coniston in Cumbria,[29] are a British speciality, so perhaps it is not surprising that such a rich culture has grown up around the tree here. Ecologically, too, these woods are exceptional, a rare temperate-zone equivalent of the evergreen cloud forests of South America and northern China.

There is immense variety in both woods and individual trees. In the ancient wood-pasture at Staverton in Suffolk gigantic holly trees grow among thousands of contorted oak pollards (see p. 87). There is what is believed to be one of the biggest hollies in the kingdom (74 feet high and 7 feet 2 inches in girth in 1969), as well as some of the most elevated: in many of the crucks of the oak pollards, holly saplings have taken root amongst the ferns and humus, 20 feet above ground level.

Some hollies carry yellow berries, or variegated leaves. (I once found a prostrate, golden-leaved tree sprawling across a rock in the remote limestone wastes of the Burren in County Clare.) Occasional specimens have nothing but spineless leaves, of the kind that are normally confined to the top, unbrowsed reaches of the tree. This is called 'free' or 'slike' holly in Shropshire: 'When dealers at Christmas were buying holly, they'd rather have slike holly – there was just a bit of prickle at the end. They'd give more for slike holly than real prickle holly.'[30]

A few trees sucker weakly, forming dense multi-stemmed clumps, or root along the line of low, whippy shoots which become buried under leaf litter. Some have down-curving, 'weeping' branches, which can take root at the tip and create a kind of bower round the trunk. Birds and mammals often use these as shelters in the winter. Humans, too: 'One den I remember well was a domed holly tree, whose branches touched the ground leaving a spacious room in which to play. We painstakingly paved the floor with a mosaic of stones.'[31]

The weather in spring and summer seems to affect the flowering and fruiting of some individuals, and there are always trees which hold on to their berries into summer, or flower in winter (as in the Derbyshire Dales in 1992, and the Chilterns in 1994 and 1995).[32] One idiosyncratic flowerer, which has a girth of over eight feet, is in Broaks Wood, Suffolk: 'This venerable tree has some interesting – though largely illegible – graffiti on it (none of it recent). Another curiosity is its habit of starting to flower in January.'[33]

But it is the clusters of scarlet berries and the darkly monumental foliage that make holly such a dramatic and conspicuous tree, and one that would inevitably lend its name to places. Hollington in Derbyshire and Hollingworth in Cheshire come from the Old English *holegn* – and both still have plenty of trees.[34] Cullen in Banffshire is probably a derivation of the Gaelic

'The holly bears a berry' … but only on female trees.

word for holly, 'cuillioon'.[35] The village of Hulver in Suffolk shares the Middle English name for the tree, though there are now 'only 18 trees left in the village',[36] and Hollybush in Herefordshire, despite being in one of the holly heartlands, seems to have virtually none remaining. Holmstone (from *holm*, also Middle English) in Kent is a unique wood of stunted hollies growing on the shingle beach at Dungeness, which was documented as early as the eighth century. There were 224 bushes at the last count in 1992: 'As the holly was used to construct sea defences (groynes) it must have been a very highly valued commodity, and this could be the reason why Lydd folk, who have always been threatened by inundation by the sea, have always and indeed still are striving to keep their Holly Forest.'[37]

But holly elements in place names can be difficult to distinguish because of their similarity to

other common components such as holy, hollow, and 'holm' meaning 'island'. Hollytreeholme in Yorkshire looks like the ultimate in holly place names, but actually means 'island with a holy tree'. Hollingbourne, Kent, is probably 'the stream of Hola's people'. Christmas Common in the Chilterns, on the other hand, may well be 'holly common' as Christmas tree is an early local name for the species, which is common in the region.[38]

Another puzzling suite of names crops up elsewhere in the Chilterns, between Chipperfield and Sarratt. This is an ancient and densely hollied landscape. Hollies spread in dark copses and commons. Thick holly hedges line the narrow switchback lanes. One of these lanes, threading through this woody enclave for a mile and a half, is called Holly Hedges at one end and Olleberry at the other. This seems straightforward enough – except that there is a farm called *Hollow* Hedges half way along the lane, and records of a seventeenth-century family called Olbury living in the area. Like many persistent place names, the roots of these names are probably complex, converging and reinforcing each other, and maybe encouraging the preservation of holly as well as being prompted by it.

The most common and reliable ancient holly name is the Middle English *hollin*, which also came to stand for a group or grove of hollies that were regularly lopped for cattle feed. Holly seems an improbable and unpalatable form of browse. But feeding it to stock (sheep especially) during the winter is an ancient practice that doubtless goes back into prehistory. Its leaves have one of the highest calorific contents of any tree browsed by animals, and are rich in nutrients.[39] Martin Spray, who has done a historical survey of the use of holly as cattle food, believes that it was a widespread, if not always well-documented practice up until the eighteenth century. It seems to have been particularly prominent

Hollies are often retained when hedgerows are cleared or lowered. They are used as guide-marks by ploughmen and combine drivers in many areas.

on the grits and sandstone of the Pennine foothills, roughly in the triangle formed by Derby, Leeds and Manchester. Spray has traced a conspicuous concentration of surviving 'hollin' and 'holly' place names in this area, and even an abundance of the same words as family surnames (noted from telephone directories) which exactly matches the place-name distribution.[40]

Reminders of old hollins are frequent in place names in the north, as for instance in this cluster near Oldham in Lancashire:

'As you can see from my address [Hollingreave Farm, Holly Grove], hollies are reasonably common in this area. But, although the moorland peat contains roots of prehistoric trees and there were said to be many more trees in the past, it is not an area of many old trees. The hollies by the cottages have very thick trunks, sometimes divided at the base, so possibly cut back at some time. Although our house was only built about 1800, the hamlet of Holly Grove is very old – there are church records of a Richard de Hollingrave in 1272.'[41]

'Next to my house, Hollin Hall, there stood a "Red Hall", and if you look over Ordnance Survey Maps you will often find abodes called Hollins and Red Hall close to each other, and often a tannery close by, as the holly wood was used in the tanners' fires.'[42]

'The name of my farm is "Hollinroyd", meaning holly clearing. The land was cleared c. 1450, but we still have holly which cows eat in winter.'[43]

But there are large surviving hollins too. One well-dispersed group is in the Olchon valley in Herefordshire, where the gnarled pollards stand in a landscape of Celtic fields and ancient stones.[44] Another is in Needwood Forest, Staffordshire – despite 150,000 trees being felled to make bobbins for the Lancashire cotton mills in 1802.[45] The most intact is probably the open woodland of almost pure holly at the southern edge of the Stiperstones in Shropshire. This is a remote area of heather ridges and splintered quartzite, where the commoners were part miners and part graziers (a way of life described in Mary Webb's novel *Gone to Earth* in 1917). The

Ancient coppiced holly, Yarner Wood, Devon.

has played in the landscape and local economy. Groups of self-sprung hollies – known locally as 'holms' or 'hats' – mixed with thickets of gorse, often provide the cover through which new oak and beech seedlings grow, in the slow process by which the Forest regenerates itself. And holly branches are still cut for the ponies and cattle when there is snow on the ground, though not as extensively as in the past.[47]

But it is a measure of just how confined plant-based traditions can be that a farmer from Eardiston, Worcester, just 20 miles from the famous hollins on the Stiperstones, could express disbelief about this particular practice: 'I have lived on a farm most of my life, apart from the last war. I have reared pigs, sheep, cattle and horses, but have never known of holly being fed to farm animals . . . The holly was known to be shade in the summer, and shelter in the winter. Many years ago the true gipsy women were known to give birth under a holly tree.'[48]

It is a custom which the stock themselves often followed: 'We have a very old holly tree. Over 100 years ago it was grafted with three different types of holly on the same trunk. We are 859 feet above sea level [in the Mendips], and have a lot of holly about around the farm. We always protect it because as a livestock farmer it is the best shelter for the animals. We find if a cow is calving out, she will always calve under a holly tree. But we have never fed holly to the livestock and have never known them eat it. We find it is the cold winds which will kill it back.'[49]

But on some farms a more superstitious attitude persists, as on the fells around Lancaster: 'In a new building or one where an animal has died a sprig of holly should be hung up (too high for the animals to reach) to remove and keep away evil spirits. The sprig should be at least two feet long and should be changed from time to time and the old one burnt.'[50]

This echoes a practice in France, in which the 'evil spirits' are replaced by more tangible parasites: 'In France, many farmers will hang branches of holly just above the height of their cattle when they are housed. The aim is to prevent ringworm.'[51]

local trees, some of which are probably 400 years old, were a source of winter browse, and they have been repeatedly cut at between three and five feet above the ground. Down in one of the valleys there are the remains of the old grinding machines once used to make the spinier leaves more palatable (as with gorse, see p. 78).

Holly boughs are still cut for sheep and occasionally cattle in Dumfries, Derbyshire and Cumbria.[46] But the most extensively used hollins are in the New Forest, where an abundance of holly place names – e.g. Holmsley, Holmhill, Holly Hatch – testify to the important role holly

Holly has had other practical uses, many of them touched by the tree's slight aura of magic. Like the elder, holly was believed to have power over horses, and its white, pliable wood made it the favourite timber for whips: 'The second largest use of holly in the late eighteenth and all the nineteenth centuries was as the best stocks for driving whips. When one realises that the carriage, coach, van, gig and pony and trap were used (as we use cars) in their hundreds of thousands, some 210,000 holly whips were made in the kingdom at the peak of the horse-drawn era each year.'[52]

'In the time of plough horses, holly was used for handles for horse whips by the ploughmen. The trees were established in deep burnsides, coppiced to produce many long straight stems. This would seem to be a Stirlingshire tradition, according to my forestry colleagues … (Incidentally, roe deer crop the lower leaves in a neat cut but red deer chew the next branches up in an easily identified, ragged manner.)'[53]

There are echoes of this in the Hertfordshire mummer's practice of using holly twigs as the horns of his hobby horse;[54] and in the notes of 'Ratcatcher' (an aspiring 'rune-master') on his apprenticeship: 'I am trying to become a rune-master. Holly is one of the best woods to make runes with. The holly is a very powerful and magical tree. If you want to use the wood, you must first ask the tree if you can use some of it. (You will get a feeling of it if the tree says "yes".) Then you must provide a useful gift for offering to the tree. Then you will be given all the power you need in the wood. It is also important to cut your holly on a night when there is a full moon. This adds more power to your runes.'[55]

There are several customs in which holly seems to be regarded as a proof or deterrent against fire (despite the fact that it is extremely inflammable in leaf, and as green timber): 'I remember being told when I lived in a village on the Isle of Wight with constant thunderstorms, that holly trees were often planted on either side of a building as a form of lightning conductor.'[56]

Up to the end of the last war, young hollies were used to sweep chimneys by being hauled through them on a rope. 'In Essex I had to struggle to keep my little tree from a neighbour who wanted it for that purpose.'[57]

'When I was a young gamekeeper in south Devon, I was told that the large number of holly trees locally were grown to meet the demand for tea-pot lids and handles. I believe they were rarely cracked by heat.'[58]

In Culmhead in Devon, there is even a pub called the Holman Clavel, which means a 'holly-beamed open fireplace'.[59]

But the most persistent, *trusting* use of holly is as a boundary tree. Across Britain, in every kind of landscape, hollies are looked on as constants in the landscape. One walker has noted how often they grow close to stiles, perhaps 'assisting in locating the stile and hence indicating the line to walk'.[60] Another used the evergreen leaves as reliable shelters on a fixed route to school: 'A life long friend of mine spent his childhood in the New Forest, for several years walking some two miles to school. Between the two locations every holly tree was known, and on days of frequent showers a dash from tree to tree was made, for it took a long time for the rain to penetrate the canopy.'[61]

In Cornwall, an inspector of mines has recorded holly trees being used to mark the overground course of a tin lode: 'Back at the beginning of the nineteenth century a mine called Wheal Pool (wheal is work in Cornish) near Helston was closed, and to mark the course of its lode, holly trees were planted along it. Most of them have long since disappeared, but what appear to be replacement trees are on the site … As far as I know this is the only recorded case in Cornwall of holly trees being used to mark the line of a lode; the common custom in the Helston area was to use thorn or elder trees, depending on whether the mine was wet or dry.'[62]

Holly trees sometimes appear to be deliberately left standing when hedges are grubbed out, and a down-to-earth explanation for this – suggested from several arable areas – is that ploughmen use their conspicuous, dark shapes as sightlines during winter ploughing.[63] At Inverary a particularly venerable holly was saved in 1861, when the Duke of Argyll 'insisted that an awkward bend be put in the line of a public road to avoid the necessity of cutting it down'.[64] And in the absence of any firmer physical or legal evidence, even Ordnance Survey map-makers regard mature hollies as being the best pointers to the course of old boundaries. Holly, it seems, is widely regarded as capable of outliving changes in ownership and farming practice, and of echoing the contours of ancient estates. (Though the enduring protection given to one tree by a family in Gloucester was exceptional. When they sold off part of their garden, they inserted a restrictive covenant in the contract, prohibiting the felling of the male holly tree it contained, so that the female tree that grows in their own garden would continue to be pollinated and set berries.)[65]

Why should holly have this special indemnity? It is, of course, a reliable, stock-proof tree, and very visible as a marker. But it seems that many hedge and boundary hollies survive because of the stubborn persistence into the late twentieth century of the belief that cutting down holly trees brings bad luck. In Suffolk and Worcestershire, for instance, professional forestry contract workers are still reluctant to fell hollies, just in case.[66] I have seen the same reaction from scientifically trained ecologists in my own wood. And from every part of the country people have written with stories of illness, heartbreak and disaster which ensued – with a time-lag of as much as forty years – when the taboo was broken and a holly was cut down.

In farming areas there sometimes seems to be a clear religious rationale behind the superstition – either orthodox or pagan:

'There is a suspicion here [Buckinghamshire] about felling hollies. Legend still has it that witches appear instead.'[67]

'[In East Sussex] holly is left as standards, in hedgerows, to prevent the passage of witches, who are known to run along the top of hedges.'[68]

'When I was rector of Iping and Linch near Midhurst, Sussex, I noticed hollies left to grow above hedge level. One answer was given to me by a Linch parishioner who was a professional woodman as his father had been before him. He told me that his father had taught him that he must not cut hollies "because they are the King's tree". He considered the "King" to be the King of England, though it did cross my mind to wonder whether the reference was to the King of Kings, cf. in "The Holly and the Ivy": "Of all the trees that are in the wood, the holly bears the Crown"'[69] (see p. 227).

The odd thing is that this superstition should coexist with the sanctioning of the cutting of holly *branches* for Christmas. Bringing in evergreen boughs to deck out barns and houses in midwinter is a custom which goes back to pre-Christian times. Holly, especially, with its sharp spines and red berries held throughout the winter, was seen as a powerful fertility symbol and a charm against witchcraft and house goblins. (It was, ironically, also seen as a masculine plant, despite the berries being carried solely on female trees.) The custom was easily accommodated by Christianity, holly standing for the crown of thorns and the berries for Christ's blood. Yet echoes of the old religion linger, and there is still a fixed – and widely respected – routine for taking down the Christmas greenery, though the date has shifted from early February (now Candlemas) to Twelfth Night. These are some of the customs – often contradictory – in different families' holly calendars:

'A holly branch is often used instead of a Christmas tree in Cornwall.'[70]

'My father (from Dorset) would never allow holly to be put up as decoration before 25 December.'[71]

'In my childhood home [Yorkshire] every Christmas, leaves were taken from the decoration holly and dispersed around the house, one leaf to each room, usually into ornaments or vases.'[72]

'Our family custom in Shropshire involves leaving a sprig of holly to dry after all the Christmas decorations have been taken down on Twelfth Night. This holly is kept. Usually it is stuck behind the clock or over a picture rail. Then, come Shrove Tuesday, it was taken down and put onto the fire over which the first pancake was cooked.'[73]

'If a leaf falls out of a vase of holly never put it in the fire to get rid of it.' (Lancashire)[74]

'I was always taught that any holly used in decorations should be burned in the garden afterwards, for continual good luck through the year.' (Hampshire)[75]

Even commerce is not immune. At Brakspear's Brewery in Henley, a bush of holly and mistletoe is suspended from the eaves each Christmas and left there all year to ward off misfortune. No one knows when this custom began, but the bush is visible in a photograph from 1910.

The commercial trade in holly itself has long had one of its main centres in the market at Tenbury Wells in Worcestershire, where during the four weeks leading up to Christmas there is a special arena devoted to holly and mistletoe sales (see p. 210). Much of the holly taken to market is cut on a small scale on local farms and commons. A woman brought up on the Shropshire borders remembers taking over her grandfather's patch when he was ill after the war:

'Months before, during the summer, my grandfather would go to various farms and look over the trees, and the bargain would be made; which trees he could cut, and how much he would pay the farmer. Holly trees are very slow growing, so having cut one this year, it could be three or four years before the tree would be ready for cutting again. And cutting holly trees, let me say, is quite an art. It is no good going in and cutting great lumps out of the side. You can easily ruin a tree by hacking at it, and not treating it with care and respect ... Down below, my husband was busy packing pieces of holly still covered with frost. The sack must be filled just right, not too loose, or the branches move about and the berries fall off; and not too tightly, or they all jam together and knock the berries off. The merchant in Manchester, to whom the holly was sent, would grumble if it didn't arrive in the right condition and would reduce the price ... My grandfather was full of questions on our return. All these farms and fields and trees had been a big part of his life

every Christmas time. He knew the names of all the fields and the very trees which grew there. He knew when to expect two sacks from a tree and half a sack from a much bigger tree, the tree by the stile in Cae Mawr, the two trees by the gate in Ty Gwyn, and on and on, he knew them all.'[76]

Alas, this modest husbanding is becoming a thing of the past. In some areas holly is illegally 'poached' on a large scale, with whole trees often being chain-sawed just for their berries. Yet in

Intertwined oak and holly, Pinnick Wood, New Forest. Holly provides protection for regenerating trees in the Forest.

contrast to the 1960s, when holly was widely believed to be becoming scarcer, it is now un-questionably spreading. In hill-country woods and commons where grazing has ceased, the browsed clumps have started to sprout into more substantial trees. In the south, especially in the Chiltern and Hampshire beechwoods, the slowing-down of thinning has favoured this shade-tolerant tree. Bird-sown seedlings are pro-liferating (in my own wood they occur most commonly under a pigeon roost in a stand of beeches) and in many woods holly is now the commonest shrub in the understorey. In a few decades, given its persistence and ability to form a closed canopy, it may become the dominant tree, and we may have a new generation of pure holly-woods.

Holly has held a place in popular affection through all its swings of fortune. It has been a talisman for the woman who found a young holly on a child's grave at Walkden Moor church, near Manchester, sprung from a berry on a holly wreath.[77] And for Mrs Berry too, who named her daughter Holly, 'so we don't burn the dead holly after Christmas (nor the Rosemary – that's my name). I have no worries cutting the holly to bring it in at Xmas, but I never burn it, always compost it.'[78] And for the teacher in Leeds, one of 'hollin's' ancestral haunts, for whom the tree has been a kind of mascot throughout her life:

Ivy, a gothic, softening cover for a dead tree (Gresham, Norfolk) ...

'One of my first teenage Christmas dresses –
holly-green with green velvet trim and red buttons – really felt right for the time of year – holly
on cakes – 1970, moved to Leeds, and a holly was
growing in our garden – 1984, moved to Adel,
Leeds, and though I shouldn't have, I brought a
small growing shoot back from Adel Wood to
plant in our back garden – At least six "hollins"
addresses in Leeds 16 …'[79]

Ivy, *Hedera helix*. Attitudes towards ivy have
been ambivalent since classical times. In the days
of sympathetic magic, ivy's ability to smother
grape-vines persuaded early herbalists that its
berries could overcome the malign effects of
alcohol. Goblets were sometimes made out of
ivy-wood to neutralise the toxic effects of bad
(or poisoned) wine. In medieval times ivy and
drink became such bosom companions that ivy-
covered poles, known as 'ale-stakes' or 'bushes',
were used to advertise taverns. The bigger the
ale-stake, the more ambitious the inn-keeper.
(Hence the expression 'Good wine needs no
bush'.) In 1375 an Act of Parliament was passed
to restrict their height to seven feet.[80] But, though
it was a toper's mascot, ivy was also seen as a
weak, 'feminine' plant, contrasted in mythology
and poetry with the red-blooded, prickly holly.

During the fashion for the Picturesque in the
eighteenth century, ivy became a token of melancholy, especially when draped over ruins. But
at the same time it was included in the festive
garlands brought into houses at Christmas
time. Today, it divides geographical regions and
professions. In the gale-dashed West Country
and the territories of commercial foresters it is
regarded as a curse and a killer of trees. In less
turbulent eastern regions and amongst more
easy-going gardeners and naturalists it is looked
on benignly, as an ornament to buildings and
woods and a boon to birds and bees.

Myths about the plant persist, and the facts of
its life-style are worth setting down at the outset.
Ivy is our only evergreen liana, a clinger and
hanger-on. But it is not even a partial parasite and
manufactures all its own nourishment in the
same manner as other plants. Although it is most
often seen as a climber, it is perfectly happy to

creep about the ground and in its maturity to
stand on its own roots. It uses trees and walls
simply as scaffolding, clamping itself on by
means of a mat of adhesive suckers. Only when
these encounter soil or deep crevices does it put
out true, feeding roots. But when ivy reaches the
top of a tree (and it has been known to climb
more than 100 feet) it begins to bush out and can
then begin to cause trouble by the sheer weight
of its foliage or by shading out the tree's own
leaves. This is when it also begins to bring out
our own loyalties and prejudices:

'I was raised on a moorland farm on the Bod-
min Moors, and I was taught that there were two
types of ivy. The type that competed with the

… a garden gate (Coverack, Cornwall) …

tree for food below ground, but only used the tree for support. And the type that not only competed for food below ground but also sunk its aerial roots/clingers into the tree and sucked the sap from the tree, thus weakening it.'[81]

'It is a somewhat sweeping statement that ivy does no harm to trees. Here in the West Country [Cornwall], one important factor is the wind, and in a gale a tree that is heavily laden with ivy is like a fully-rigged ship, unable to lower its sails. Over it goes!'[82]

'When clearing ivy from fallen trees I have found that the weight of ivy exceeds the weight of its host.' (Dorset)[83]

'As a Tree Surgeon I dislike ivy and she doesn't like me. It will take 30 years to smother a tree and I have seen trees killed off by too much ivy. Its roots will strangle its host and it will in time almost ring-bark it, causing the branch to swell up on either side. The dead leaves can't drop from the host and the ivy will put its roots into the rotting debris. Any cavities are covered over … It grows nearly eighteen inches a year. Its dark growth stops the light coming through even in winter. As you can see I like taking ivy off trees to give them freedom.'[84]

'I spent several weeks climbing into the yew trees in our churchyard and cutting down the ivy, which had such a grip that in some cases I had to use a crowbar to remove it . . . It had left deep weals where it was wrapped round the branches.' (Dorset)[85]

One parish priest from central Wales – perhaps seeing similarities between ivy and the serpent – would go even further: 'Throughout England and Wales, hundreds of thousands of trees can be seen in various stages of total destruction by ivy. How futile it seems for people to be asked to plant a tree when the present trees are being killed. I challenge honest people to open their eyes as they travel through every part of England and Wales to see this terrible

… and a headstone (Burnham Overy, Norfolk).

destruction of precious trees … It would be splendid and so merciful to trees if there could be a campaign to kill the ivy around our trees to save them.'[86]

But there are more sympathetic views, even amongst tree surgeons: 'Although ivy is a superb groundcover, creeper and wildlife habitat, it can and does cause problems for trees … Our solution is: where ivy is heavy within the crown, we remove it. On the trunks, we trim it back and leave it. Only in certain situations where there is a possible risk to the public do we remove it completely from the tree. In parkland and where the public do not often go, it is quite alright to leave ivy on trees as a wildlife habitat.' (Derbyshire)[87]

Ivy completely capping the wall of a derelict church at Ufton Nervet, Berkshire.

'As a bee-farmer, I have found that ivy provides the last main source of nectar and pollen for bees to top up their winter stores in mid-September, when the heather has finished flowering.'[88]

The late-flowering of ivy from September to November (when it can roar with bees as loudly as a lime tree in July) and the dark berries that last through until spring have made it attractive to gardeners as well as to insects and birds. In the eighteenth century it was regarded as the classic Gothic plant, and the landscaper Thomas Whately's description of Tintern Abbey graphically captures its contribution to the genius of the place: 'The shapes even of the windows are little altered; but some of them are quite obscured, others partially shaded, by tufts of ivy,

John Ruskin's 'Study of Ivy', c. 1872.

and those which are most clear, are edged with its slender tindrils, and lighter foliage, wreathing about the sides and the divisions; it winds round the pillars; it clings to the walls; and in one of the isles, clusters at the top in bunches so thick and so large, as to darken the space below ... No circumstance so forcibly marks the desolation of a spot once inhabited, as the prevalence of nature over it.'[89]

'The Victorians loved ivies and encouraged them to cover their summer houses and garden bowers. They trained and trailed them all through their homes, growing them outside and then encouraging them to grow through an open window ... Queen Victoria as a young wife wore a

wreath of real Osborne Ivy, interwined with diamonds, in her hair.'[90]

'House-ivy' is now viewed as ambivalently as that on trees. One taken into a house in Manchester as a tiny cutting has 'grown right across the fireplace, round the pictures. We are wondering if it will ever stop.'[91]

'I live in a semi-detached house which has been "taken over" by ivy. It has grown up the walls over many, many years and is now covering the roof. I cannot get rid of any of it, as it is firmly attached to the pebble-dashing. If I saw off the trunks at the base it will be brown and look unsightly, and I cannot remove the individual branches as they pull off the pebble-dash in great lumps.'[92]

'We have a rather superb ivy hedge; it must be about eight to nine feet tall; it was obviously planted to cover a fence. It is now holding the fence UP! It is wide; a fox has been seen to climb up through it and sunbathe on the top.'[93]

'[We have] an "ivy tree" – about nine feet in diameter and about ten times the height of a man. It is surrounding a hazel tree – hidden inside it, but still healthy, because its branches stick out all around it. Everyone round here calls it the "ivy tree".'[94] (The ability of ivy to survive as a free-standing shrub has long been known by gardeners, as is the fact that it can be deliberately propagated in this form. Cuttings taken from an ordinary, ivy-leaved climbing or scrambling shoot produce a climbing or scrambling plant. But cuttings from the flowering branches produce a so-called 'tree-ivy', which makes a small, upright, self-supporting bush with simple oval leaves.)[95]

Ivy's heartwood is a glossy cream and dries to the tint and surface texture of ivory. Branches are often used to give a driftwood effect in flower arrangements. In several craftshops in Wales, sculpture is made from thick sections of the trunks.[96] Being naturally forked, it is often used to make rough pitchforks, especially on the continent.

'Some time ago I came across a large trunk of ivy cut through at ground level and hanging from an oak tree. A friend told me that ivy was once used for pastry rolling pins, so as he used a lathe I asked him to spin three and keep one himself. They are still in use and pastry does not stick to them as much as to other wood.'[97]

Ivy berries and leaves have also had decorative and domestic uses: 'As a child during the war when cultivated holly was difficult to obtain, and the wild species practically non-existent in the Fen country, it was common practice to collect ivy for Christmas decoration and paint the berries red. However, I have discovered this painting of ivy berries was a much earlier practice in this area. John Clare, the Northampton-shire poet and a great recorder of the flora and fauna of his native heath and fen, makes the following observation: "hasten to the woods to get ivy branches with their chocolat berries which our parents used to color with whiting & the bluebag sticking the branches behind the pictures on the walls".'[98]

In Chudleigh, Devon, ivy from woods and hedges was called 'coloured ivy' because of the different leaf-shades, which were sought after for home decoration.[99]

'When my mother was born in 1885 at Inverkip, Ayrshire, her father was a policeman. I was told that my grandmother used to boil up ivy leaves to use as a colour restorer when his uniform looked shabby.'[100]

'In the early years of my married life (in the 1940s) I used to press my husband's suits with a damp cloth wrung out in a solution made from boiling water and ivy leaves. It certainly took the shine off suits, which had to last for ever – clothes coupons and finances making that necessary then. I think Gilbert Harding in a Brains Trust Programme on the wireless passed on that tip.'[101]

'As a child I attended a school in Wales where we had to wear navy blue serge gym slips as a school uniform – saddle, yoke, and three box-pleats back and front. I never remember these being washed, but during the school holidays we gathered the darkest green ivy leaves and our mothers poured onto them boiling rainwater, left it to steep overnight and sponged down our tunics with the liquid. Garments were cleaned of

Ivy, painted with flowers and berries in Frampton, Gloucestershire, c. 1840.

all grease and looked like new.'[102]

'I am 70 years of age. When I was about 10 or 12 years of age I had verrucas on one of my feet. Each morning I was sent to a neighbour's back yard to get two ivy leaves. These I put inside my white school sock. I wore this all day at school. This continued for about two weeks, and then there were two small very clean holes in the sole of my foot where the verrucas had been, no pain at all.'[103]

'Ivy was used to charm warts away in Essex up to the 1950s. A hole was pricked for each wart in an ivy leaf, which was then impaled on a thorn in a hedge or bush.'[104]

But the most frequent uses of ivy which still seem touched by ancient beliefs about its magical powers are in cattle-farming. Ivy has always been browsed by domestic animals, and it is some-times still used as emergency winter food, but it is seen as having a protective role as well:

'In the Highlands and Islands ivy was plaited into wreaths with rowan and honeysuckle as a good-luck charm. It was especially good at keeping evil away from milk, butter and cows, and

Ivy flowers are one of the few plentiful sources of nectar for late-flying butterflies and bees in September and October.

would be hung up on the lintel of the byre or hidden beneath the churn. In the Hebrides, people went to great lengths to collect the necessary plants, one man in the Uists swimming out regularly to an island in the Loch.'[105]

'My husband (a livestock farmer) tells me that sick animals suffering from poisoning, e.g. through eating yew or ragwort, will eat ivy when they refuse all else. We wonder, therefore, whether ivy has a medicinal or purgative property. In his experience livestock when healthy will only eat ivy when no other forage is available.' (Shropshire)[106]

'In the sick pen of the lambing shed I place a branch of ivy leaves to entice a ewe to find her appetite after a difficult birth or illness.' (Devon)[107]

'I have found that my cattle do exceptionally well when they have access to ivy. Also about four years ago I had an outbreak of New Forest Eye, and the cattle were moved into a wooded area with a lot of ivy and the eye trouble cleared up very quickly.' (Isle of Wight)[108]

A 'false spruce' – the framework of the dead tree totally cloaked by evergreen ivy.

'[In the 1930s] on Xmas morning, as soon as milking was over, we had to go out collecting ivy, and every animal, young stock as well, had to have a piece before 12 o'clock. The belief was that kept the Devil away for 12 months.' (Shropshire)[109]

The inclusion in Christmas greenery and rituals is the high point of ivy's ceremonial year. But it has been used in children's games and divinations:

'An Ivy leaf left on New Year's Eve in a dish in water and left untouched till 6th Jan. had some significance. If it was fresh or green the year would be happy. Black spots meant illness – according to where they were found – near the point, pain in feet and legs; near the middle, pain in stomach, etc. If it withered, the one who played it would die.'[110]

'When I taught at a school in Ruthin, Clwyd, on May 1st I found many children wearing an ivy leaf: "First of May is pinching day." The ivy leaf was to prevent being pinched by another child.'[111]

At Denbigh (also Clwyd) 'you could hide your ivy leaf and, if someone pinched you, you could reveal your leaf (usually hidden down a sock) and pinch the pincher ten times!'[112]

'When I was young in Rosneath village, schoolgirls used leaves of Irish ivy [see below] as a forecaster of their marriage prospects, singing the verse collected by the Opies from all over England and Scotland, and beginning "Ivy, ivy, I love you".'[113] (The full rhyme, as quoted by the Opies, is 'Ivy, ivy, I love you,/ In my bosom I put you./ The first young man who speaks to me/ My future husband he shall be.')[114]

But the best known of all ivy rhymes, the carol 'The Holly and the Ivy', remains something of a conundrum:

> The holly and the ivy,
> When they are both full grown,
> Of all the trees that are in the wood,
> The holly bears the crown.

On the surface it is almost a nonsense verse. Holly is one of the smaller woodland trees; as a model for the crown of thorns it is beaten easily by blackthorn and hawthorn. Ivy is not a tree

'Coloured ivy' – often used in flower arrangements.

and makes no other appearance in the full carol, which is devoted to the Christian symbolism of holly. The editors of *The New Oxford Book of Carols* believe that the best known stanza was the chorus from an older carol, tacked on as a verse by a Birmingham broadside publisher around 1710.[115]

A white witch from Yorkshire suggests, on the other hand, that the carol is a satire on the battle of the sexes; also that ivy is banned as a decoration in churches.[116] Although this was undoubtedly true in a few parishes because of ivy's traditional associations with drink, there are fine medieval carvings of it on supporters in both Westminster Abbey and Wells Cathedral.[117]

But there are secular medieval poems which do suggest that the red-berried, festive holly was seen as a man's plant, and the entwining, black-berried ivy as a woman's. One contains the stanzas:

> *Ivy bereth beris*
> *   As blak as any sloe.*
> *There commeth the woode colver [pigeon],*
> *   And fedeth her of tho;*
> *She lifteth up her taill*
> *   And she cakkès or she go;*
> *She wold not for an hundred pound*
> *   Serve Holly so.*
>
> *Holly with his mery men*
> *   They can daunce in hall;*
> *Ivy and her jentell women*
> *   Can not daunce at all,*
> *But like a meine of bullokès*
> *   In a water fall,*
> *Or on a hot somers day*
> *   Whan they be mad all.*[118]

How would the medievals have coped with the knowledge that holly's berries are borne on the female tree?

Atlantic or **Irish ivy**, *H. helix* ssp. *hibernica*. This is the commoner plant in many places in the extreme west and south-west of Britain. Its large and uniform leaves, rapid growth and lack of inclination to climb walls and trees have made it popular as ground cover with gardeners and landscapers. In the wild it can cover cliffs, and even grow on shingle banks.[119]

Box, *Buxus sempervirens*. Box is an anomaly amongst plants which have lent their names to settlements. It is a drab, malodorous and not especially useful shrub confined to the southern chalk, but in southern England it has as many places named after it as the elm. There are some 20 English place names which begin with the 'Box' prefix – 25 if you include the formations Bexhill and Bexley, Kent; Bexington ('settlement amongst box'), Dorset; Bix, Oxfordshire; and Bixley ('box woods'), Norfolk.[120] (Though half a dozen of these almost certainly have no connection with the shrub: e.g. Boxholme in Lincolnshire – beyond its possible natural range;

Boxted Green and Cross in Essex – perhaps from OE *Boc-hamstede* ('homestead among beeches'); Boxworth, Cambridgeshire – 'Bucc's worth' (enclosure); Boxford, Suffolk; and Box near Minchinhampton in Gloucestershire – perhaps after Julia de la Box.[121]) Box also appears as a boundary shrub in medieval charters for Ecchinswell and East Meon, both in Hampshire.[122]

Why should such a subfusc shrub have proved so compelling to the people who settled near it? One myth can be put aside at the outset. Box is not some exotic import from the Mediterranean, whose presence here can be traced to escapees from Elizabethan knot gardens or to coverts planted by Victorian landscapers. It is unquestionably native in scrub and open woodland on calcareous soils in southern England, forming dark, dense, elfin thickets amongst the paler-leaved deciduous shrubs, which are visible from long distances. This, together with the distinctive smell of the leaves (politely likened to foxes, but really more like tom cats' urine) and the remarkable hardness of the wood, is enough, I think, to account for its fascination. The best evidence of all is the surviving stands of wild box in places which have borne the shrub's name for the best part of a thousand years. Boxley, in Kent, is one of the famous sites, and local people have unearthed some fascinating details of the village's connections with the box tree:

'It does appear that the "ley" in Boxley is derived from the Anglo-Saxon word "leah" which has the fairly definite meaning of a permanent glade or clearing in woodland. This, linked to the fact that the village still supports fairly natural-looking populations of box in the surrounding countryside, proves the link between the village name and the box tree fairly conclusively. Indeed such Anglo-Saxon place names provide some evidence that the box is a native tree – more recent evidence comes from finds of box-wood charcoal in association with Neolithic camps on the South Downs.

Conditions for the box tree are almost perfect at Boxley with its position on the south-facing slopes of the calcareous North Downs. A few straggly natural-looking trees may still be

The dark outlines of box bushes on the Chequers Estate, Buckinghamshire.

found even within woodland on the steep slopes above the village … A pair of box trees also flank the war memorial in front of the church (and there are several large ones inside the churchyard) and though they were almost certainly planted around 1919 it does show that a perception of the historical links between the village and the tree has existed for some time … As for the future, it was agreed at a recent Parish Council meeting [1993] that as part of our centenary celebrations we will plant a box grove somewhere in the parish – well away from our precious natural population of course and perhaps in combination with other trees and shrubs characteristic of the locality such as whitebeam and wayfaring tree.'[123]

Sixty miles to the west, at the Surrey end of the North Downs, is Box Hill, with the best-known of the native boxwoods. They cover the cliff-like banks above the River Mole with a density that permits very little else to grow underneath. John Evelyn wrote about the hill in 1706: 'The *Ladies*, *Gentlemen* and other *Water-drinkers* from the neighbouring *Ebesham-Spaw* [Epsom Spa], often … *divert* themselves in those *Antilex* natural Alleys, and shady Recesses, among the *Box-trees*; without taking any such offence at the Smell, which has of late banish'd it from our *Groves* and *Gardens*; when after all, it is infinitely to be preferr'd for the bordering of *Flower-beds*, and Flat *Embroideries*, to any sweeter less-lasting *Shrub* whatever …'[124]

A century later, William Gilpin wrote of 'shivering precipices, and downy hillocks, every-where interspersed with the mellow verdure of box, which is here and there tinged, as box commonly is, with red and orange'.[125]

In West Sussex, box is quite common, native or naturalised in woods and on the downs. But Boxgrove (whose name appears in the Domes-day Book) is the only settlement named after it.[126] Box must once have been common in the Chilterns too, from Bix, near Henley in the south, through Boxmoor, Hertfordshire, to, per-haps, Box End in Bedfordshire. There are still scattered individual bushes in apparently wild situations throughout this range – for instance

near Ivinghoe Beacon in Buckinghamshire. These may be remnants of the much larger populations reported between Tring and Dunstable by many writers, including the philosopher John Stuart Mill in 1855. A century before, Pehr Kalm had stated that these were planted by the Duke of Bridgewater, and the wood sold to London craftsmen. (The exceptional hardness of box timber made it a valuable raw material, and it was used for chessmen, rulers, rolling pins, pestles, and especially for printing blocks: the nineteenth-century engraver Thomas Bewick claimed that one of his blocks was still sound after 900,000 printings. The wood was also used for cleaning rings.)

The dark, sprawling hummocks on Shirburn Hill, east of Watlington, look natural, though the presence of exotic species such as cork oak nearby suggest they too may have been part of a planted landscape. But there is not much doubt about the provenance of the most extensive stands of box in Britain, eight miles to the north-east of Shirburn in Ellesborough Warren and the Chequers Estate. The trees are tall and ancient and occupy three steep-sided coombes. The at-mosphere amongst the twisted trunks is extra-ordinary: humid and dark from the closed, evergreen canopy overhead and filled with that pungent but powerfully nostalgic smell. In one of the coombes, known as Happy Valley, there is an area of young regenerating box on a steep, stony slope.

The early history of the Ellesborough and Chequers colonies is not well known. But, up to the beginning of the nineteenth century, the area was apparently commonland, and local people coppiced the box for firewood. The Enclosure Award of 1805 stopped this practice, and a local tenant wrote that 'the box increases in beauty and value and forms a very picturesque appear-ance'.[127] Now some coppicing has been reintro-duced, to try to prevent the box shading out too much of the chalk grassland. But this long rota-tional cutting is not entirely compatible with what has become the commonest modern use for box: the harvesting of young shoots for florists' wreaths.

The grove at Boxwell in Gloucestershire, also in a steep-sided coombe, is much smaller than those in Ellesborough, but the trees are older and the site has a much longer documented history. John Aubrey described the Boxwell trees in 1685 as 'a great wood ... which once in ... [unspecified] yeares Mr. Huntley fells, and sells to the combe-makers in London'.[128] A distinctive feature of the Boxwell boxwood is that it merges with the nearby beechwoods, forming an understorey as the tree often does on the continent. And close to the drive up to Boxwell Court the wild trees are progressively trimmed, so that by the Lodge they are in the form of a neat box hedge. (In southern France, where box is a common shrub, topiary is practised even on wild trees. A couple holidaying in the Corbières Hills in the Languedoc in 1992 were mystified to find artfully clipped box bushes out in wild *maquis*, miles from any settlement. It was some days later that they traced the sculptors: local road-menders with time on their hands after lunch.)[129]

Box, like other sombre evergreens, has long been a plant of grave decorations and funerals. A considerable thicket of box – mixed with yew and snowdrops – surrounds the memorial cross which marks the site of the execution of Piers Gaveston at Blacklow Hill in Warwickshire. The inscription on the cross reads: 'In the hollow of this Rock, was beheaded, On the 1st Day of July 1312, By Barons lawless as himself, PIERS GAVESTON, earl of Cornwall, The Minion of a Hateful King: In Life and Death, A Memorable Instance of Misrule.'[130]

Wordsworth describes a north-country funeral custom of filling a basin with sprigs of box, and placing it by the door of the house from which the coffin was taken. Each person who attended the funeral would take a piece of box and throw it into the grave after the coffin had been lowered.[131] The custom persisted in the region well into the late nineteenth century. In 1868, a *Daily Telegraph* reporter sent to cover the aftermath of a colliery disaster at Hindley Green near Wigan wrote: 'I find an old Lancashire custom observed in the case of this funeral. By the bedside of the dead man, the relatives, as they took their last

Box Hill, Surrey. The hardwood of box is used to make woodcut blocks.

look at the corpse, have formed a tray or plate, upon which lay a heap of sprigs of box. Each relative has taken one of these sprigs, and will carry it to the grave, many of them dropping it upon the coffin. Ordinarily the tray contains sprigs of rosemary or thyme: but these poor Hindley people not being able to obtain these poetical plants, have, rather than give up an old custom, contented themselves with stripping several trees of boxwood.'[132]

Beauties and Prodigals

BEAUTY, uncertain origins, romantic histories, can all give a species a cultural *frisson*. The striking wild peony, which grows only on the island of Steepholm, may be a relic of a medieval monastic herb farm; so may be the birthwort at Godstow Abbey in Oxfordshire.

There are species, too, which lure plant-hunters because of their secretiveness. The wild gladiolus is not only restricted to a single area of England – the New Forest – but hides itself even further by growing almost exclusively under bracken. The cryptic asarabacca lurks under dark hedgerows. Lady's-slipper and monkey orchids are found each year in just one or two sites – as is the military orchid, whose fortunes in this country have had the character of an epic drama.

There is the special attractiveness of rarities of extreme habitats, such as Jacob's-ladder on the limestone cliffs of Malham Cove, or Cheddar pink, which grows nowhere else in Britain except in the Mendip gorges. The distinguished botanist J. H. Balfour caught well the allure of scarce and beautiful plants growing in remote places when writing of alpines in 1847: 'There is moreover, something peculiarly attractive in the collecting of alpine plants. Their comparative rarity, the localities in which they grow, and frequently their beautiful hues, conspire in shedding around them a halo of interest far exceeding that connected with lowland productions. The alpine *Veronica* displaying its lovely blue corolla on the verge of dissolving snows; the Forget-me-not of the mountain summit, whose tints far excel those of its namesake of the brooks; the *Woodsia* with its tufted fronds adorning the clefts of the rocks; the snowy Gentian concealing its eye of blue in the ledges of the steep crags ...'[1]

Part of the spectacular colony of Jacob's-ladder at Malham Cove, which mounts the scree like a 'ladder to heaven'.

Peony, *Paeonia mascula*. Britain is a thousand miles from the wild peony's native home in the Mediterranean scrublands. Yet this handsome shrub with its luscious crimson flowers has had at least two newsworthy 'wild' appearances on these shores.

The first was possibly a seventeenth-century 'urban myth', or a simple confidence trick. In the original edition of his *Herball* (1597), John Gerard claims to have found peony growing 'wilde vpon a conie berrie [rabbit warren] in Betsome, being in the parish of Southfleete in Kent'.[2] But

Wild peony, in Britain known only from the island of Steepholm.

the editor of the second edition, the scrupulous Thomas Johnson, adds a sceptical, reproving footnote to Gerard's entry: 'I haue beene told that our Author himselfe planted that Peionie there, and afterwards seemed to finde it there by accident: and I doe beleeue it was so, because none before or since haue euer seene or hard of it growing wilde since in any part of this kingdome.'[3] If this was a 'plant', so to speak, it is one of a long history of botanical hoaxes, though none of them has ever achieved the notoriety of the fake skull of Piltdown Man.

But in 1803 a small clump of naturalised peonies was found growing on the uninhabited island of Steepholm, in the Bristol Channel. The discovery of this exotic beauty in such a desolate place caught the imagination of the Romantics, and one of Coleridge's mentors, William Lisle Bowles, composed a poem to this 'one flower, which smiles in sunshine or in storm, there sits companionless, but yet not sad'.[4] The lateness of its discovery is curious, given that the island had been a magnet to botanists since the middle of the sixteenth century. William Turner, author of the first serious study of British plants, *A New Herball* (1551), may have visited it in 1562, followed by de l'Obel (1581), Sir Joseph Banks and John Lightfoot (1770s). They recorded many of the southern European herbs that still crowd the island's craggy slopes – henbane (a hypnotic), caper spurge (the 'katapuce' in Chaucer's 'Nun's Priest's Tale', an ingredient in a potent laxative), coriander, wild leek, greater celandine and alexanders. Such a suite of foreign medicinals growing together is a strong hint that there was once a physic garden on the island. A community of Augustine monks, an order noted for their medicinal and gardening skills, lived there between 1166 and 1260, and John Fowles believes they may have deliberately exploited Steepholm's equable oceanic climate for the bulk growing of Mediterranean herbs.[5] Yet despite the fact that peony was one of the most prized and frequently grown wild herbs, and has flamboyant red flowers up to five inches across, not one of Steepholm's early botanisers – a distinguished and observant company – mentions so much as a glimpse of it. This has tempted some sceptics (remembering Gerard's sleight of hand, perhaps) to speculate that it might have been slipped in to the island by a visitor later – and less reverent – than the Augustinians.

Yet the wild peony is in flower for only seven days, and could easily have been missed; and a twelfth-century monkish herb-farm is still the most plausible explanation for its presence, given its importance in the medieval *materia medica*. Gerard provides a prodigious list of ailments for which it was effective – jaundice, 'torments of the belly', falling sickness, and 'the disease of the minde'. Perhaps there was just a tinge of guilt in his long description of its most effective use, for those afflicted by '*Ephialtes* or nightMare, which is as though a heauie burthen were laid vpon them, and they opressed therewith'.[6]

Mezereon, *Daphne mezereum*. Mezereon was once known as 'paradise plant' because of the heady fragrance of its February flowers, and was widely planted close to cottage doors. It is now a national rarity, and the two facts are probably connected. Although it is conspicuous in late winter – the close-packed pink flowers appearing on leafless woody stems up to four or five feet in height – it can never have been common. It was not recorded growing in the wild in Britain until 1752, when it was found in some woods near Andover in Hampshire.[7] A few years later, Gilbert White found it on Selborne Hanger, not far from the same site, and as is evident from his journals, he transplanted some to his garden.[8]

Mezereon now occurs very scarcely in calcareous woods from Sussex and Hampshire to Yorkshire, and elsewhere as a bird sown casual or relic of cultivation. (There is a small colony in the chalk-pit near Mildenhall, Suffolk, where the military orchids grow, see p. 242.) But it is worth saying that it is not universally admired. The scent of the flowers has been likened to 'Windolene',[9] and the bright red berries are exceedingly poisonous. A. A. Forsyth relates a sad and ironic story of how a litter of piglets was accidentally killed by them:

'During the last war [I] investigated the sudden death of six out of a litter of seven young pigs,

about ten weeks old ... All had vomited before death and their stomachs were empty of ingesta. An evacuee child, unused to the country, had picked mezereon berries from a bush in the garden thinking that they were red currants, and after tasting one and finding that it burned his mouth and tongue had ejected it again quickly without swallowing it. He threw the remainder of the berries into a trough, from which the pigs were feeding at the time. The surviving pig was the "rickling" or "runt" of the litter, which had apparently been kept away from the trough by the others while the berries were eaten.'[10]

Jacob's-ladder, *Polemonium caeruleum*. Truly native sites for this beautiful species, with its spires of bright blue (or, rarely, white) flowers, are confined to grassland, scree and rocky ledges in the Derbyshire and Yorkshire Dales and one place in Northumberland. Its most famous and long-lasting site is at Malham Cove in Yorkshire, where John Ray first saw it in 1671.[11]

Specimens appearing elsewhere are almost invariably garden escapes. Jacob's-ladder is a popular border plant, though the varieties in cultivation are usually continental in origin, with larger, earlier-flowering blooms.

The name 'Jacob's-ladder' (recalling the story in Genesis, Chapter 28) probably derives from the pinnate leaves, which have rows of rung-like leaflets.

Fairy foxglove, *Erinus alpinus* (VN: Roman Wall plant). This is a tufted, purplish-pink alpine, introduced at an unknown time from the mountains of south west Europe and now naturalised on a scatter of old walls, ruined castles, bridges and stony places (especially on calcareous rock) throughout Britain. As with many species of uncertain history and evocative settings, myths have gathered about its origins. Because of a long presence on Hadrian's Wall, it is widely known on both sides of the border as 'the Roman Wall plant', and its arrival is attributed to the Romans, despite evidence that it was probably sown in the wall in the nineteenth century.[12] One family have meticulously worked out the route the seeds might have followed, stuck to the boots of the legionaries:

'The seeds of *Erinus* could have been accidentally picked up by the men of the Twentieth Legion on their arduous march through the high passes of the Pyrenees and transported to Hadrian's Wall, where there would be plenty of suitable habitats and a climate imposed by northern latitudes not altogether different from the much higher altitudes of the Pyrenees.'[13]

Fairy foxglove is currently expanding its British range, and the most plausible explanation for its welcome arrival in new sites is simply that it has escaped from a nearby cottage garden or rockery. But what has all the appearance of an urban myth about its migrations has recently begun to be passed on in botanical circles. The story concerns two botanists who met at a fairy foxglove site, fell in love, married and ever since have carried *Erinus* seeds to sow as a memento at any site they visit together – hence the species' seemingly uncanny preference for nature reserves and romantic ruins!

Among the most flamboyant of all British natives are two rare cow-wheats. **Crested cow-wheat**, *Melampyrum cristatum*, has crimped yellow and purple flowers stacked as elaborately as a Christmas table decoration. It is a rare annual of edges and clearings in ancient woods in East Anglia and adjacent counties, sometimes appearing after coppicing. It is also occasionally found on chalky hedge-banks. **Field cow-wheat**, *M. arvense*, is its even more extravagant equivalent in arable land, with a flower-spike 'like a purple, rose and yellow pagoda'.[14] It was formerly quite widespread as a weed of arable fields on dry and chalky soils, but now survives precariously in north Essex, Bedfordshire and the Isle of Wight.[15] On the fields above the Undercliff between Ventnor and St Lawrence, it was once so abundant that it was called 'poverty weed' because of the way its seeds reduced the market value of corn. Its first record on the Isle was in 1823:

Left: fairy foxglove – naturalised from south-west Europe on many romantic ruins.
Right: field cow-wheat. The flowers have been described as 'like a purple, rose and yellow pagoda'.

'A few years later Dr Bromfield … carefully investigated its history. Local tradition asserted that the plant was imported with wheat-seed from "foreign parts" – some said Spain, some Jersey, others, with more probability, from Norfolk. He learnt that it was the custom at harvest time to pull up the weed with the greatest care, and carry it off the fields in bags, and to burn it, picking up the very seeds from the ground wherever they could be perceived lying. The bread, he was told, made from the wheat on the farms above the Undercliff was

the vivid floral memories many people bring back from Mediterranean holidays. Occasionally, naturalised specimens of this species turn up in southern Britain, usually as relics of cultivation on old bulb fields. (In the Isles of Scilly, where feral gladioli are common, they are known as Slippery or Whistling Jacks.)

These are plainly all escapes. But in 1856, a clergyman discovered a closely related gladiolus species, *G. illyricus*, growing wild in the New Forest.[17] It is still there, in more than 50 sites, and has the look of a genuinely wild species. On the European mainland it grows in scrub and light woodland, and it is a woodland edge species in the Forest too – though always under a canopy of bracken fronds. It seems that only under such unpalatable cover can the gladioli escape grazing by the local ponies and cattle.[18]

Lady's-slipper, *Cypripedium calceolus*, is one orchid that is genuinely rare, and now reduced to a single, heavily guarded site in Yorkshire. Collectors have played a role in its decline, though it was probably never a common plant in Britain. It formerly grew wild in open woods on the Pennine limestones, from Derbyshire[19] to Cumberland and Durham. Its best-known stations were in the valleys of the upper Wharfe in the West Riding, especially between Litton and Grassington; on the southern slopes of the Cleveland Hills in the North Riding; and in the craggy ravine known as Castle Eden Dene, near Hartlepool in Durham.[20]

The remarkable flowers – claret-coloured petals crowning a large, bright-yellow pouch, rather like a garden calceolaria – make the lady's-slipper the only native orchid that, even to an amateur, plainly belongs to the same group as the tropical species sold by florists. So it is perhaps worth meditating on the fact that the flowers most frequently mistaken for this rare prodigy by non-botanists are the gaudy but not dissimi-

not so dark coloured and "hot" as it used to be, and that the "droll" plant was less plentiful than formerly.'[16]

Wild gladiolus, *Gladiolus illyricus*. The ancestors of our blowsy cultivated gladioli were first introduced to Britain from southern Africa in the mid-eighteenth century. They could hardly be more different from the wild European species, the 'corn flags' of seventeenth-century gardens, slender, well-proportioned plants, only a foot or so tall with magenta, lily-like flowers. **Eastern gladiolus**, *G. communis* ssp. *byzantinus*, is one of

Above: lady's-slipper orchid, the rarest species, known now at just a single site in Britain.
Right: wild gladiolus, found only in the New Forest, and almost invariably under bracken.

Satyrium Hircinum.
Lin: XX....1.

Lizard, *or* Great Goat Orchis.
J.Robins Del. Bath *1784.*

240

larly shaped blooms of that much maligned and impetuous immigrant, the Indian balsam (see p.164)!

Lizard orchid, *Himantoglossum hircinum*. The lizard orchid has the most bizarre appearance of any of the 'mimic' species. It can grow up to three feet tall, and the spike carries sometimes as many as 80 closely packed flower-heads. The flowers begin to open from late June, and passable imitations of small lizards begin to uncoil, with the petals and sepals forming the head, and the lip dividing into two legs and an impressively long (up to two inches) and twisted tail. They are greenish purple in colour, spotted with darker purple on the tail, and smell distinctively of goat.

The lizard orchid is a sun-loving, continental species, and though it may take many years to grow from seed to flower, it is abundant in road-verges, field edges, vineyards and rough grassland throughout southern Europe. It has, till recently, been a rare plant in Britain, occurring sporadically on chalk and limestone grasslands in the south and east of England. Its populations have fluctuated notoriously. It was thought to be extinct in 1900, then expanded rapidly in the warm spell between 1920 and 1940, then went into another decline.[21] But in the six years between 1988 and 1994 – responding perhaps to global warming – the number of flowering plants tripled from 962 to more than 3,000.

Military orchid, *Orchis militaris*. The story of the military orchid's decline, fall and subsequent resurrection in England could be a parable for the fortunes of all our wild flowers. Up to the nineteenth century, to judge from the records, it had been comparatively widespread in the chalk country of southern England. There had been a colony at the bottom of the slope beneath the Duke of Bridgewater's monument at Ashridge, Hertfordshire.[22] In Essex, in 1738, it was found

Left: lizard orchid, painted in Bath in 1784. The illustration shows the testicle-like root tubers which gave plants of this family the Latin name Orchis. Above: military orchid, known from just two sites, in Suffolk and the Chilterns.

in 'Belchamp Walter Parish, on a little hillock in the corner of a ploughed field adjoining the way leading from Goldington Hall by the lime kiln towards Gestingthorpe'.[23]

But 'Souldiers Cullions' as Gerard called it (literally, 'soldiers' testicles'),[24] is a plant of the warm south, on the edge of its range here, and it has always been temperamental. Some years it would flower, other years not even show itself above ground, and during the cool summers of the second half of the nineteenth century it began to disappear from one district after another. By about 1914 it seems to have been extinct.[25] For the next 30 years the orchid was not seen, or at least not reported, by a single soul. But the possibility that an isolated specimen of this handsome flower – it is a little like a compact lady orchid – might be blooming in some remote corner of the Chiltern Hills turned searching for lost 'soldiers' into an insatiable quest for some orchid lovers (and probably some collectors, too).

In the end, the military orchid was found again almost by chance. The botanist J. E. Lousley had gone to the southern Chilterns in May 1947 ostensibly for a picnic. But, as he put it, 'I selected our stopping places on the chalk with some care, and naturally wandered off to see what I could find. To my delight I stumbled on the orchid just coming into flower.'[26] But, aware of the threat collectors might pose to the plant, he never made the location of his find public. In 1948 the writer Jocelyn Brooke made the fruitless search for military orchids the theme of the first volume of his trilogy of autobiographical novels.[27] It was not until the 1960s that the colony (or possibly another in the same region) was refound in Buckinghamshire. The site was Homefield Wood near Marlow, and the occasion was announced by a now legendary coded telegram from its discoverers: 'The soldiers are safe in their home field.'

In 1975, the naturalists' trust that managed the site decided to go public, and announced the mysterious orchid's return amidst high security and not a little melodrama. I wrote about it at the time:

'This time local naturalists took steps to ensure that it would not vanish again because of any human agency by setting an electric fence around it. There were rumours of round-the-clock watches and of a warden who carried a shotgun with his sandwiches. Souldiers Cullion was about to be restored to the public, but on rather different terms from those it had enjoyed in Gerard's day. When the press were finally told about the return of this prodigal to an idyllic woodland glade only 50 miles from London, they knew they had a story. For the *Daily Mirror*'s photographer it meant "a pledge

of secrecy, a rendezvous in a car park off a lonely country road … A long walk, an electrified fence, a last few careful steps." And there, "The Beauty that Must Blossom in Secret", the headline in the shadows. More people must have seen the rather smudgy black-and-white picture of *Orchis militaris* the following morning than had seen the plant in its whole history in this country. Yet it seemed a far cry from "the little hillock in the corner of a ploughed field" and the chance of finding it for yourself on a spring picnic.'[28]

Happily, this over-protective stance was abandoned at the end of the 1980s. A summer warden was installed at Homefield Wood and the general public welcomed. Far from leading to their immediate demise at the hands of rapacious pickers, the scheme has been a huge success. The population has grown to over 50 plants (with more than 20 flowering in 1993), and thousands of people have seen them and the 11 other species of orchid that grow close by. The only fencing seen these days is to protect the plants from trampling and rabbit-grazing.

But there is a certain amount of low-key 'gardening' at the site. Trees have been thinned and patches of chalk downland grazed by sheep, in order to create the dappled mosaic of scrub and grass that the military orchid prefers. And, since no pollinating insect has yet been firmly identified, visitors in May stand a chance of witnessing a touching act of symbiosis between orchid-lovers and needy plants: the voluntary wardens, on their knees, delicately extracting pollen from the flowers with proboscis-like stalks of grass, and ferrying it to other clumps.[29]

Military orchids also grow in some numbers in a chalk-pit near Mildenhall in Suffolk, where they were first found in 1955. They are larger and more vigorous than the Chiltern flowers and seem to have more in common with continental plants.[30] As there is no history of the orchid in Suffolk, this does suggest that they may be introductions or windblown colonists.

Calendar of Plant Folklore

New Year's Day *1 January*
On this day, until the early 1900s, the 'Burning the Bush' fertility ceremony was held in Herefordshire. The Bush was made of twisted hawthorn twigs and a bunch of mistletoe which had hung in the farmhouse all year. Early on New Year's Day it was taken to the first sown wheatfield and either burned on a large straw fire or dragged burning round the fields (p. 206).

Twelfth Night *6 January*
'Old' Boxing Day (before the calendar change of 1752). This is the day when Christmas greenery must be taken out of the house (p. 203).

The Feast of Candlemas *2 February*
Snowdrops are the traditional ornament and symbol of this Christian feast day which commemorates the Purification of the Virgin Mary (p. 138).

Lent-tide
In the north Pennines, this is the customary season for eating a bitter springtime pudding made from bistort leaves, oatmeal, egg and other herbs.

Palm Sunday
Boughs of yew or pussy willow are carried to some churches as substitute 'palm'.

Easter Day
Easter eggs are sometimes coloured by boiling with wild flowers. Gorse gives a yellow, pasque-flower a mauve.

Fritillary Sunday
last Sunday in April or first Sunday in May
On this day some of the few meadows still growing snake's-head fritillary – e.g. at Ducklington, Oxfordshire – are opened to the public. When the plant was more common, picking was permitted in return for donations to charity.

May Day *1 May*
The date of the old Celtic festival of Beltain, which is echoed in spring festivals associated with flowers in many parts of Britain (pp. 44–5).

In Oxford, for example, at six o'clock on May morning a Jack-in-the-Green cloaked in hawthorn leaves cavorts with Morris Dancers, while the choir sings from the top of Magdalen College Tower. In Padstow, Cornwall, cowslip is the favoured decoration of participants in the Obby Oss procession.

Garlands are still made in many country schools (and some villages). At Charlton-on-Otmoor, Oxfordshire, children make garlands in the form of small crosses, which are then taken into the church.

Obby Oss procession, Padstow, Cornwall.

The Furry Dance, Helston, Cornwall.

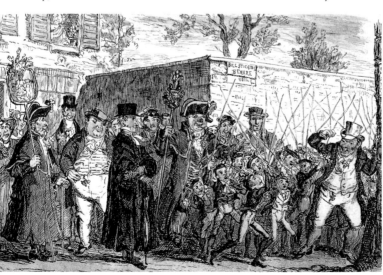

Well dressing, Derbyshire.

'May birching' is largely obsolete, but involved fixing sprigs of plants to people's doors. The plants were chosen because of their symbolic associations or because their names rhymed with the epithet regarded as most apt for the householder. So, plum, holly and briar meant, respectively, glum, folly and liar.

The Furry Dance *8 May*
On this day houses in Helston, Cornwall, are decked with branches of sycamore, beech and evergreens. The dancers in the street wear lily-of-the-valley, the traditional flower of the festival.

Rogationtide and Ascension Day
fifth week after Easter
This is the traditional date for Beating the Bounds. Plants are invariably involved in these ritual processions, being the most frequent natural features marking boundaries, as well as instruments (in the form of elm or willow wands) for 'beating' them (p. 45).

The custom of dressing Derbyshire wells with pictures made of flowers usually begins at this date and continues throughout the summer in different villages. The flowers are pressed into bases of clay.

'Beating the Bounds' by George Cruikshank. The schoolboys – here being encouraged to pound a point on the bounds with their willow wands – were sometimes larruped themselves to impress the boundaries on their memories.

Grovely Forest Rights, Great Wishford, Wiltshire.

Oak Apple Day *29 May*

Many festivals which began as May Day rites for encouraging growth in the fields and woods have migrated to this date at the end of the month, joining with Oak Apple Day, the civic commemoration of the Restoration of Charles II.

In Clun, Shropshire, the festival is Arbor Tree Day, when a local black-poplar is dressed with flags (p. 108).

In Great Wishford, Wiltshire, the ceremony of Grovely is held. The villagers cut oak boughs from the Grovely Forest, set them in front of houses, and carry them in processions through the village (and eventually to Salisbury). The ceremony affirms the villagers' ancient common rights to gather firewood in Grovely (p. 88).

Oak Apple Day itself celebrates the triumphant return of Charles II to London at the Restoration of 1660. Charles declared the day should be set aside as a public holiday for the dressing of trees. Today, it is still commemorated in some schools and military establishments by the wearing of sprigs of oak (p. 89).

Midsummer's Day *24 June*

A day of ancient pagan festivals, when bonfires were lit all over Europe to magically strengthen the waning sun. St John's-wort – a 'sun herb' from its bright yellow star-like flowers – was nearly always a crucial ingredient of the fires. Midsummer fires are still lit in many regions of Spain, Sweden and Eastern Europe, as well as in parts of Cornwall.

Old Midsummer's Day *5 July*

The Tynwald Ceremony on the Isle of Man occurs on one of the most important days in the Manx calendar, when every law which has been passed in the Manx parliament during the preceding year has to be promulgated to the public from Tynwald Hill. Sprigs of mugwort – 'Bollan Bane' – are traditionally worn at the assembly (p. 52).

Bawming the Thorn. In Appleton, Cheshire, what is presumed to be a descendant of the Christmas-flowering Glastonbury Thorn is still dressed with red ribbons and flags.

Rush-bearing ceremonies *early July to August*

Rush-bearing ceremonies are held in several parishes – e.g. Grasmere and Ambleside in the Lake District; Bishops Castle in Shropshire; Saddleworth, West Yorkshire; Liskeard, Cornwall; and Hull. The ceremony commemorates the time when the stone or earth floors of churches were strewn with a mixture of rushes, sweet-flags and herbs. This fragrant carpet was renewed at least once a year, usually at the time of the local Wakes week.

The Burry Man parade *second Friday in August*

On this day a man dressed in a suit entirely covered in burdock burs parades through the streets of the Royal Burgh of Queensferry, Edinburgh, visiting houses and receiving gifts and greetings (p. 50).

Apple Day *21 October*

This is a new festival, inaugurated in 1991, for celebrating orchards and the huge variety of cultivated apples.

Hallowe'en *31 October*

This is another day when apples (including wild crab-apples) are celebrated and become the subject of many rites – especially divination games.

It is also known as 'Nutcrack Night' in a few districts, because it was the evening when hazel nuts, stored away to ripen, were first opened. In some parishes there was a custom for the nuts to be taken into church the following Sunday and cracked noisily during the sermon (p. 68).

Christmas Eve *24 December*

This is traditionally the day when houses are decorated with winter greenery.

Rush-bearing ceremony, Grasmere.

Source Notes

SELECT BIBLIOGRAPHY

Allen, David Elliston, *The Victorian Fern Craze*, 1969

Aubrey, John, *Memoires of Naturall Remarques in the County of Wilts*, 1685 (edited by John Britton and first published in 1847 as *The Natural History of Wiltshire*)

Bates, H. E., *Through the Woods*, 1936

Beales, Peter, *Roses*, 1992

Betjeman, John, *Collected Poems*, 3rd edn, 1970

Brewis, Anne *et al.*, *The Flora of Hampshire*, 1995

Bromfield, W. Arnold, *Flora Vectensis*, 1856

Bunce, R. G. H. and Jeffers, J. N. R., *Native Pinewoods of Scotland*, 1977

Burton, Rodney, M., *Flora of the London Area*, 1983

Cave, C. J. P., *Roof Bosses in Mediaeval Churches*, 1948

Chambers, E. K. and Sidgwick, F., *Early English Lyrics*, 1907

Clare, John, *The Midsummer Cushion*, Ann Tibbles (ed.), 1978

Cloves, Jeff, *The Official Conker Book*, 1993

Cooke, M. C., *A Fern Book for Everybody*, 1867

Cornish, Vaughan, *The Churchyard Yew and Immortality*, 1946

Culpeper, Nicholas, *The English Physician*, 1699 edn

Curtis, William, *Flora Londinensis*, 1777–99

Dakers, Caroline, *The Countryside at War*, 1987

Dallimore, William, *Holly, Yew and Box*, 1908

Deering, C., *Catalogus Stirpium*, 1738

Dickson, J. H., *Wild Plants of Glasgow*, 1991

Dony, John, *Flora of Hertfordshire*, 1967

Druce, George Claridge, *The Flora of Oxfordshire*, 1886; 2nd edn, 1927

———, *The Flora of Berkshire*, 1897

———, *The Flora of Buckinghamshire*, 1926

Ekwall, Eilert, *The Concise Oxford Dictionary of English Place-names*, 4th edn, 1960

Evelyn, John, *Sylva, or a Discourse of Forest-trees*, 1664; 2nd edn, 1670; 3rd edn, 1679; 4th edn, 1706

Forsyth, A. A., *British Poisonous Plants*, 1968

Fowles, John, *The Tree*, 1979

Fowles, John and the Kenneth Allsop Trust, *Steepholm: A Case of History in the Study of Evolution*, 1978

Friend, Revd Hilderic, *Flowers and Flower-lore*, 1883

Gelling, Margaret, *Place Names in the Landscape*, 1984

Gerard, John, *The Herball*, 1597

———, *The Herball*, 2nd edn enlarged and amended by Thomas Johnson, 1633

Gibbons, Euell, *Stalking the Wild Asparagus*, 1962

Gilbert, O. L., 'The ecology of an urban river', in *British Wildlife*, 3(3), 1992

———, *The Flowering of Cities*, 1993

Gillam, Beatrice (ed.), *The Wiltshire Flora*, 1993

Gilpin, William, *Remarks of Forest Scenery*, 1791

———, *Observations on the Western Parts of England*, 1808

Gimingham, C. H., *Ecology of Heathlands*, 1972

Goody, Jack, *The Culture of Flowers*, 1993

Greenoak, Francesca, *God's Acre*, 1985

Grigson, Geoffrey, *Gardenage*, 1952

———, *The Englishman's Flora*, 1955 and 1987

———, *A Herbal of All Sorts*, 1959

——— (ed.), *Dictionary of English Plant Names*, 1974

Grindon, L. H., *The Trees of Old England*, 1868

———, *The Shakspere Flora*, 1883

Hadfield, Miles, *British Trees*, 1957

Hartley, Dorothy, *Made in England*, 1939

Hickin, Norman E., *The Natural History of an English Forest*, 1971

Hole, Christina, *British Folk Customs*, 1976

Hoskins, W. G., *The Common Lands of England and Wales*, 1963

Jackson, Kenneth (ed.), *A Celtic Miscellany*, 1971

Jefferies, Richard, *Wild Life in a Southern County*, 1879

Jermyn, Stanley T., *Flora of Essex*, 1974

Johns, Revd C. A., *Flowers of the Field*, 1853

Kent, Douglas H., *The Historical Flora of Middlesex*, 1975

Keyte, Hugh and Parrott, Andrew (eds), *The New Oxford Book of Carols*, 1992

Krüssmann, Gerd, *Roses*, 1982

Leather, E. M., *The Folk-lore of Herefordshire*, 1912

Lees, Edwin, *The Botany of Worcestershire*, 1867

Lightfoot, John, *Flora Scotica*, 1777

Loudon, J. C., *An Encyclopaedia of Trees and Shrubs*, 1842

Lousley, J. E. *Wild Flowers of Chalk & Limestone*, 1950

Lyte, Henry, *A Nievve Herball*, 1578

Mabey, Richard, *Plants with a Purpose*, 1983

——— (ed.), *The Frampton Flora*, 1985

——— and Evans, Tony, *The Flowering of Britain*, 1980

Miles, Roger, *The Trees and Woods of Exmoor*, 1972

Miller, Philip, *The Gardeners Dictionary*, 3rd edn, 1737; 6th edn, 1752

Milner, J. Edward, *The Tree Book*, 1992

Mitchell, Alan, *A Field Guide to the Trees of Britain and Northern Europe*, 1974

Morris, M. G. and Perring, F. H. (eds), *The British Oak*, 1974

Morton, John, *The Natural History of Northamptonshire*, 1712

North, Pamela and the Pharmaceutical Society of Great Britain, *Poisonous Plants*, 1967

Opie, Iona and Peter, *The Lore and Language of Schoolchildren*, 1959

———, *Children's Games in Street and Playground*, 1969

Perring, F. H., Sell, P. D., Walters, S. M., and Whitehouse, H. L. K., *A Flora of Cambridgeshire*, 1964

Perring, F. H. and Farrell, L. (eds), British Red Data Books: 1. *Vascular Plants*, 2nd edn, 1983

Pevsner, Nikolaus, *The Leaves of Southwell*, 1945

Pollard, E., Hooper, M. D., and Moore, N. W., *Hedges*, 1974

Preston, T. A., *The Flowering Plants of Wilts*, 1888

Rackham, Oliver, *Hayley Wood: Its History and Ecology*, 1975

———, *Ancient Woodland*, 1980

———, *The History of the Countryside*, 1986

Raven, John and Walters, Max, *Mountain Flowers*, 1956

Ray, John, *Catalogus Plantarum circa Cantabrigiam nascentium*, 1660

Rendall, Vernon, *Wild Flowers in Literature*, 1934

Richens, R. H., *Elm*, 1983

———, 'Studies on *Ulmus*'. The first paper, 'The range of variation of East Anglian elms', is in *Watsonia*, 3(3), 1955; the remaining six are in *Forestry*. A full list is given with 'Essex elms' in *Forestry*, 40, 1967

Riddelsdell, H. J. *et al.*, *Flora of Gloucestershire*, 1948

Robinson, William, *The Wild Garden*, 1870

Roden, D., 'Woodland and its management in the medieval Chilterns', in *Forestry,* 41, 1968

Roper, Patrick, 'The British Service Trees', in *British Wildlife,* 6(1), 1994

Ruskin, John, *Proserpina*, 1874-86

Salisbury, Sir Edward, *Weeds and Aliens*, 1961

———, *Weeds and Aliens*, 2nd edn, 1964

Salmon, Charles Edgar, *Flora of Surrey*, 1931

Sinker, C. A. *et al.*, *Ecological Flora of the Shropshire Region*, 1985 and 1991

Stevens, H. M. and Carlisle, A., *The Native Pinewoods of Scotland*, 1959 and 1996

Summerhayes, V. S., *Wild Orchids of Britain*, 1951

Tubbs, Colin R., *The New Forest*, 1986

Wallis, J., *The Natural History and Antiquities of Northumberland*, 1769

Walters, Max, *Wild and Garden Plants*, 1993

Webb, R. H. and Coleman, W. H., *Flora Hertfordiensis*, 1849

White, Florence (ed.), *Good Things in England*, 1932

White, Gilbert, *The Natural History of Selborne*, 1789

———, *The Antiquities of Selborne*, Sidney Scott (ed.), 1950

Wilkinson, Gerald, *Trees in the Wild*, 1973

———, *Epitaph for the Elm*, 1978

Wolley-Dod, A. H., *Flora of Sussex*, 1937

NOTES

Introduction

1 Barbara Tocher, Exhibition Florist, Tamworth, Staffs.
2 David Underdown, *Revel, Riot and Rebellion: Popular Politics and Culture in England, 1603–1660*, 1985
3 See for example Mary Roberts, *Flowers of the Matin and Even Song*, 1845; James Neil, *Rays from the Realms of Nature, or Parables of Plant Life*, 1879
4 Goody, 1993
5 John Vidal, *Guardian*, 10 December 1993
6 Caroline Smedley, Newton Regis, Staffs.
7 Alison Rutherford, Helensburgh, Strath.
8 Ronald Blythe, 'An inherited perspective', in *From the Headlands*, 1982
9 M. K. Farmer, Petersfield, Hants.

Local Names

1 Grigson, 1955
2 Forsyth, 1968
3 Bryn Celan, ADAS, Newtown, Powys
4 C. Walker, Condover, Shrops.; Ursula Bowlby, Ullinish, Isle of Skye
5 Robin Page, *Daily Telegraph*, 10 September 1993
6 'The Ragwort', in Clare, 1978
7 Colin Jerry, Peel, I. of M.; D. C. Fargher, Port Erin, I. of M.
8 Druce, 1886
9 Druce, 1927
10 Peter Casselden, Chesham, Bucks.
11 S. A. Rippin, Fforest Coalpit, Gwent
12 J. E. Lousley, 'A new hybrid *Senecio* from the London area', in *Report of the Botanical Society and Exchange Club of the British Isles*, 12, 1946
13 Ray, 1660
14 Ekwall, 1960
15 quoted in Rendall, 1934
16 Meg Stevens, Llanfrynach, Powys
17 W. Teasdale, Corby Hill, Cumb.
18 Janet White, Great Totham, Essex
19 Gerard, 1597
20 Jane Allan, Hawick, Roxburghshire; Chris Alsop, Buckley, Clwyd
21 Pamela Michael, Lostwithiel, Corn.
22 Edward Deville, Hertford, Herts.
23 D. Moore, Solihull, W. Mids
24 Paul Jackson, Aberystwyth, Dyfed
25 Carol Bennett, Sprowston, Norf.
26 Sheila Evans, Llanfwrog, Clwyd
27 Barbara Penman, Hever, Kent
28 Rosemary Teverson, Cornwall Trust for Nature Conservation
29 E. M. Porter, *Cambridgeshire Customs and Folklore*, 1969
30 Gelling, 1984; Ekwall, 1960
31 Ruth Ward, Culham, Oxon.
32 Caroline Giddens, Minehead, Somer.
33 Gillam, 1993
34 Gerard, 1597
35 Curtis, 1777–99
36 Druce, 1897
37 Ruth Ward, Culham, Oxon.

Plants as Emblems

1 Grigson, 1959
2 Allen, 1969
3 Culpeper, 1699
4 Len and Pat Livermore, Lancaster, in *BSBI News*, 61, 1992
5 Caroline Male, Halesowen, W. Mids
6 M. H. Beard, Little Wilbraham, Cambs.
7 Ida Turley, Ty Gwyn, Clwyd
8 Bill Chope, Baden Powell Scouts Association, King's Heath, Birmingham
9 Chris Walker, Condover, Shrops.
10 Lightfoot, 1777
11 'Stack silage made from bracken', in *Transactions of the Highland Society of Scotland*, 20, 1988
12 Whybrow, *c.* 1920
13 C. Walker, Condover, Shrops.
14 Dorothy Mountney, Harleston, Norf.
15 Martin Spray, Ruardean, Glos.
16 A. J. Cherrill and A. M. Lane, 'Bracken … infestation of rough grazing land in the catchment of the River Tyne, northern England', in *Watsonia*, 20(2), 1994
17 S. A. Rippin, Fforest Coalpit, Gwent
18 P. M. and Madeline Reader, Horney Common, E. Susx
19 Dr Jack Oliver, Lockeridge, Wilts.
20 S. M. Walters, 'Cambridgeshire ferns – ecclesiastic and ferroviatic', in *Nature in Cambridgeshire*, 12, 1969
21 C. C. Babington, *Flora of Cambridgeshire*, 1860; Perring, Sell, Walters and Whitehouse, 1964
22 Charlotte Chanter, *Ferny Combes. A ramble after ferns in the glens and valleys of Devonshire*, 1856
23 Cooke, 1867
24 Rickard, Martin, 'Ferns – a case history', in *The Common Ground of Wild and Cultivated Plants*, A. Roy Perry and R. Gwynn Ellis (eds), 1994
25 *ibid.*
26 Cooke, 1867

27 *The Times*, 28 March 1992
28 H.W., London W1
29 Salisbury, 1961
30 Friend, 1883
31 Grigson, 1955
32 Clement Scott, *Poppy-land Papers*, facsimile edn, Christine Stockwell, 1993
33 Dakers, 1987, quoting Ivor Gurney
34 Edmund Blunden, *Undertones of War*, 1928
35 William Orpen, *An Onlooker in France 1917–19*, 1924
36 Salisbury, 1964
37 Pamela Francis, Letterston, Dyfed
38 Ruskin, 1874–86
39 Hazel Sumner, St Weonards, Here.; and many other contributors, including S. A. Rippin, Fforest Coalpit, Gwent, and Margaret Pilkington, Lindfield, W. Susx
40 John Presland, Winsley, Wilts., per Martin Cragg-Barber, Hullavington, Wilts.
41 *Gardeners' Chronicle*, March 1889
42 P. Tickner, Shirley, Croydon, Surrey
43 Mrs Ethel Kerry, Irby, Wirral, Lancs., in Roy Vickery, in *Folklore*, 94(2), 1983
44 Mrs D. Wakeham, Bebington, Lancs., in Roy Vickery, *op. cit.*
45 Hole, 1976
46 E. H. W. Crusha, Charlton-on-Otmoor, Oxon.
47 Ruth Wheeler, 'The wild flower garlands', in *The Bampton Beam*, April 1993; also Ruth Ward, Culham, Oxon.
48 George Herbert, *A Priest to the Temple*, 1652

Games and Rituals
1 Jane Arnold, Bishopstone, Wilts.
2 John Josselyn, *New-Englands Rarities Discovered*, 1672
3 J. H. G. Grattan and C. Singer, *Anglo-Saxon Magic and Medicine*, 1952. Version in Grigson, 1955
4 T. T. Freeston, Wellington, Somer.
5 Elizabeth Telper, Selkirk, Borders
6 The Church of Christ's Women's Fellowship, Selston, Derby.
7 Pam Gorman, Dartington, Devon; University of Sussex Natural History evening class, per Margaret Pilkington, Lindfield, W. Susx
8 H. G. B. Coast, Chatham, Kent
9 Peter Marren
10 Elizabeth Telper, Selkirk, Borders
11 Margaret Bennett, School of Scottish Studies, Edinburgh
12 C. Walker, Condover, Shrops.

13 Betty Dow, Frampton Coterell, Avon
14 Peter Marren
15 Daphne Cooper, Shrewsbury, Shrops.
16 Tony Bayfield, Eastbourne, E. Susx
17 Tony and Faith Moulin, Yatton, Bristol
18 Peter Gateley, Maghull, Liverpool, per 'Plants, People, Places' project, Liverpool Museum
19 The Curator, City of Edinburgh Museum
20 Hole, 1976
21 Mark Powell, Riseley, Beds.
22 A. G. Barr (Soft Drinks) plc
23 Hilda Evans, New Tredegar, Gwent
24 Val Gateley, 'Plants, People, Places' project, Liverpool Museum
25 Margaret Trevillion, Germoe, Corn.
26 Nancy Girdler, Hurst, Berks.; also Christine Butcher, Holt, Wilts.
27 Dr Larch Garrad, Manx Museum, Douglas, I. of M.
28 Colin Jerry, Peel, I. of M.
29 William Cobbett, *Cottage Economy*, 1823
30 White, 1789
31 Mabey, 1983
32 Ida Turley, Ty Gwyn, Clwyd
33 Simon Leatherdale, Halstead, Essex
34 Jonathan and Wendy Cox, Kingston St Mary, Somer.
35 Philip Oswald, Cambridge
36 I. O. Jones, Ashley Heath, Shrop.
37 Martin Spray, Ruardean, Glos.
38 Dorothy Mountney, Harleston, Norf.
39 Sandra Woodman, Clutton. Avon
40 Jane Hall, Romsey, Hants.; also Caroline Smedley, Newton Regis, Warw.; Harry Triggs, Gwern-y-Brenin, Shrop.; Anne Newcombe, Churchstoke, Powys; Jonathan Curry, Crosspool, Sheffield
41 Hugh McAllister, Deputy Director, Ness Gardens, Ches.
42 Francesca Greenoak, Wigginton, Herts.
43 Bill Chope, Baden Powell Scouts Association, King's Heath, Birmingham
44 Friend, 1883
45 Grigson, 1974; C. E. Hubbard, *Grasses*, 3rd edn, revised by J. C. E. Hubbard, 1984
46 James Robertson
47 Hartley, 1939
48 Elizabeth and Rachel Stevens, Fleetwood, Lancs.
49 Cameron Crook, Preston, Lancs.; Aaron Woods, Milton Keynes, Bucks.; also Ray Woods, Llandindrod Wells, Powys, per Mary Briggs, in *BSBI News*, 60, 1992
50 Grigson, 1974
51 Pauline Conder, West Cross, Swansea

52 Joan Johnson, Guildford, Surrey
53 'John', Herne Bay, Kent
54 Jonathan and Wendy Cox, Kingston St Mary, Somer.
55 Caroline Giddens, Exmoor Natural History Society, Minehead, Somer.

Plants as Resources

1 Madeline Reader, Horney Common, E. Susx
2 Peter Marren
3 Loudon, 1842
4 Peter Marren
5 Barbara Mellish and Helen Beet, Handcross WI, W. Susx
6 Rackham, 1980
7 Jackson, 1971
8 Una Cosgrove, Balmaclellan, Kirkud.
9 Dr Larch Garrad, Manx Museum, Douglas, I. of M.
10 Ian and Victoria Thomson, Bentworth, Hants.; Roy Fussell, Chirton, Wilts.
11 Tony Hare, London
12 Mark Powell, Riseley, Beds.
13 Adrian Harris, Dragon Project, London
14 Meg Game, 'Cobnuts and conservation', in *British Wildlife*, 6(6), 1995
15 Meg Game, Kent
16 Aubrey, 1685
17 quoted in Rackham, 1980
18 Alma Pyke, Great Houghton, Northants.
19 M. J. Yates, Saltburn, Cleve.
20 The Revd Peter Gilks, Upper Clatford, Hants.
21 per C. I. P. Denyer, Chief Clerk to the Queen's Remembrancer, Royal Courts of Justice, London
22 Nigel Ashby, Greatford, Lincs.
23 Maggie Colwell, Box, Glos.
24 Anita Jo Dunn, Charlbury, Oxon., in *BSBI News*, 66, 1994
25 Daniel Keech, Common Ground, London
26 Ida Turley, Ty Gwyn, Clwyd
27 Geoff Locke, Rockhampton, Glos.
28 William Berry, Brook Farm, Chediston, Suff.
29 Jill Goodwin, Ashmans Farm, Kelveden, Essex
30 Gimingham, 1972
31 Hoskins, 1963
32 N. W. Norman Moore, 'The heaths of Dorset and their conservation', in *Journal of Ecology*, 50, 1963
33 Phyllis Somes, Fawley, Hants.
34 James Robertson
35 Colin Jerry, Peel, I. of M.
36 Madeleine Reader, Horney Common, E. Susx
37 M. R. Newman, St Leonards on Sea, E. Susx
38 Mary Beith, Melness, Sutherland
39 Joyce Dunn, Bridge of Allan, Stirling
40 Bruce Williams, Broomhill, Glasgow
41 *ibid.*
42 Mrs Jean Williamson, Whitby, Cleve.
43 Mike Coyle, Stoke, Devon; A. Hosier, Northchurch, Herts.
44 John Fishenden, Bolton-le-Sands, Lancs.
45 James Robertson
46 Ruth Ward, Culham, Oxon.
47 Mary A. Coburn, Harpenden, Herts.
48 George H. Whybrow, *The History of Berkamsted Common*, c. 1920
49 Geoff Brown, Cockermouth, Cumb.
50 Ursula Bowlby, Ullinish, Isle of Skye
51 Colin Jerry, Peel, I. of M.; also D. C. Fargher, Port Erin, I. of M.
52 per Danny Hughes, Beaford Arts Centre, Devon
53 Gailann Keville-Evans, Shirley, Hants.

Trees

1 D. Flitney, Barnet, Herts.
2 Evelyn, 1664
3 Nick Delaney, Honorary Warden, Sladden Wood, Dover District Council, Kent
4 Mrs Jackson, Caton, Lancs.
5 Jean Sharples, Eardisley, Here.
6 Susan Telfer, East Cowes, I. of W.
7 Peter Marren
8 Bob Mills, ATS Tree Surgeons, per *West Sussex County Times*
9 Michael Sumpster, Farley Hill, Berks.
10 Andy Patmore, Ranger, Salcey Forest, Northants.
11 David Morfitt, Coventry, W. Mids
12 Sue Paice, Great Barrington, Northants.
13 Zoë Upchurch, Hartley Wintney, Hants.
14 Geoff Marsh, Lytchett Matravers, Dorset
15 Evelyn Smith, Norfolk Society, Norwich
16 Brewis, 1995
17 Rackham, 1980
18 Fowles, 1979
19 Cave, 1948
20 George Hayward, Oak Apple Club, Great Wishford, Wilts.; also C. C. G. Ross, *The Story of Oak Apple Day in Wishford Magna*, 1987; Hole, 1976
21 Friend, 1883
22 Pamela Michael, Lostwithiel, Corn.
23 Glenys Lund, Moreton, Lancs.
24 Robin Ravilious, Chulmleigh, Devon
25 Morris and Perring, 1974
26 Rackham, 1980
27 Miles Hadfield, 'The oak and its legends', in Morris and Perring, 1974

28 The Revd R. M. Robertson Stone, *A Short History of the Bale Oak*, 1993
29 Roden, 1968
30 White, 1789
31 Gilpin, 1791
32 Peter Webb, Suffolk County Council
33 Anon., Ingleby Greenhow, Cleve.
34 Glenys Lund, Moreton, Lancs.
35 R. H. Mills, Regional Director, National Trust, High Wycombe, Bucks.
36 Joan Poulson, per Ruth Ward, Culham, Oxon.
37 Anthony Bayfield, Eastbourne, E. Susx
38 Phil Gates, Crook, Durham
39 John Chinery, Hayes, Middx; A. McRae, Holmbrook, Cumbr.; Roger Deakin, Mellis, Suff.; G. D. Bridges, Wiveliscombe, Somer.; Kevin Pyne, Burley, W. Yorks.; B. Stewart, Hastings, E. Susx
40 Sheila Evans, Llanfwrog, Clwyd
41 Brian Cave, Longhope, Glos.
42 John A. Dolwin, Crowborough, E. Susx, in *Quarterly Journal of Forestry*, January 1994
43 F. L. Forbes, Watford, Herts.; A. V. B. Flecchia, Croydon, Surrey
44 Dorothy Mountney, Harleston, Norf.
45 Hazel Sumner, St Weonards, Here.
46 Vera Gleed, Wooton Bassett, Wilts.
47 Betjeman, 1970
48 Wilkinson, 1978
49 Sheila Beosham, Greenstead Green, Essex; Roy Fussell, Chirton, Wilts.; David M. Norfitt, Coventry, W. Mids; Barbara Penman, Hever, Kent; Mark Powell, Riseley, Beds.
50 Rackham, 1986
51 Richens, 1967
52 Rackham, 1986
53 Janey Rimington, Brighton, E. Susx
54 Humberside County Council, Kingston upon Hull, Humbs.; Faith Moulin, Yatton, Avon
55 Richens, 1983
56 The Revd Edward Houston, Paulesbury, Northants.
57 Canon T. Barnard, Lichfield Cathedral, Staffs.
58 David Wall, The Cathedral School, Lichfield, Staffs.
59 J. N. Rounce, Great Walsingham, Norf.
60 Rackham, 1986
61 Peter Levi, Frampton on Severn, Glos.
62 Edgar Milne-Redhead, Great Horkesley, Essex
63 *ibid*.
64 Charles Watkins, University of Nottingham, Notts.
65 Desmond Hobson, Wantage, Oxon.
66 Edgar Milne-Redhead, Great Horkesley, Essex
67 David Bleasdale, Trawden, Lancs.
68 E. Milne-Redhead, 'The B.S.B.I. Black Poplar survey, 1973–88', in *Watsonia*, 18(1), 1990
69 John Kirkpatrick, Aston on Clun, Shrops.
70 Dr Daffydd Huws, Caerffili, Clwyd; Hazel Harrison, Llanbedr, Gwynedd; Judith Fearnall, Hope, Clwyd
71 Riddelsdell *et al.*, 1948
72 Sonia C. Holland, *The Black Poplar in Gloucestershire*, 1992
73 Graham King, Norfolk County Council, Norwich
74 Peter Webb, Suffolk County Council, Ipswich
75 Barbara Wilson, Marlesford, Suff.
76 Mary Taylor, Bardwell, Suff.
77 B. Kelsey, Worstead, Norf.
78 Margaret Wingrove, Aylesbury, Bucks.
79 Susan Cowdy, The Lee, Bucks.
80 G. F. Peterken and F. M. R. Hughes, *Restoration of Floodplain Forests*, 1994 (from ICF Discussion Meeting on Forests and Water); Jonathan Spencer, *The Native Black Poplar in Britain: An Action Plan for its Conservation*, 1994
81 Roger Lines, High Ham, Langport, Somer.
82 Mrs Linford, Watford, Herts.
83 Rackham, 1980
84 Pevsner, 1945; T. C. Burnard, Corsham, Wilts.
85 White, 1789
86 Rackham, 1980
87 Katrina Porteous, Beadnell, Northum.
88 Alistair Scott, Forestry Commission, Edinburgh
89 Franklyn Perring, Oundle, Northants.; Roger Deakin, Mellis, Suff.
90 Eleanour Brown, Coulter, Lanark.
91 J. Roberts, Rhiw, Gwyn.
92 Roy Fussell, Chirton, Wilts.
93 Simon Leatherdale, Forest Enterprise, Woodbridge, Suff.
94 Jane Allen, Hawick, Roxburghshire
95 Nancy Roberts, Weybridge, Surrey
96 Terry West, Cranbrook, Kent
97 Rackham, 1980
98 Lynn Fomison, Ropley, Hants.
99 Desiree Merican, Shoreham-by-Sea, W. Susx

Plants as Historic Landmarks

1 Stevens and Carlisle, 1959; Bunce and Jeffers, 1977
2 Max Sinclair, Avoncroft Museum of Building, Bromsgrove, W. Mids
3 E. Morris, Minsterley, Shrops.
4 S. Healey, Hoarstone Farm, Wribbenhall, Here.
5 Barbara Barling, Yatton, Here.

6 Andy Patmore, Forest Ranger, Salcey Forest, Northants.; P. C. McE., Berkhamsted, Herts.

7 G., Stonegrave, N. Yorks.

8 Dorothy Halliday, Wantage, Oxon.

9 Kenneth Watts, 'Scots Pine and droveways', in *Wiltshire Folk Life*, 19, 1989

10 T. J. Flemons, Luston, Here.

11 D. I. H. Johnstone, *In Search of Scotch Ale*, 1984

12 Mitchell, 1974; also Hadfield, 1957

13 Peter Webb, Suffolk County Council

14 Robin Hamilton, Hitcham, Suff.

15 Rackham, 1980

16 Edgar Milne-Redhead, Great Horkesley, Essex

17 A. J. L. Fraser, Conservation Manager, Worcestershire Nature Conservation Trust, Worcs.

18 Rackham, 1980

19 C. D. Pigott, 'Factors controlling the distribution of *Tilia cordata* at the northern limits of its geographical range, IV', in *New Phytologist*, 1989

20 David Esterley, 'Out of the ashes', *Independent Magazine*, 4 July 1992

21 Bob and Margaret Marsland, Hallwood Green, Glos.

22 Dr Donald Pigott, University Botanic Garden, Cambridge

23 Lloyd James, Stratton St Margaret, Wilts.

24 N. Owens, Corton Denham, Somerset

25 Peter Lewis, Ewell, Surrey

26 Anne McKean, Forty Hill, Middx

27 Rackham, 1976

28 Alistair Scott, Forestry Commission, Edinburgh

29 Pam Gorman, Dartington, Devon

30 Ekwall, 1960; Gelling, 1984

31 Grigson, 1952

32 W. E. Foster, Epping, Essex

33 J. B. Hurry, *The Woad Plant and its Dye*, 1930

34 Edwin Lees, *Pictures of Nature*, 1856

35 Dorothy Hilton, Tewkesbury, Glos.

36 Jill Goodwin, Kelvedon, Essex; Jane Wise, Stogumber, Somer.; R. M. Wickenden, Staplecross, E. Susx

37 The Revd R. Addington, Charsfield, Suff., per Suffolk Naturalists' Society

38 Clare, 1978

39 Patrick Roper, 'The distribution of the wild service tree … in the British Isles', in *Watsonia*, 19(4), 1993

40 Geoff Locke, Rockhampton, Glos.

41 D. Blissett, Solihull, W. Mids

42 Grindon, 1868

43 Richard Jackson, Brooks Green, W. Susx

44 Bromfield, 1856

45 E. M. Crampton, Tenterden, Kent

46 Howarth Greenoak and Alice Kilpatrick, Wigginton, Herts.

47 H. G. B. Coast, Chatham, Kent

48 Barbara Penman, Hever, Kent

49 Patrick Roper, Sedlescombe, W. Susx; see also Roper, 1994

50 Simon Leatherdale, Halstead, Essex

51 Nigel Ashby, Greatford, Lincs.

52 Daniel Keech, Common Ground, London

53 Judith Marshall, Gedney Dyke, Lincs.

54 B. Heath-Brown, Welwyn Garden City, Herts.

55 Roper, 1994

56 Hickin, 1971

57 Roper, 1994

58 Quentin Kay, Llanmadoc, W. Glam.

59 Gerard, 1597

60 Burton, 1983; Salmon, 1931

61 Wolley-Dod, 1937

62 North, 1967

63 F. Morris, Minsterley, Shrops.; also Janet Preshous, Lydham, Shrops.

64 Anne Sandford, Stoke St Milborough, Shrops.; Jonathan and Wendy Cox, Kingston St Mary, Somer.

65 Geoff Brown, Cockermouth, Cumb.

66 Rose Macdonald, Llangain, Dyfed; Maura Hazelden, Crymych, Dyfed

67 James Robertson

68 Kevin and Susie White, Hexham, Northum.

69 Mrs and Mrs Heard, Othery, Somer.; Betty Don, Frampton Cotterell, Avon; Rollo and Janie Clifford, Frampton on Severn, Glos.; Anne Jeffery, Stroud, Glos.; Ruth Ward, Culham, Oxon.

70 The Revd Lynne Mayers, Anfield, Liverpool

71 Hilary Forster, Sedbury, Gwent

72 Jefferies, 1879

73 Deering, 1738

74 Hazel Wilson, Abergele, Clwyd

75 Denny Ingram, Huntspill, Somer.; P. M. Sharp, Upton, Somer.; Hilary Stephenson, Bicton Heath, Shrops.

76 William Withering, *A Botanical Arrangement of British Plants*, 1776; *Oxford English Dictionary*, 1933; Gerard, 1633 and 1597

77 Eileen Plume, Leominster, Here.

78 Mrs Legge, Donhead St Andrew, Dorset

79 Eddie Smith, Wraysbury, Middlesex

80 Irene Payne, Donnington, Berks.

81 Grace Moynan, Dover, Kent

82 P. Hill, Clifton, N. Yorks.; Patrick King, Walsingham, Norf.; G. E. Watts, Abbotskerswell, Devon; Eva James, Carmlington, Northum.;

G. B. and A. M. Maddison, Hainault, Essex
83 A. Knapton, Reighton, N. Yorks.
84 V. M. Cook, Park Gate, Southampton, Hants.; also Joan D. Owen, Fareham, Hants.
85 Valerie Burgess, Sible Hedingham, Essex; Sallie Duckitt, Kirk Bramwith Parochial Church Council, Moss, S. Yorks.
86 M. W. B. Hunter, Lower Bourne, Surrey; Jacquie Moon, Puddingstone, Ches.; Mandy Archer, Kirton, Suff.; L. Mould, Southampton, Hants.; Margaret Hale, Sandown, I. of W.; Patricia D. Newnes, Chepstow, Gwent; E.D., London; Margaret Long, Wadsley, S. Yorks.
87 Ingrid Foster, Monkton, Wilts.
88 Mary Hignett, Oswestry, Shrops.
89 Pamela Michael, Lostwithiel, Corn.
90 Roy Fussell, Chirton, Wilts.
91 Clare Jones, Norwich, Norf.
92 Webb and Coleman, 1849
93 per Ruth Ward, Culham, Oxon.
94 H. Whiting, Redhill, Surrey
95 Friend, 1883
96 Mary A. Coburn, Harpenden, Herts.
97 Viv Street, Hemsworth, W. Yorks.
98 M. O'Sullivan, Middleton St George, Durham
99 Rackham, 1986
100 David Morfitt, Coventry, W. Mids.
101 Pollard, Hooper and Moore, 1974
102 Ann Tate, 'Squatters' hedges break the rules', in *Countryman*, 1993
103 Vikki Forbes, Bushey, Herts.
104 Mark Purdey, Lydeard St Lawrence, Somer.

Immigrant Plants
1 Grown by and presented to me by that great geographer David Lowenthal
2 Dony, 1967; also S. A. Rippin, Fforest Coalpit, Gwent; Kathleen Coleman, Castleford, W. Yorks.
3 Vanessa Baker, Colliers Wood, Gtr London
4 Audrey Allan, Netherthong, W. Yorks.
5 Jill Lucas, Fixby, W. Yorks.; also John Ackroyd, Dewsbury, W. Yorks.
6 Trevor Moxom, Huddersfield, W. Yorks.
7 H. G. B. Coast, Chatham, Kent; Dickson, 1991
8 Gilbert, 1992
9 Robinson, 1870
10 R.W.R., Sway, Hants.
11 'Village green', in *Devon Community Council Newsletter*, December 1992
12 Robin Ravilious, Chulmleigh, Devon
13 Martin Spray, Ruardean, Glos.
14 Judith Cheney, University Botanic Garden, Cambridge

15 Gibbons, 1962
16 Maura Hazelden, Crymych, Dyfed; Sheila Evans, Ruthin, Clwyd
17 P. Lock, Kingsdown, Bristol
18 Burton, 1983
19 *ibid*.
20 David Bevan, Warden, Railway Fields Nature Reserve, Harringay, Essex
21 Colin Jerry, Peel, I. of M.
22 M. Trayner, Knaresborough, N. Yorks.
23 Philip and Janet Oswald, Cambridge
24 Gareth Pearce, Woodlavington Primary School, Somer.
25 Cloves, 1993
26 Lyte, 1578
27 Gerard, 1597
28 Gerard, 1633
29 Mrs Healey, Wribbenhall, Here.
30 Ernest Law, *The Chestnut Avenue*, 1919
31 Helen Steinlechner, Hampton, Middx
32 Opie and Opie, 1969
33 Cloves, 1993
34 Opie and Opie, 1969
35 Nigel Mussett, Head of Biology, Giggleswick School, N. Yorks.
36 Opie and Opie, 1969
37 *ibid*.
38 Ernest Worthington, Calverton, Notts.; A. Baxter, Ilkley, W. Yorks.
39 Eleanor Nesbitt, Coventry, W. Mids.
40 Evelyn, 1706
41 Peter Casselden, Chesham, Bucks.
42 Gerard, 1597
43 Thomas Sharp, *Oxford Replanned*, 1948
44 George Tinkler, Carlisle, Cumb.
45 D. Parsons, Countryside Officer, City of Bradford Metropolitan Council
46 Paul Lipscombe, Beaminster, Dorset
47 V. Smethurst, Penistone, S. Yorks.
48 Peter Branney, Cumbria Broadleaves, Bowness, Cumb.
49 Julia Upton, Youlgreave, Derby.
50 Miles, 1972
51 Edna Mallett, Wigginton, N. Yorks.
52 J. Morton Boyd, 'Sycamore and conservation', in *Tree News*, Summer 1993; also R. C. Steele, 'Sycamore in Britain', in *Quarterly Journal of Forestry*, April 1992
53 John Taylor, Causewayhead, per Joyce Dunn, Bridge of Allan, Stirling.
54 James Robertson; Paul Jackson, Aberystwyth, Dyfed
55 White, 1932

56 E. Crouch, Liskeard, Corn.
57 J. N. Rounce, Great Walsingham, Norf.; also J. Lawmon, Cyncoed, Cardiff; Ida Turley, Ty Gwyn, Clwyd
58 Peter Marren
59 Robin Ravilious, Chulmleigh, Devon
60 Heather Paul, Royal Botanic Gardens, Edinburgh
61 Valerie Hetherington, North Berwick
62 Hadfield, 1957
63 Burton, 1983
64 A. O. Hume, in *Journal of Botany*, 1901
65 Diana Harding, Dulverton, Somer.
66 J.M., Sheffield
67 R. Butler, Maidenhead, Berks.
68 Brett Westwood, Cookley, Worcs.
69 Jo Pasco, Tarewaste, Corn.
70 Anne Emmett, Warrington, Ches.
71 Sue Goss, Bucks.; Barbara Penman, Hever, Kent.
72 Godfrey Nall, Shirley, W. Mids
73 Deirdre Barrett, Wetheringsett, Suff.
74 Kathleen Frith, FRCOG, Romford, Essex
75 The *Gardener's Magazine*, 12, 487, 1836
76 James Fenton, Elgin, Moray, in *BSBI News*, 58, 1991
77 per E. Charles Nelson, National Botanic Gardens, Dublin, in *BSBI News*, 57, 1991
78 Robinson, 1870
79 Peter Morris, Hampton-in-Arden, W. Mids
80 Allan Harris, Colinsburgh, Fife
81 Peter Marren; also Bruce Philp, West of Scotland College of Agriculture
82 E. O. Holdsworth, Blackburn, Lancs.
83 M.L.D., Overstrand, Norf.
84 D.H., Scorton, N. Yorks.
85 Mandy Barwell-Parker and Simon Rogers, Coventry, W. Mids
86 Denis Malsher, Hanworth, Middx
87 Y. Howe, Stockbridge, Hants.
88 M. H. O. Hoddinott, Chester
89 M. Murray, Wolverhampton, W. Mids
90 Richard Stewart, Ipswich, Suff.
91 J. B. Foster, Arnside, Lancs.
92 Stephen Alton and Sarah Ausberger, Letchworth, Herts.; Jane Coles, Berrynarbor, Devon; K. Davis, Saltash, Corn.; Audrey Harrison, Launceston, Corn.; B. J. White, New Ollerton, Notts.; Penny Anderson, Chinley, Lancs.
93 Dickson, 1991
94 Peter Marren
95 Roy Fussell, Chirton, Wilts.
96 Rachel Hamilton, Hitcham, Suff.
97 Walters, 1993
98 M. H. O. Hoddinott, Chester
99 Gilbert, 1993
100 William Baxter, *British Phaenogamous Botany*, 1833–43
101 Anon., Runcorn Visitors' Centre, Ches.
102 Robinson, 1870
103 Robin Ravilious, Chulmleigh, Devon; D. J. and K. O'Connor, Exeter, Devon
104 Jill Lucas, Fixby, W. Yorks.
105 A. P. Mead, Kingston St Mary, Somer.
106 Krüssmann, 1982
107 Pam Sinfield, Milton Keynes, Bucks.
108 per Ronald Blythe, Wormingford, Essex; also William T. Stearn, 'The Five Brethren of the Rose: An old botanical riddle', in *Huntia*, 2, 1965
109 Krüssmann, 1982; Beales, 1992
110 M. J. Yates, Whitby Naturalists' Club, Saltburn, Cleve.
111 Evangeline Dickson, Westerfield, Suff.
112 Margaret Crichton, Helensburgh, Dunbarton.; G. Tinkler, Flimby, Cumb.; Michael Bradford, Penwithick, Corn.
113 A. E. Burrows, Dringhouses, York
114 Ray Veerman, Horticultural Adviser to the Crime Prevention Office, Essex Police
115 Wallis, 1769
116 Webb and Coleman, 1849
117 Mabey, 1985
118 Johns, 1853
119 Preston, 1888
120 Lees, 1867
121 Berkhamsted Citizens Association, Herts.
122 Riddelsdell *et al.*, 1948
123 T. G. Tutin, 'Natural factors contributing to a change in our flora', in *The Changing Flora of Britain*, J. E. Lousley (ed.), 1953
124 Salisbury, 1961
125 Susan Cowdy, The Lee, Bucks.
126 Colin Twist, A. Culverhouse, Chris Poulson, Sam Hallett, Peter Gateley, 'Plants, People, Places' project, Liverpool Museum
127 Druce, 1926
128 Kent, 1975; Gerard, 1597
129 James Bolam and Susan Jameson, Wisborough Green, W. Susx

Urban Commons

1 Richard Mabey, *The Unofficial Countryside*, 1973
2 Gilbert, 1993
3 Barry Hunnett, Scunthorpe, Humbs.; Carol Woodward, Hucknall, Notts.; Ian Hartland, Worksop, Notts.; F. A. Niker, Frogpoool, Truro,

Corn.; J. Groves, Chepstow, Gwent; B. Huggins, Tunley, Bath; Dr Peter Shaw, Dept of Environmental Sciences, Roehampton Institute, London

4 Madge Goodall, Otterbourne, Hants.; also Lilian Endsell, Horley, Surrey

5 David Monks, Llanddulas, Clwyd

6 Mary Bradbury, Cockermouth, Cumb.; Derek Sodo, Burnley, Lancs.; Nigel Northcott, Sandford-on-Thames, Oxon.; Anne Lee, Seascale, Cumb.; Sally Edmondson, Lancashire Wildlife Trust

7 Penny Anderson, Chinley, Ches.

8 John Tucker, Chippenham, Wilts.

9 Ian Dunnett, Gipping Valley Countryside Project, Suffolk County Council; also Mrs Doney, Needham Market, Suff.; C. M. Twyman, Claydon, Suff.

10 David Binstead, Sully, S. Glam.; Barry Hannett, Scunthorpe, Humbs.

11 S. A. White, Leighton Buzzard, Beds.

12 A. Chowns, Berkhamsted, Herts.; Rhoda Downes, Poole, Dorset

13 J. A. Webb, Kidlington, Oxon.

14 Antony Galton, Exeter, Devon

Churchyards

1 Pevsner, 1945

2 Greenoak, 1985

3 John Spencer, Churchwarden, Studley, Warw.

4 Wilkinson, 1973

5 Cornish, 1946

6 Robert Turner, *Botanologia: The Brittish Physician*, 1664

7 Aubrey, 1685

8 Sir Thomas Browne, *Hydriotaphia*, 1658

9 White, 1789; also White, 1950

10 Robert Hardy, *Longbow*, 1976

11 Friend, 1883

12 Leather, 1912

13 Cornish, *op. cit.*

14 Milner, 1992

15 White, 1950

16 Allen Meredith, Bushey, Herts.; also Allen Meredith, *Touchwood* (in preparation); Milner, 1992

17 Wordsworth, 'Yew-Trees', composed 1803

18 L. Harris, Low Lorton, Cumbr.; Scott Henderson, Keswick, Cumbr.

19 Jill Burton, *The Element Iw in Cheshire Place-Names*, 1987

20 Ruth Ward, Culham, Oxon.

21 Madeline Reader, Horney Common, E. Susx; also

C. M. Maudslay, Duddleswell, E. Susx

22 Susan Cowdy, The Lee, Bucks.

23 Julia Upton, Derbyshire County Council

24 Professor G. I. Ingram, Hastingleigh, Kent

25 Ida Turley, Ty Gwyn, Clwyd

26 James Anderson, *The Selborne Yew*, 1993

27 David Allen and Sue Anderson, *The Great Yew Excavation: February 1990*, Hampshire County Museums Service Interim Report, 1990

28 White, 1789

Midwinter Greenery

1 Paul Jackson, Aberystwyth, Dyfed

2 Colin Jerry, Peel, I. of M.

3 Hole, 1976

4 Ayers Cleaners, per Common Ground, London

5 *Transactions of the Woolhope Naturalists' Field Club*, 1864

6 Hole, 1976

7 Leather, 1912

8 Grigson, 1952

9 Miller, 1737

10 Alfred Lord Tennyson, 'Morte D'Arthur', 1842

11 Blyton, 1944

12 *Transactions of the Woolhope Naturalists' Field Club*, 1870

13 Bryan Hay, Chesterfield, Derby.

14 Jill Lucas, Fixby, W. Yorks.

15 G. Wildon, Malvern, Worcs.

16 D. McKirgan, Weston-super-Mare, Somer.; Maggie Colwell, Box, Glos.

17 Graham Talbot, Maidenhead, Berks.

18 Mary Gay, Ledbury, Here.; Joan Dickinson, Twyning, Glos.; Peter Hill, Ross-on-Wye, Here.; T. J. Flemons, Luston, Here.; P. Powell, Hereford; J. Madeley, Monkhopton, Shrops.; A. P. Radford, West Bagborough, Somer.

19 Morton, 1712

20 Helen Mayo, Chepstow, Gwent; Jean Churchill, Blandford, Dorset; Jo Dunn, Charlbury, Oxon., in *BSBI News*, 70, 1995; Joy Barnes, Taunton, Somer.; R. Booty, Galleywood, Essex

21 Sinker *et al.*, 1985 and 1991

22 S. A. Rippin, Fforest Coalpit, Gwent

23 Mrs Holbrow, Yeovil, Somer., in *Plant-lore Notes and News*, April 1992

24 Simon Leatherdale, Halstead, Essex; M. Tucker, Warborough, Oxon.; Mrs Copper, Cowes, I. of W.; Constance Swain, Lostwithiel, Corn.

25 Jermyn, 1974

26 Angus Idle, Wycombe Urban Wildlife Group, High Wycombe, Bucks.

27 Pam Tickner, Shirley, Surrey

28   C. M. Langstaff, Home Farm, Winkburn, Notts.

29   Daniel Keech, Common Ground, London

30   Stone House Recall Group, Bishops Castle, Shrops.

31   Hazel Brecknell, Quarndon, Derby.

32   Grace Wheeldon, Bakewell, Derby., in *BSBI News*, 63, 1993

33   Simon Leatherdale, Forest Enterprise, Woodbridge, Suff.

34   Ekwall, 1960

35   Mary Jannetta, Cullen, Banff.

36   Dianne Harvey, Haddiscoe, Norf.

37   Dorothy Beck, Lydd, Kent; also G. F. Peterken and J. C. E. Hubbard, 'The shingle vegetation of southern England: the holly wood on Holmstone Beach, Dungeness', in *Journal of Ecology* 60, 1972

38   Ruth Ward, Culham, Oxon.

39   Nature Conservancy Council, 'The Food and Feeding Behaviour of Cattle and Ponies in the New Forest', 1983

40   Martin Spray, 'Holly as a fodder in England', in *Agricultural History Review*, 1981; see also J. Radley, 'Holly as a winter feed', in *Agricultural History Review*, 1961

41   Lorna Gartside, Saddleworth, Oldham, Lancs.

42   Mary Aitkenhead, Greenfield, Oldham, Lancs.

43   Geoff Boswell, Oldham, Lancs.

44   Bob and Margaret Marsland, Hallwood Green, Glos.

45   P. H. Nicholls, 'On the evolution of a forest landscape', in *Transactions of the Institute of British Geography*, 56, 1972

46   B. R. Oakley, High Yewdale Farm, Windermere, Cumb.

47   Tubbs, 1986

48   E. V. Reece, Eardiston, Worcs.

49   A. Rich, Whitnell Farm, Binegar, Somer.

50   Mrs Mary Taylor, Botton Head, Taham Fells, Lancs.

51   Paul Ottard, Walford College of Agriculture, Shrops.

52   Norman Chalk, North Walsham, Norf.

53   Stan Tanner, Dumf. and Galwy

54   P. J. Rollason, Hitchin, Herts.

55   'The Ratcatcher', Basingstoke, Hants.

56   Susan Gogarty, Nettlecombe, I. of W.

57   Norma D'Lemos, Truro, Corn.; also Jill Hill, Lower Peover, Ches.

58   G. MacKay Smith, Rothesay, Isle of Bute

59   T. T. Freston, Wellington, Somer.

60   Ken Procter, Wilmslow, Ches.

61   Bill Shephard, Newport, I. of W.

62   Justin Brooke, Marazion, Corn.

63   Tess Baker, Legant, Corn.; Ronald Blythe, Wormingford, Essex; Geoff Marsh, Lytchett Matravers, Dorset

64   Dallimore, 1908

65   Margaret Stump, Berkeley, Glos.

66   Simon Leatherdale, Forest Enterprise, Woodbridge, Suff.; C. Walker, Condover, Shrops.

67   Susan Cowdy, The Lee, Bucks.

68   Madeline Reader, Horney Common, E. Susx

69   The Revd F. Vere Hodge, Glastonbury, Somer.

70   Rosemary Teverson, Corn.

71   P. Mead, Kingston St Mary, Somer.

72   B. P. Major, Huntington, N. Yorks.

73   Patty Jackson, Mold, Clwyd

74   Elspeth Wrigley, Holden Clough, Lancs.

75   D. G. Grant, Lee on Solent, Hants.

76   Alwen Byer, Shrewsbury, Shrops.

77   Beth Howell, Walkden, Lancs.

78   Rosy Berry, Marlborough, Wilts.

79   Sue Jenkins, Leeds, W. Yorks.

80   Duncan Ross, Newton Popppleford, Devon

81   Michael Morgan, Canvey Island, Essex

82   Jennifer Sandy, Gunnislake, Corn.

83   N. J. Burrell, Wareham, Dorset

84   Simon Russell, Sevenoaks, Kent

85   R. Chilver, Shaftesbury, Dorset

86   The Revd E. Pearson, Penrhos, Gwent

87   Matthew Edmonds, Midland Tree Surgeons, Sudbury, Derby.

88   Major D. A. Pudsey, The Hampshire Honey Farm, Sutton Scotney, Hants.; also M. L. Somers, Surrey Beekeepers' Association, Churt, Surrey

89   Thomas Whatcly, *Observations on Modern Gardening*, 1770

90   Jane Burse, Bentham, Lancs.

91   S. Barlow, Watersheddings, Lancs.

92   E. J. Saynor, King's Lynn, Norf.

93   Jacqueline Brook, Selly Park, Birmingham

94   Irene Tait, Caversham, Berks.

95   Walters, 1993

96   Glynys Morgan, Ammanford, Dyfed

97   K. W. Gilbert, Otterbourne, Hants.

98   Jill Betteridge, Cottenham, Cambs.

99   Ernie Marshall, per Michel Hughes, Chudleigh, Devon

100   Beth Veale, Herne Bay, Kent

101   Mary Sutch, Bardwell, Suff.

102   Wyn Lawrence, Farnborough, Hants.

103   Jennie Lancaster, St Helens, Lancs.

104   C. Walker, Condover, Shrops.

105   Peter Marren

106   E. Morris, Minsterley, Shrops.

107 John Pike, Copplestone, Devon
108 J. Ellis, Ventnor, I. of W.
109 C. H. Williams, Shrewsbury, Shrops.
110 P. Mann, Bristol
111 Eluned Davies, Tremeirchion, Clwyd
112 Gwen Redshaw, Rhewl, Clwyd
113 Alison Rutherford, Helensburgh, Dunbarton.
114 Opie, 1959
115 Keyte and Parrott (eds), 1992
116 Amanda, Hessle, Humbs.
117 Jill Lucas, Fixby, W. Yorks.
118 Chambers and Sidgwick, 1907
119 H. A. McAllister and A. Rutherford, 'Hedera helix … and H. hibernica … in the British Isles', in Watsonia, 18(1), 1990
120 Ekwall, 1960; Gelling, 1984
121 John Bullman, Parish Council, Boxford, Suff.; J. F. Wilkinson, Box, Glos.
122 Rackham, 1986
123 Tony Harwood, Boxley Parish Councillor, Maidstone, Kent
124 Evelyn, 1706
125 Gilpin, 1808
126 C. J. L. Farmer, Petersfield, Hants.; the Vicar of Boxgrove, W. Susx
127 Internal documents, Nature Conservancy, Monks Wood, 1972
128 Aubrey, 1685
129 Bernard and Carla Phillips, Wells, Norf.
130 Shirley Warnes, Lillington, Warw.
131 Friend, 1883
132 'Plants, death and mourning', in Daily Telegraph, 1 December 1868, quoted in Vickery, 1984

17 William A. Clarke, First Records of British Flowering Plants, 2nd edn, 1900
18 Tubbs, 1986
19 W. R. Linton, Flora of Derbyshire, 1903
20 Summerhayes, 1951
21 Philip Oswald, Cambridge
22 Webb and Coleman, 1849
23 quoted in Jermyn, 1974
24 Gerard, 1597
25 Ronald Good, 'On the distribution of the Lizard Orchid (Himantoglossum hircinum Koch)', in New Phytologist, 35, 1936
26 Lousley, 1950
27 Jocelyn Brooke, The Military Orchid, 1948
28 Mabey, 1980
29 Belinda Wheeler, Homefield Wood Warden, BBONT, Oxford; see also the annual reports on the site published by the Chiltern Military Orchid Group
30 Perring and Farrell, 1983; also Summerhayes, 1951

Beauties and Prodigals

1 quoted in Raven, John and Walters, 1956
2 Gerard, 1597
3 Gerard, 1633
4 W. L. Bowles, Banwell Hill, 1829, quoted by Grigson, 1955
5 Fowles, 1978
6 Gerard, 1597
7 Miller, 1752
8 White, 1789
9 Sue Goss, Bledlow Ridge, Bucks.
10 Forsyth, 1968
11 C. E. Raven, John Ray, Naturalist, 1950 and 1987
12 M. E. Braithwaite, Hawick, Roxburghshire
13 Anne McKean, Forty Hill, Enfield, Middx
14 Grigson, 1955
15 Perring and Farrell, 1983
16 John Vaughan, Flowers of the Field, 1906

Acknowledgements

To the Countryside Commission, English Nature, the Ernest Cook Trust and Reed Books for so generously supporting the research stage of the project.

To Common Ground – and Sue Clifford and Angela King especially – who acted as charitable host to the project and who were unfailing in their support and encouragement whenever my own enthusiasm showed signs of wilting. And to Daniel Keech and John Newton, who worked as full-time information and research officers, principally from Common Ground's office, but who also did invaluable and original fieldwork beyond the call of duty.

To Peter Marren, James Robertson and Ruth Ward, who co-ordinated research for us in Scotland, Wales and Oxfordshire respectively.

To Roz Kidman Cox, editor of *BBC Wildlife* Magazine, and Patrick Flavelle, producer of BBC TV's *CountryFile*, who gave us space and time (and encouragement) to recruit contributors.

To the many societies and associations, national, regional and local, whose members and staff were amongst the principal contributors:

Botanical Society of the British Isles, British Bryological Association, British Association for Nature Conservation, British Naturalists' Association, British Trust for Conservation Volunteers, Butterfly Conservation Society, Churchyard Conservation Project, John Clare Society, Council for Protection of Rural England, Countryside Council for Wales, Folklore Society, Forest Enterprise, Help the Aged, Herb Society, Learning through Landscapes, Local Agenda 21, National Association for Environmental Education, National Association of Field Studies Officers, National Farmers' Union Scotland, National Federation of Women's Institutes, National Trust, Open Spaces Society, Plantlife, Poetry Society, Ramblers' Association, the Royal Botanic Gardens at Kew and Edinburgh, Royal Forestry Society, Royal Society for Nature Conservation, Scottish Environmental Education Council, Scottish Natural Heritage, Tree Council and the Parish Tree Wardens network, Watch, Youth Hostels Association.

Arthur Rank Centre, Association of Leicestershire Botanical Artists, Bioregional Development Group, Bolton Museum, Cheshire Landscape Trust, Cleveland Community Forest, Cobtree Museum, the County Wildlife Trusts of: Berkshire, Buckinghamshire and Oxfordshire; Cambridge and Bedfordshire; Cleveland; Cornwall; Derbyshire; Gloucestershire; Hampshire and Isle of Wight; Hertfordshire and Middlesex; Kent; Lancashire; London; Norfolk; Northamptonshire; North Wales; Nottinghamshire; Scotland; Suffolk; Surrey; Wiltshire. Cymdeithas Edward Llywd, Derbyshire Ranger Service, Deeside Leisure Centre, Flora of Dunbartonshire Project, Groundwork Trusts of Merthyr and Cynon, Kent Thames-side and Amber Valley, Humberside County Council Planning Department, Liverpool Museum, Manchester Herbarium, Mid-Yorkshire Chamber of Commerce, Montague Gallery, Norfolk Rural Life Museum, Norfolk Society, North York Moors National Park, Social and Education Training Norfolk, Ted Ellis Nature Reserve, South-east Arts, University of Sussex Centre for Continuing Education, Warwickshire Rural Community Council, Wildplant Design.

Boxley Parish Council, Bradford City Council Countryside Service, Buchan Countryside Group, Thomas Coram School, Cumbria Broadcleaves, Dragon Environment Group, Embsay with Eastby Nature Reserve, Giggleswick School, Great Torrington Library, Greenfield Valley Heritage Centre, Mike Handyside Wildflowers, Harehough Craigs Action Group, Hedingham Heritage Group, Hexham Nursery, Horsham Natural History Society, Ingleby Greenhow Primary School, Graham Moore Landscape Works, Lee Parish Society, Little Wittenham Nature Reserve, Oakfield Methodist Church, Paulersbury Horticultural Society, Pytchley Parish Sunday School Group, St Mary's Church Kirk Bramwith, Spiral Arts, Wealden Team Conservation Volunteers, West Bromwich Albion Football Club, White Cliffs Countryside Management Project, Whitegate and Marton Parish Council.

My personal thanks for their support to Charles Clark, Gren Lucas, Sir Ralph Verney and the late Sir William Wilkinson, and to the Leverhulme Trust for their generous award of a Research Fellowship to help fund my own researches.

To the friends and colleagues who gave me hospitality, company and much stimulating information during my own research trips: Elizabeth Roy and Nigel Ashby, Ronald Blythe, Hilary Catchpole and the pupils of Thomas Coram School, Berkhamsted, Rollo and Janie Clifford, David Cobham, Mike and Pooh Curtis, Roger Deakin, the late Edgar Milne-Redhead, Robin and Rachel Hamilton, Anne Mallinson, Richard Simon, Jane Smart, Jonathan Spencer, Ian and Vicky Thomson. And to Liza Goddard, who acted as guinea-pig contributor whilst I was still refining the idea of the project and who accompanied me on some of the early field-trips, and to Pattie Barron for her patience.

To Penelope Hoare, my publisher, and the directors of Reed Books, who gave unflagging support to the project over what, in the modern book world, was a very long gestation period.

To Robin MacIntosh, my personal assistant, who helped in so many ways, especially with the awesome task of putting the contributions into some order. To Vivien Green, my agent, especially for bolstering me up during the low periods of the writing. To Douglas Matthews, for the speed and accuracy with which he produced the lengthy indexes. To Philip Oswald, whose vast background knowledge and meticulous attention to detail not only gave the text botanical respectability but added a wealth of anecdotes, historical notes and stylistic improvements. And to Roger Cazalet, my editor, for his diligence, dedication, patience and care.

And finally, the warm thanks of all of us go to the many thousands of people who contributed to *Flora Britannica* and without whom it would not exist. Those of you whose stories and notes have found their way into the text are individually acknowledged in the Source notes. But every single contribution helped form the entries and the overall flavour of the book. Please keep contributing, as we hope that the first edition of *Flora Britannica* will not mark the end of the project so much as the beginning of a new phase.

Picture credits

Bob Gibbons: 11, 13, 14-15, 16, 18-19, 20, 22, 23, 24b, 25, 26, 27, 31, 35, 36, 37, 42, 43, 45, 49, 53, 54-5, 56, 57, 60-1, 62, 65, 66, 70, 71, 74, 75, 78, 80r, 81 (both), 89, 96, 106-7, 109, 111, 113, 114-15, 118, 119, 122, 123, 127, 128, 130, 131, 133, 135, 137, 139, 141, 143, 144-5, 147, 149, 152, 153, 156r, 157, 160, 162, 164, 166, 168, 172, 173, 174, 175, 176, 177, 178, 181, 182-3, 186, 187, 188, 189, 191, 195, 199, 202-3, 205, 206, 208-9, 211, 213, 216, 226 (both), 231, 232-3, 234, 236, 237, 238, 239, 241.

Gareth Lovett Jones: 6-7, 21, 28-9, 50, 59, 63, 64, 69, 72-3, 77, 80l, 82-3, 88, 92, 94, 97, 99, 101, 103, 104, 117, 125, 150, 155, 158-9, 171, 192, 193, 196-7, 214, 219, 220, 221, 222, 223, 229.

Heather Angel: 85.

Ashmolean Museum: 161.

Bridgeman Art Library: 68.

British Museum: 224.

Carlisle City Museum and Art Gallery: 91.

Ian Collins: 8.

Common Ground: 12, 44.

Tony Evans © Timelapse Library: 17, 38, 120, 227.

Hulton Getty Picture Collection: 121, 204.

A. F. Kersting: 148.

London Transport Museum: 156l.

Richard Mabey: 32-3, 95, 184.

Margaret Marsland: 126.

Mercury Gallery: 41.

Natural Image: (Peter Wilson) 24t, 58, 86; (Robin Fletcher) 134, 163.

National Trust Photographic Library (John Bethell): 30l.

Katrina Porteous: 112.

Royal Horticultural Society: 240.

Eddie Ryle-Hodges: 30r, 180, 201, 225.

Edwin Smith: 124, 179.

Homer Sykes: 46-7, 243, 244tl and tr, 245, 246.

The Board and Trustees of the Victoria & Albert Museum (Bridgeman Art Library): 100, 108.

Index of Places

General Index